The Cockapoo Handbook

LINDA WHITWAM

Copyright © 2015 Linda Whitwam

ISBN-13: 978-1517733285

Acknowledgements

My sincere thanks go to all the Cockapoo organisations, breeders, owners and canine experts who have generously contributed their time and expertise. Without them, The Cockapoo Handbook would not have been possible. Special thanks to: the British Cockapoo Society, American Cockapoo Club, The Doodle Trust, Diana Hoskins, Mary Gosling, Dave and Linda Zarro, Jessica Sampson, Rebecca Mae Goins, Karol Watson Todd, Chloe and Pat Pollington, Jeanne Davis, Jackie Stafford, Julie Shearman, Eileen Jackson, Julie and Nigel Houston, Judy and Greg Moorhouse, Dr Sara Skiwski and all the Cockapoo owners who participated. Details of contributors are listed at the back of the book.

Copyright

Table of Contents

1. Meet The Cockapoo

The Cockapoo has been known and loved in North America since the 1950s. More recently, it has shot through the canine ranks to become one of the most familiar dogs in the UK, as well as being increasingly seen in countries across the world. You won't go far without spotting one of these appealing dogs; they are in most neighbourhoods and nearly everybody knows somebody who's got one.

The Cockapoo - also known as the Cockerpoo, Spoodle (if you're in Australia) and even Cockadoodle - is the original designer dog, and is the result of crossing a Cocker Spaniel with a Poodle. Fans say that the Cockapoo brings together the best qualities of both parent breeds, combining the intelligence and sensitivity of the Poodle with the desire to please and happy disposition of the Spaniel. And the Cockapoo often outlives both parent breeds, with a lifespan of 15 to 17 years not uncommon – some have been known to live to 20 years old.

The Cockapoo is not a purebred or pedigree, but a crossbreed or hybrid. There was a time when mixed breeds were looked down on by certain sections of the canine fraternity. But over the last couple of decades, they have seen an explosion in popularity. As far as the Cockapoo is concerned, this is largely due to two reasons. Nobody knows the exact origins of this crossbreed in the United States and whether it happened by design or accident. But these days, Cockapoos are most definitely born by design – due to these two great attributes.

The first is the 'hypoallergenic' coat, and the second is the sweet, happy temperament. The Cockapoo will naturally get along with everything and everybody and has earned a well-deserved reputation as an excellent family pet.

Most have a soft, wavy coat which sheds little or no hair – unless they are first generation (F1) crosses which happen to take after the Spaniel parent, which does shed. This has made the Cockapoo a popular choice with families where one or more people have allergies or asthma. However, a word of caution, as the Kennel Clubs on both sides of the Atlantic will tell anybody who will listen: there is no such thing as a non-shedding dog! All dogs shed a little. Also, allergic reactions are usually caused by canine dander (like dandruff) and saliva, rather than hair. Many allergy sufferers do live perfectly well with Cockapoos, but there is no guarantee - every dog is different, every human is different. See **Chapter 4. Cockapoos for Allergy Sufferers** for further details.

The coat can be sleek if the puppy takes after the Spaniel, although most Cockapoos combine the attributes of both parent breeds and have a soft, low shedding and wavy coat, like the dog pictured. How much it sheds varies from one dog to another. However, as the coat often loses hardly any hair, regular brushing and trips to the grooming parlour – unless you can clipper a dog yourself – are a must.

I can't think of another dog which has such a variety of coat colours: black, blond, red, chocolate, apricot, buff, sable, tan, brown, silver, brindle, tri-colours, partis (one colour and white), roan, merle (mottled or 'splashed with paint' effect), to name but a few. Then there are variations within the colours and coat patterns: 'dilute' is when the base colour is diluted with hints of another colour, and a 'tuxedo' is not a dinner jacket, but a patch of white on the chest, while 'ticking' is little spots of colour. The skin and nose colour of a Cockapoo vary according to coat colour.

Unfortunately, the coat's hypoallergenic trait (which means "**less** likely to cause an allergic reaction") has led to some unscrupulous breeding to cash in on the craze – but none of this is the fault of the dog. If you haven't got your puppy yet, make sure you spend the time to find a reputable, ethical breeder who health tests her dogs. Cockapoos come in various sizes, shapes and colours as well as with different coat types, but one thing is generally agreed – an ugly Cockapoo has yet to be born! So, do your research BEFORE you view any puppies, as the sight of a litter of cute Cockapoo pups will almost certainly be too hard to resist.

The Cockapoo Club of Great Britain says: "The coat type of the Cockapoo will vary as characteristics are inherited from both the Poodle and the Cocker Spaniel. There may even be some variety within a litter. The three possible coat types are a tight curly coat, a loose wavy/ringlet coat and a straighter coat. An experienced breeder will be able to advise you what the likely coat type of a puppy will be from their Cocker Spaniel/Poodle mix that they breed, and when the puppies are just a few weeks old, it is possible to see the coat type starting to develop. The texture of the Cockapoo coat usually consists of dense, soft or silky fur, unlike the coarser fur found on many dogs, and all three coat types of the F1 Cockapoo will be low-shedding/dander with low-allergen qualities."

The second outstanding feature of the Cockapoo is his excellent temperament. These dogs are highly intelligent, easy to train, extremely affectionate and loyal, eager to please their owners, have a sunny disposition and get along well with other dogs and people - from children to the elderly.

Given sufficient exercise and mental stimulation, Cockapoos are relatively uncomplicated and suitable for first-time owners. They excel at agility and other canine competitions where they are physically and mentally challenged and can be trained to a high level. Their intelligence, even-tempered nature and love of humans mean that they make excellent therapy, service and assistance dogs – one of the few crossbreeds to be trained in this manner. In order to better understand your Cockapoo, it helps to understand what went into his or her genetic make-up, so let's take a look at the parents and grandparents.

Cockers and Poodles

A Cockapoo is the result of mating a Cocker Spaniel with a Poodle. The size and, to some extent, temperament and energy levels, of a Cockapoo depend on which type of Poodle and which type of Cocker Spaniel he or she was bred from and which parent, if any, the puppy favours.

The parents or grandparents could be one of three types of Spaniel. The English Cocker Spaniel (pictured) could have been bred either for the show ring or work in the field. Cockapoos from working Cockers often have a higher energy drive and exercise requirements than show Cockers. The third type is the American Cocker Spaniel. Both English and American Cockers are used as breeding stock in the UK and North America.

Spaniels are one of the oldest breeds of dog - they have certainly been known for hundreds of years. They are classed in the Gundog Group in the UK and are the smallest breed in the Sporting Group in the US. They were bred to flush game birds out of dense undergrowth during the hunt. In the late 1800s, the Cocker was recognised in the UK as a separate breed from the larger Field and Springer Spaniels. Originally called the "Cocking" Spaniel, the breed took its name from the woodcock, which it was specifically bred to flush out.

Although the Kennel Club does not distinguish between show and working Cocker Spaniels, there are some differences between the strains. The English show Cocker is the largest of the three types and is characterised by its domed head, long ears and thick, wavy coat. The working Cocker is smaller and more athletic, having been bred to run all day. He has a shorter coat, ears set higher on the head and a slightly shorter muzzle.

The American Cocker Spaniel (pictured) is slightly smaller than its British cousins; the other main differences being the shorter muzzle, longer ears and the shape of the head. The American Cocker's coat is denser and longer than the English, but still retains that silky texture. Referred to simply as the "Cocker Spaniel" in the US, some have a calmer disposition and lower energy requirements than a working English Cocker.

The trademark characteristic of all three types of Spaniel is their constantly wagging tail. They are affectionate and enthusiastic and they love learning, with scent work being high on their agenda, as they love using their noses. The greatest desire of all three types of Cocker is to please their owners. They are listed in the top 20 of 110 dogs tested for psychologist Stanley Coren's Intelligence of Dogs List.

The other breeds which make up the Cockapoo are the Poodle – usually the Toy or Miniature. We may think of the Poodle prancing around a show ring with elaborate hairstyles, but people often forget that the Poodle was bred as a working dog. It is a water dog which originated in Germany, where its name – Pudelhund – meant 'splash in water dog'. The Standard Poodle is considered the original and was a gundog used mainly for hunting duck and sometimes upland birds.

Apart from his unique appearance, the Poodle has two other outstanding features: his coat and his intelligence. Yes, the Poodle has beauty AND brains! After the Border Collie, this is the most intelligent canine on the planet, according to the Intelligence of Dogs List. The non- or low-shedding qualities of the breed's wool coat have led to the Poodle becoming the Number One choice for dam or sire when it comes to creating hybrid puppies. Today there are oodles of Doodles and piles of Poos in the canine world, thanks to the Poodle.

All Poodles – even small ones - like to run, play and swim, and exercise is a necessity for their happiness. They excel at agility and obedience classes, being both athletic and highly intelligent. The breed has a reputation for being 'intuitive', picking up on their owner's moods. Because of this, some Poodles do not respond well to stress, tension or loud noises.

What the Breeders Say

A number of Cockapoo breeders have kindly given their time to share their experiences in this book and we asked them to tell us about their dogs. This is what they said, starting in the UK:

Pat Pollington, of Polycinders Cockapoos, Devon, has been breeding dogs for 35 years and Cockapoos for 11. She said: "My Cockapoos are from show strain parents. We believe the show strain Cockapoos are calmer, less energetic, more of a family pet. The working Cockapoos are more hyperactive and need a family that is very active and like walking all the time.

"The working Cockapoo needs to be exercised more than the show Cockapoo. The show strain Cocker Spaniels are bred for the show ring so they are more relaxed, whereas the working Cocker Spaniels are bred to work all day and do a job, i.e. beating, picking up and working on farms, so they like to be on the go a lot.

"Both strains have lovely temperaments, if bred from the right parents. They are brilliant with children. Every Cockapoo wants to be a lapdog and sleep on your lap, but unfortunately they grow to be a touch too big! "Every time a Cockapoo needs telling 'NO', they give you the big soppy Cockapoo eyes and it is impossible to not give them a big cuddle. They love other dogs and they make brilliant family pets." Pictured is Pat's three-month-old F1 pup, Lucy, enjoying a walk in the countryside.

"They fit into everyone's lifestyle. If you like walking a lot, they will love that too, but if you fancy a pyjama day watching movies, they will join you on the sofa and enjoy the snacks with you! They are very good at training. If you put your time into a Cockapoo, you will have a well behaved, trained, loyal and loving family pet.

"The Cockapoo is a very special breed thanks to its fantastic coat. We have had many Cockapoos go to people that are extremely allergic and they have never had any problems. They are just over the moon because they never believed they would be able to own their own dog. If you buy from the right parents, you will have a Cockapoo with a long wavy, shaggy coat that's the softest thing you can touch. They are low to non-moulting." NOTE: Not every Cockapoo is suitable for every allergy sufferer.

Karol Watson Todd, KaroColin Cockapoos, Lincolnshire: "Our Cockapoos are bred from both working and show Spaniels, and I find adult show Cockers to be lazier and less biddable! The working stock is more honest and eager to please in attitude. With the puppies, those from show Spaniels do not always get on as well together, while puppies from working Cockers are better at co-operative play from the beginning. I make my own rag toys and working puppies will take an end each and have a great game, while show Cocker puppies will try to get the other puppy to release the toy. It's very interesting!

"Even though people think puppies from show Cockers require less exercise, I haven't found this to be true. I also find that working puppies simply need more mental stimulation, rather than exercise. I always pop a Kong-style toy into my puppy packs for this reason."

Julie Shearman, Crystalwood Cockapoos, Devon: "We breed from show Spaniels. We have found them to be slightly calmer and needing a little less exercise, so better suited to family life. The typical temperament is loving, loyal, intelligent, energetic and fun with a happy disposition, and the most appealing thing is their affection towards people."

Jackie Stafford, Dj's Cockapoo Babies, Texas, US: "Cockapoos are the best family dogs that there are. They are loving, kind and the smartest of all hybrids. They are unique because they are very smart and yet happy-go-lucky at the same time. They are happy in their owner's lap all the time and are always looking to their owner for ways to please them. They are sweet and loving, yet playful and energetic for a moderate timespan. They live to please their owners and the only fault in their temperament is the possibility of separation anxiety."

Jeanne Davis, Wind Horse Offering, Maryland: "The typical Cockapoo temperament? Wonderful! Smart, great companions and easy to train. I breed from working Spaniels and I do find there is a difference in temperament between them and other Spaniels. I find working Spaniels are more serious and show Cockers like to be pampered a bit more."

Rebecca Mae Goins, MoonShine Babies Cockapoos, Indiana: "Most of our Cockers, Poodles and Cockapoos are from the heavy-coated show type, but we do have a few that are more towards the working type. The working type does seem to require more exercise and be harder to keep in a home setting, unless the family is very active. The typical Cockapoo temperament is very loyal and loving to their family and very smart; easy to train to become a perfect loving family pet. They also do very well as therapy and service dogs. The Cockapoo is very playful and can be comical and a true joy to be around. The temperament is first imprinted on the puppy when it is still with the breeder, and the new family has to help their new Cockapoo by continuing with the training and socialisation.

"If you see a Cockapoo that is happy and loves to play and meet new people in public and in their home, then the breeder and family did their jobs well and socialised the puppy properly from Day One. Now if you see a Cockapoo that is overly shy or aggressive with either a family member or stranger, then this Cockapoo was not properly socialised and will require professional training to overcome this obstacle."

Jessica Sampson, Legacy Cockapoos, Ontario, Canada: "All our Cockapoos descend from American Cocker Spaniels. We chose them for their calm, affectionate and eager-to-please temperament. I have not had a lot of experience with working Spaniels here in Canada, but the little I have seen of them, I have noticed they have a lot more energy than your typical show Cocker, which, of course, would be needed for working in the field." Pictured relaxing at home with a favourite toy is Jessica's F2 chocolate stud Karl.

"The typical Cockapoo is a happy, merry dog that knows no stranger. They are very intelligent and eager to please. Also, they have the unique gift of being able to sense one's emotional state and are extremely forgiving. "The forgiving nature makes the Cockapoo unparalleled as a family dog and has also made it one of the top picks as a therapy dog, especially when children are involved - particularly those with autism. I would say that the best and most appealing thing about the Cockapoo is that it is loving and eager to please, and thus easily trained."

Sizes and F Numbers

As well as the different coat colours and parentage, there are other factors to consider when considering a Cockapoo; namely size and F numbers.

Size

The size and weight of a Cockapoo depends on which type of Poodle went into his or her make-up. The most popular sizes of Cockapoo are Toy and Miniature, bred – unsurprisingly - from Toy and Miniature Poodles. The sizes are:

➢ A **Teacup** (seen in the US) is less than six pounds in weight and under 10 inches in height

➢ A **Toy** Cockapoo weighs less than 12 pounds and can reach 10 inches in height, but has a sturdier build

➢ A **Miniature** ranges in weight from 13 to 18 pounds and stands from 11 and 14 inches high

➢ A **Standard** or **Maxi** Cockapoo (bred from a Standard Poodle) is less common and weighs more than 19 pounds. It stands at least 15 inches high

These sizes and weights are not written in stone. If you are considering a Cockapoo puppy, find out exactly what the parent breeds are and ask to see both parents, if possible. This will give you a good idea of the size of the adult dog.

'Teacup' varieties of many different breeds and hybrids have sprung up in the US and are miniaturised versions of the original breed. There have been some recorded health issues with Teacups, notably regarding adverse effects on the dog's skeleton. I am currently not aware of any documented issues with Teacup Cockapoos. However, there is anecdotal evidence of health problems and shortened lifespans with some Teacup Poodles (which is not a breed recognised by the Kennel Clubs). Whatever size of Cockapoo you get, the important thing is to check the health history and certificates of the parents.

F Numbers

In the canine world, F numbers have nothing to do with photography or Formula One motor racing. They are used to describe the generation of a crossbreed dog. The F comes from the Latin *filius* (son) and means "relating to a son or daughter."

So, an **F1** Cockapoo is a **first generation** cross - one parent was a purebred Cocker Spaniel and the other was a purebred Poodle.

This first generation cross often – but not always - produces a puppy which combines attributes from both parents, including the coat, which may have the soft, silky feel of the Spaniel's coat, but will be virtually non-shedding, like the Poodle's coat. F1 crosses may benefit from 'hybrid vigour' and can grow up to one inch taller than either of their parents.

So far, so good...but then it gets a little more complicated. The next generations are worked out by always **adding one number to the parent with the lowest F number.** So if two F1 Cockapoos are mated, they will produce F2 Cockapoos puppies. They might also produce something called the 'Granddad Effect - this doesn't mean that all the puppies are wrinkly - although they are when they are new-born! It is when some pups take on the physical characteristics of either a Poodle or a Spaniel – while others look like a Cockapoo; all within the same litter. So, an F2 Cockapoo will have one F1 parent, the other could be an F1 F2, F3, F4, etc. Cockapoo. Similarly, an F3 Cockapoo is the produce of mating one F2 Cockapoo with another F2 or with an F3, F4 etc.

As well as an F, you might see a **'b'** next to an advertised puppy, for example F1b or F2b. The 'b' stands for 'backcross' and it occurs when a Cockapoo has been mated with a purebred Spaniel or, more often, a Poodle. With a Poodle, this is usually done to increase the likelihood of the puppies having a hypoallergenic coat. It is not so common for breeders to backcross to a Spaniel, so a typical F1B might be one-quarter Spaniel and three-quarters Poodle.

Hybrid Vigour

Hybrid vigour is the principle that the first cross between two unrelated purebred lines (e.g. a Cockapoo) is healthier and grows better than either parent line (e.g. the Cocker Spaniel and Poodle parents). The theory is that the puppy may be stronger and healthier as he is less likely to inherit the genetic faults of either purebred parent.

Many purebred (pedigree) breeds have health problems which have been bred in over the years. For example, some Dalmatians are deaf, some Labradors have hip problems, Dachshunds may suffer from back problems and some Cocker Spaniels have inherited eye problems. This is because as well as breeding the good points into a pedigree dog, the faults have also been inadvertently passed on, often through inbreeding or breeding from a very small gene pool.

Although the gene pool is larger with crossbreeds like the Cockapoo, it is vital that health checks are still made on the parents, which is why it is so important to get your puppy from an ethical Cockapoo breeder who health tests her breeding stock. For example, if a Cockapoo puppy has a Poodle or Spaniel parent or ancestor with eye problems, there is a chance that your puppy will inherit that fault, just as with a purebred.

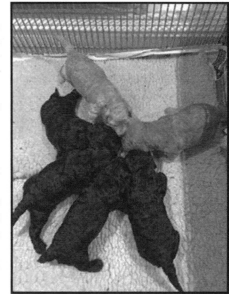

The one important fact to remember with hybrid vigour is that **it only truly applies to first generation (F1) dogs.** In other words, to Cockapoos who have one purebred Poodle parent and one Cocker Spaniel parent. Provided they have parents free from genetic issues, Cockapoos are often extremely healthy, robust dogs that live to a ripe old age. Pictured is a litter of healthy Cockapoo pups bred by Karol Watson Todd.

Breed Standard

The Cockapoo is a crossbreed, not a purebred (North America) or pedigree (UK). It is the product of crossing two breeds of dog and, because the Cockapoo is a hybrid, you cannot get Kennel Club or AKC registration papers with your dog - although you can register him or her with one of the Cockapoo clubs in your country (see back of book for details). You should, however, always find out about your dog's parents and ancestors because, provided you care for him well, his genes will be the major factor in deciding how healthy he will be.

The breed clubs for purebred dogs have a written set of guidelines which govern how all dogs of that breed should look and move and what sort of temperament they should have. This blueprint is called a **breed standard** and it ensures that all dogs of the same breed conform.

The breed standard is registered with the Kennel Club or AKC and all approved breeders produce dogs which conform to these guidelines. They are then allowed to register their puppies with the Kennel Clubs and receive a family tree certificate for the puppy - this is called a pedigree.

However, in the past it has also led to some breeders using a very narrow gene pool to breed for certain exaggerated traits – for example the very flat nose on a Bulldog – and sometimes this has led to health issues. It's fair to say that the Kennel Club in the UK has relaxed some of the breed standards and, along with the breed clubs, is making great strides to improve the health of pedigree (purebred) dogs.

Because the Cockapoo is a crossbreed, there is no Kennel Club or AKC breed standard. The Cockapoo Club of Great Britain (CCGB) promotes a '**breeding standard**' - rather than a breed standard – which promotes ethical breeding and allows for variations in appearance. The CCGB says that "healthy and fit for purpose" should be the main consideration for Cockapoo breeders. The American Cockapoo Club does have a written breed standard, and this is it:

The American Cockapoo Club Breed Standard

General Appearance. Cockapoos have a sturdy, squarely-built appearance. The length from the body measured from the breastbone to the rump is approximately the same-to-slightly longer than the height from the highest point of the shoulder to the ground. He stands up well at the shoulder on straight forelegs with a top line that is level-to-slightly sloping toward moderately-bent hindquarters. He is a dog capable of great speed and endurance, combined with agility. The body must be of sufficient length to permit a straight and free stride. Cockapoos should never appear low and long, or tall and gangly, but should always be in proportion.

Size and Weight. Size of Cockapoos can be influenced by either parent's recent background. Adult dogs 10" at the shoulder or less are toy size. Dogs 11"-14" at the shoulder are considered mini size, and those 15" at the shoulder and over are standard size. Cockapoo size is judged by their height, not their weight. Two dogs that are the same size can vary considerably in weight depending both on their overall build and whether one is fat or thin. Weights of individuals will depend on the factors explained above. To give a general idea of weight, a toy would ideally weigh under 12 pounds, a Mini 13-20 pounds and a Standard 21 pounds and up.

Head, Expression. Large, round, well-set, well-spaced eyes with a keen, soulful, endearing and intelligent expression. The color of the eyes should be dark brown on dogs with black noses. Brown dogs have brown noses. Dogs with light-colored noses may have lighter (i.e.: greenish, hazel) eyes. The eyes should not have a droopy appearance. Hair should be scissored back so as not to obstruct the eyes or vision. The ears should hang fairly close to the head, starting above the eyes and hanging to well below eye level. They should be well-feathered, but never erect or carried up over the head. Ideally the bottom of the ears should be level with the beard. The skull is moderately rounded but not exaggerated, with no tendency towards flatness.

Bite. Aligned bite, with neither over- nor under-bite. Level bites (incisors striking edge to edge) are acceptable, but scissors bite (lower incisors striking just behind the uppers) is preferred.

Neck, Top Line, Body. The neck rises strongly from the shoulders and arches slightly as it tapers to join the head. Carried high and with dignity, the neck is never pendulous (no throatiness - skin tight). The top line is level- to-slightly sloping toward the hindquarters. The chest is deep and moderately wide, with well-sprung ribs, its lowest point no higher than the elbow.

Tail. The tail is set on line with the back and carried on line with the top line or higher; when the dog is in motion the tail action is merry. The tail can be left long or docked like the parent breeds; both are acceptable. The tail should be well feathered and full coated when left long. If not docked, the tail is to be curled up over the back and left long, never shaven. If docked, tail should be no more and no less than 4 inches.

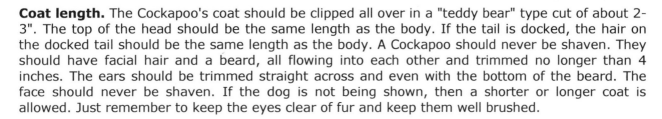

Forequarters. The shoulders are well laid back, forming an angle with the upper arm of approximately 90 degrees, permitting easy movement and forward reach. When viewed from the side with the forelegs vertical, the elbow is directly below the highest point of the shoulder blade. Forelegs are parallel, straight, with strong pasterns. Legs should be set close to the body. Front dew claws can be left or removed, back dew claws should be removed. Feet should be in balanced proportion with the dog; however, the feet should be compact, with arched toes and turn neither in nor out.

Hindquarters. When viewed from behind, the legs are parallel when in motion and at rest. Moderately angled at the stifle, and clearly defined thighs. When standing, the rear toes should be behind the point of the rump.

Coat Types. As with many other breeds, Cockapoos have three different coat types. There is the tight curly coat, the medium curl, and the flat coat. While we strive for the medium curl, all three coat types are acceptable. It is very common to see all three types within the same litter of pups. This can happen with 1st, 2nd, 3rd (etc). generation litters.

Coat length. The Cockapoo's coat should be clipped all over in a "teddy bear" type cut of about 2-3". The top of the head should be the same length as the body. If the tail is docked, the hair on the docked tail should be the same length as the body. A Cockapoo should never be shaven. They should have facial hair and a beard, all flowing into each other and trimmed no longer than 4 inches. The ears should be trimmed straight across and even with the bottom of the beard. The face should never be shaven. If the dog is not being shown, then a shorter or longer coat is allowed. Just remember to keep the eyes clear of fur and keep them well brushed.

Color and Markings. Any solid color; parti color (two or more solid colors, one of which must be white); phantom (brown, black or silver body with contrasting color on legs, under tail, eyebrows, side of face, inside ears); sable (may be black, brown, brindle, changing to silver, silver/gold mix, red, brown, other, all with darker points); tri-color (parti color with white base and tan markings over each eye, on the sides of the muzzle/cheeks, on the underside of the ears, on all feet and/or legs and optionally on the chest). Merle and/or roan are also acceptable colors. The nose and rims of eyes should be one solid color. Brown colored dogs may have brown noses, eye rims, lips, dark toenails and dark amber eyes. Black, blue, gray, cream and white dogs have black noses, eye rims and lips, black or self colored toenails and very dark eyes. In light-colored dogs, the liver-colored nose is quite common.

What the Owners Say

Breeder Karol Watson Todd, of KaroColin Cockapoos, Lincolnshire, England, asked a number of her puppy parents just what they thought of their Cockapoos. (All the dogs are under three years old). Here's what they have to say:

Keith and Diane: "Any potential owners of Cockapoos need to think very hard about why they want one. These are not dogs for just sitting at your feet all day long. They need plenty of exercise. Our Zippy has up to two or three hours a day and she always wants more. She needs grooming every day so the coat doesn't get matted and she visits a groomer's for a trim etc. once every six to eight weeks. They are wonderful companions and learn things very, very quickly. They idolise their owners, especially if they are treated correctly and are well looked after.

"Zippy is also becoming a wonderful agility dog and she loves every minute of it. They must be well trained or else they will take as many liberties with you as they possibly can. They do tend to jump up at people, but that really is part of their nature; they just love giving and receiving affection. They are a wonderful breed of dog - loving, friendly, caring, busy and we would not be without our Zippy. We may have only had her for a year, but she has completely transformed our lives, and we are loving every single minute of her being around us. She is absolutely gorgeous, but then we are big softies!"

Mal and Fiona: "Harry is EPIC! He is very greedy too, he will eat almost anything. He loves to be fussed – surprise, surprise! He's shy of people he doesn't know, but he usually gets used to them. Harry usually takes shoes, socks, underwear, teddies and more. He's a quick learner and has dog training, so he knows Sit, Lie Down, Dance, High Five, Wait, Stay, Stand, Heel, Let's Go and Get Becky, Feedies, Play, Fetch and OK. He's a very loyal and caring dog who gets very excited when he sees someone he knows. Harry loves to play and have a good run; he loves walks. Harry's a joy and has already got a girlfriend! He is growing up in Stafford and loves to go and have a run off the lead and always comes back ...well, nearly always!"

Judith and Patrick: "Daisy is beautiful. She has a lovely gentle nature and is very calm, although there is a feisty side to her, too. She loves water and getting wet and muddy, and adores jumping and climbing. In the woods we have seen her try to run up tree trunks! Daisy is going to the hairdressers next week. There is never a dull moment with Daisy, but we wouldn't have it any other way. She has a wonderful character; she gives love unconditionally and is always smiling and wagging her tail."

Lorraine and Geoff: "Our lovely girl is called Daisy Mae and she is as mad as a box of frogs, but we love her to bits! She has changed our lovely quiet lives into utter turmoil and put years on us. Only today we walked into the lounge and Daisy has pulled the Xmas tree over and had lights wrapped around her.

"Daisy Mae loves to be fussed and has to follow the same daily walk routine in the hope of seeing all the people who love to fuss her. People think she is so pretty and Daisy Mae usually rolls in her back, legs in air so she can be tickled. We have just had an eight-week-old kitten and, right from the beginning, Daisy Mae and Tuppence spend lots of time together - mostly racing up and down and stealing each other toys and sleeping together on the bed. She is so good and gentle with Tuppence. We love her to bits she brightens our lives. She loves her toys and when she's out in the fields love to chase balls, she runs and tumbles but she does like to roll in fox poo, we think because she loves a bath."

Alexia and Lindsay: Millie is an absolute joy. She can be manic, playful, cuddly and a couch potato, depending on what's going on. Her biggest disappointment in life is that our three cats don't want to play with her. She loves running across the fields, springing up and down in the scrub, following her nose or chasing birds or leaves, often jumping like a Springer. She usually comes when called or whistled and has picked up every command I've taught her very quickly, but won't always DO them. She was one of the smallest of the litter and is now 10.45kg. She loves having a shower after a walk, and constantly wags her tail. She loves people, dogs and life - a very happy, smiling, bundle of excitement and joy."

Amanda: "Barney is such a lovely little dog; great with our two girls and known by everyone in our village. He loves cuddles and generally following me around all day. Millie looks as if she gets as dirty as Barney, who has at least one bath a week. I would highly recommend Cockapoos, especially if you have children, as they are extremely loving, gentle and trustworthy. They do thrive on company and love affection. Barney loves playing with his ball and swimming."

Liz: "Alfie lives in Telford with Liz, Andy, Hannah (7) and Sam (5). Alfie is amazing - generally very chilled and, dare I say, a little bit lazy! He has his mad moments - generally with Sam (who has severe learning difficulties). Alfie has been fantastic with the children and is such a good addition to our family. He does like rolling in stinky stuff, though!"

Jo and Paul: "Jasper is a lovely dog who loves cuddles and having his tummy tickled. He is great with our children and most people who meet him liken him to a teddy bear! He loves playing rough and tumble with his brother, Alfie, and getting up to plenty of mischief if he thinks no one is looking. Alfie and Jasper live around the corner from each other."

Sarah and Debra: "We love Duffy and he's brought so much joy, fun and exercise to our family life. We own a motorhome and love to travel at any opportunity, so this year Duffy has been to Spain (twice), France, Italy, Germany, Austria and Belgium. He's dug in the sand, swum in the Med, been on a bus, a tram, a boat, the underground, a ski slope, a mountain stream...... in fact we've just calculated that he's travelled 8,500 miles since January! I think he's a walking ad for a pet passport!"

Jane and Jeremy: "We are the proud owners of Dylan, who had a huge appetite from Day One. What can we say about Dylan - lively, loyal (well, to Jeremy anyway), loving, adorable, wonderful with children and now thinks when passing anyone in the street that they are there to see him and give cuddles. I've lost count of the number of people that stop us and want to know what breed he his and cuddle him. Oh yes, and he still has a huge appetite!"

Debra: "Teddy is absolutely gorgeous and so much fun to have around. She's gentle and playful and incredibly easy-going, taking just about everything in her stride. (She's not keen on men in hats, but then I guess we've all got our little quirks!) She loves playing with other dogs and takes every opportunity to try to when we're out on a walk - most are equally happy to play with her. She was very good at puppy training - she's great at recall, unless there's a bird flying around to distract her. And she loves shoes, probably her favourite thing in the world to chew. She also loves being in the mud."

Jo: "Luna is the ultimate family dog for us and so I've realised all my photos tend to be of her rolling about on the floor with the kids! I love to walk, however, and so the other thing I love about her is her gusto and great enthusiasm to walk too. I let her off the lead from the word go and her recall now is amazing - she's busy chasing a pheasant through the undergrowth, but the moment she hears her whistle, she's back. She gives her absolute attention and loves training."

Sarah: "Cockapoos are excellent family dogs; my nine-year-old daughter and Lola are the best of friends. They are such an intelligent breed and pick up most commands easily unless distracted - Lola loves barking at other dogs and chasing cats! I think it's really important to meet the puppy's parents as we all did. Lola's friendly temperament is often commented on. Lola loves lots of exercise and running with other dogs, and enjoys new experiences, like her first visit to the beach this year. She just went off kibble and is now on a raw diet - Natural Instinct - which she is thriving on. She has the sweetest temperament and everyone loves her!"

Christine: "We are utterly delighted with our little girl. Amber has a beautiful nature and is very gentle and affectionate with everyone - even the smallest of children. She is also very clever and picks up commands very easily. But it's more than that; she is so eager to please that she seems to know what is required without you training her. Seriously, we are quite amazed at times.

"One thing that we have discovered is how much exercise Amber needs. We give her at least two hours a day on two or three walks, and she seems to have a never-ending supply of energy. Not a problem for us as we love walking, but anyone unable or unprepared for this commitment should probably think twice before parenting a Cockapoo!"

And finally, we asked breeders to sum up Cockapoos in four words:

> ➤ Wonderful, loving, carefree, loyal
> ➤ Affectionate, clever, fun, energetic
> ➤ Playful, loyal, funny, intelligent
> ➤ Cute, smart, fun, tractable
> ➤ Friendly, loyal, intelligent, perfect!
> ➤ Loyal, loving, intelligent, playful
> ➤ Friendly, family-orientated, characters, stunning
> ➤ Loving, affectionate, playful, a true family member and the best dog you will ever own (OK, so it's not four words, but you get the picture!)

Now you've met the Cockapoo, read on to find the right puppy and then learn how to take good care of the newest member of your family for the rest of his or her life.

2. Choosing a Cockapoo Puppy

Are You Ready?

With their big appealing eyes, silky soft fur and endearing personalities there are few more appealing things on this Earth than a litter of Cockapoo puppies. If you go to view a litter, the pups are sure to melt your heart and it is extremely difficult – if not downright impossible - to walk away without choosing one.

However, the best way to select a puppy is with your head and not with your heart. Do your research before you visit any litters to make sure you select a responsible breeder with health-tested parents (of the puppy, not the breeder!) and who knows Cockapoos inside out. After all, apart from getting married or having a baby, getting a puppy is one of the most important, demanding, expensive and life-enriching decisions you will ever make.

Just like babies, puppies will love you unconditionally - but there is a price to pay. In return for their loyalty and devotion, you have to fulfil your part of the bargain.

In the beginning you have to be prepared to devote several hours a day to your new puppy. You have to feed him several times a day and housetrain him virtually every hour; you have to give him your attention and start to gently introduce the rules of the house as well as take care of his general health and welfare. You also have to be prepared to part with hard cash for regular healthcare and pet insurance. Chocolate box pretty is eight-week-old Hermione (pictured), of Julie Shearman's Crystalwood Cockapoos, Devon, UK.

If you are not prepared, or unable, to devote the time and money to a new arrival – or if you are out at work all day – then now might not be the right time to consider getting a puppy. Cockapoos are, above all, dogs which physically **need** to be with their people, they stick to you like Velcro. Separation anxiety is not uncommon and if left alone too long, their natural sunny temperaments can change when they become unhappy. If you are out at work all day these are NOT the dogs for you; to leave a Cockapoo alone for long periods is just not fair on this lovable dog that is happiest when he's with you.

Pick a healthy pup and he or she will probably live well into the teens, so it is definitely a long-term commitment. Before taking the plunge, ask yourself some questions:

Have I Got Enough Time?

In the first days after leaving his - or her - mother and littermates, your puppy will feel very lonely and maybe even a little afraid. You and your family have to spend time with your new arrival to make him feel safe and sound. Ideally, for the first few days you will be around all of the time to help him settle and to start bonding with him. If you work, book a couple of weeks off, but don't just get a puppy and leave him alone in the house a few days later.

As well as housetraining, short sessions of behaviour training are also recommended to curb puppy biting and to teach your new pup the rules of the house. Before his vaccinations have finished, start the socialisation process by taking him out of the home to see buses, trains, noisy traffic, kids, etc. - but make sure you CARRY HIM. Cockapoos can be very sensitive to all sorts of things and it's important to start the socialisation process as soon as possible. The more he is introduced to at this early stage, the better.

Once he has had the all-clear after his vaccinations, get into the habit of taking him out of the house and garden or yard for a short walk every day – more as he gets older. New surroundings stimulate his interest and help to stop him from becoming bored and developing unwanted character traits. Spend some time gently brushing your Cockapoo and checking his ears are clean to get him used to being handled and groomed right from the beginning. You'll also need to factor in time to visit the vet's surgery for regular healthcare visits and annual vaccinations.

How Long Can I Leave Him?

This is a question we get asked all of the time and one which causes a lot of debate among owners and prospective owners. All dogs are pack animals; their natural state is to be with others. Being alone is not normal for them, although many have to get used to it.

Another issue is the toilet; all Cockapoos have smaller bladders than humans. Forget the emotional side of it, how would you like to be left for eight hours without being able to visit the bathroom? So how many hours can you leave a dog alone? Well, a useful guide comes from the canine rescue organisations. In the UK, they will not allow anybody to adopt if they are intending to leave the dog alone for more than four or five hours a day.

Dogs left at home alone all day become bored and, in the case of Cockapoos and other breeds which are highly dependent on human company, they may well become depressed. Of course, it depends on the character and temperament of your dog, but a lonely Cockapoo may display signs of unhappiness by being destructive, digging, chewing, barking or urinating.

A puppy or fully-grown dog must NEVER be left shut in a crate all day. It is OK to leave a puppy or adult dog in a crate if he or she is happy there, but all our breeders said the same: the door should never be closed for more than two or three hours during the day. A crate is a place where a puppy or adult should feel safe, not a prison. Ask yourself why you want a dog – is it for selfish reasons or can you really offer a good home to a young puppy - and then adult dog - for 15 years or even longer? Would it be more sensible to wait until you are at home more?

Is My Home Suitable?

Cockapoos are adaptable; they can live on a farm or in an apartment - much depends on what they get used to as puppies. However, Cockapoos generally have fairly high exercise requirements – especially those bred from working Spaniels – and so need regular access to the outdoors. Part of this time should ideally be spent off the lead. Half, or at least some, of your puppy's ancestors have been bred to run all day through the undergrowth. One of the main reasons for Cockapoos ending up in rescue centres is due to issues related to not getting enough exercise.

Cockapoos are highly intelligent and sensitive, and breeders find them one of the easiest (cross)breeds to housetrain – provided you are diligent in the beginning. See **Chapter 5** for more information on how to housetrain your puppy. If you are one of the few Cockapoo owners who lives in an apartment, it is very important to take him outside to perform his duty many times a day to start with if you don't want your pup to eliminate indoors. If you can continue to do this three or four times daily then there is no need to indoor housetrain him. And if you live in a house with a yard or garden, don't leave your puppy unattended; dognapping is becoming increasingly common, particularly with the high price of pups. Make sure there are no poisonous plants or chemicals out there which he could eat or drink. Common plants toxic to dogs include crocus, daffodil, azalea, wisteria, cyclamen, sweet pea, lily of the valley, tulips, hyacinth and lily.

Cockapoo-proofing your home should involve moving anything sharp, breakable or chewable - including your shoes - out of reach to sharp little teeth. Make sure he can't chew electrical cords – lift them off the floor if necessary, and block off any off-limits areas of the house, such as upstairs or your bedroom, with a child gate or barrier, especially as he will probably be following you around the house in the first few days.

Family and Children

What about the other members of your family? Do they all want the puppy as well? A puppy will grow into a dog which will become a part of your family for many years to come. If you have children they will, of course, be delighted. One of the wonderful things about Cockapoos is how naturally good they are with children; they love to be around them.

But remember that puppies are small and delicate, as are babies, so you should never leave babies or very small children and dogs alone together – no matter how well they get along. Small kids lack co-ordination and a young Cockapoo may inadvertently get poked in the eye or trodden on if you don't keep an eye on him or her. Often puppies regard children as playmates (just like a small child regards a puppy as a playmate) and so the young dog might chase, jump and nip with sharp teeth. This is not aggression; this is normal play for puppies. Train yours to be gentle with your children and your children to be gentle with your dog. See **Chapter 7. Exercise and Training** on how to deal with puppy biting.

Discourage the kids from constantly picking up your gorgeous new puppy. They should learn respect for the dog, which is a living creature with his or her own needs, not a toy. Make sure your puppy gets enough time to sleep – **which is most of the time in the beginning** - so don't let your children constantly pester him. Sleep is very important to puppies, just as it is for babies. Allow your Cockapoo to eat at his or her own pace uninterrupted; letting youngsters play with the dog while eating is a no-no as it may promote gulping of food or food aggression.

Another reason some dogs end up in rescue centres is that owners are unable to cope with the demands of small children AND a dog. On the other hand, it is also a fantastic opportunity for you to educate your little darlings (both human and canine) on how to get along with each other and set the pattern for wonderful life-long friendships.

Single People

Many single adults own dogs, but if you live alone, having a puppy will require a lot of dedication on your part. There will be nobody to share the responsibility, so taking on a dog requires a huge commitment and a lot of your time if the dog is to have a decent life. If you are out of the house all day as well, it is not really fair to get a puppy, or even an adult dog. Left alone all day, they will feel isolated, bored and sad. However, if you work from home or are at home all day and you can spend considerable time with the puppy every day, then great; a Cockapoo will become your best friend.

Older People

If you are older or have elderly relatives living with you, the good news is that Cockapoos are great company. They love to be with people and are affectionate, provided they get enough exercise. If you are older, make sure you have the energy and patience to deal with a young puppy. And ask yourself if you are fit enough to take your dog for a couple of walks (or paddles in the case of this man!) every day.

Dogs can be great for older people. My father is in his mid-80s, but takes his dog out walking for an hour to 90 minutes every day - a morning and an afternoon walk – even in the rain or snow. It's good for him and it's good for the dog, helping to keep both of them fit and socialised! They get fresh air, exercise and the chance to communicate with other dogs and their humans.

Cockapoos are also great company indoors – you're never alone when you've got a dog. Many older people get a dog after losing a loved one (a husband, wife or previous much-loved dog). A pet gives them something to care for and love, as well as a constant companion. However, owning a dog is not cheap, so it's important to be able to afford annual pet insurance, veterinary fees, a quality pet food, etc. The RSPCA in the UK has estimated that owning a dog costs an average of around £1,300 ($2,000) a year.

Other Pets

If you already have other pets in your household, they may not be too happy at the arrival of your new addition - although your new Cockapoo will generally get on well with other pets. However, it might not be a good idea to leave your hamster or pet rabbit running loose with your pup, most dogs have some prey instinct. In the beginning spend time to introduce them to each other gradually and supervise the sessions. Cockapoo puppies are naturally curious, lively and playful and they will sniff and investigate other pets. You may have to separate them to start off with, or put your boisterous and playful Cockapoo puppy into a pen or crate initially to allow a cat to investigate without being mauled by the hyper active pup, which thinks the cat is a great playmate.

This will also prevent your Cockapoo from being injured. If the two animals are free and the cat lashes out he or she could scratch your pup's eyes. Just type 'Cockapoo and cat' into YouTube to see what can happen if you leave them to their own devices unsupervised. A timid cat might need protection from a bold, playful Cockapoo - or vice versa. A bold cat and a timid young Cockapoo will probably settle down together quickest! If things seem to be going well with no aggression after one or two supervised sessions, then let them loose together. Take the process slowly, if your cat is stressed and frightened he may decide to leave. Our feline friends are notorious for abandoning home because the food and facilities are better down the road. Until you know that they can get on, don't leave them alone together.

Cockapoos generally get on well with other dogs. If you already have other dogs, supervised sessions from an early age will help them to get along and for the other dogs to accept your friendly new Cockapoo. If you are thinking about getting more than one pup, you might consider waiting until your first Cockapoo is an adolescent or adult before getting a second, so your older dog is calmer and can help train the younger one. Coping with, training and housetraining one puppy is hard enough, without having to do it with two. On the other hand, some owners prefer to get the messy part over and done with in one go and get two together – but this will require a lot of your time for the first few weeks.

As with all dogs, how well they get on also depends on the temperament of the individuals. With another dog, it is important to initially introduce the two on neutral territory, rather than in areas one pet deems his own. You don't want one dog to feel he has to protect his territory. If you think there may be issues, walking the dogs parallel to each other before heading home for the first time is one way of getting them used to each other.

Other Factors

You have to decide whether you want a male or a female puppy. In terms of gender, much depends on the temperament of the individual dog - the differences WITHIN the sexes is greater than the differences BETWEEN the sexes. Unless you are planning to breed your dog, the size and temperament should be major considerations – males are generally larger than females. However, one difference is that on walks a male will stop a lot to mark his territory by urinating, while a female will urinate much less frequently.

If you already have dogs or are thinking of getting more than one, you do, however, have to consider gender. You cannot expect an un-neutered male to live with an unspayed female without problems. Similarly, two uncastrated males may not get along, there will simply be too much testosterone and competition. If an existing dog is neutered (male) or spayed (female) and you plan to have your puppy neutered or spayed, then the gender should not be an issue.

If you are intending to get more than one dog, there is also the question of whether to get two puppies from the same litter or not. Some owners have done this very successfully; some animal psychologists claim that each puppy's first loyalty will always be to the other puppy, rather than you, as that initial bond from birth has never been broken.

A lot of people select a Cockapoo based on colour, and what a choice...there can be few types of dog with so many different colours and coat patterns. However, we would suggest that colour is not as important as size and temperament, and the colour can also change between puppyhood and adulthood. Chat with the breeder who knows her puppies well; discuss which puppy would best fit in with your household and lifestyle. That beautiful chocolate Cockapoo with the slightly timid disposition may not be the best choice if you have a busy house full of kids and other pets.

Top 10 Tips for Working Cockapoo Owners

We would certainly not recommend getting a Cockapoo if you are out at work all day, but if you're determined to get one when you're out for several hours at a time, here are some useful points:

1. Either come home during your lunch break to let your dog out or employ a dog walker (or neighbour) to take him out for a walk in the middle of the day

2. Do you know anybody you could leave your dog with during the day? Consider leaving the dog with a friend, relative or elderly neighbour who would welcome the companionship of a Cockapoo without the full responsibility of ownership

3. Take him for a walk before you go to work – even if this means getting up at the crack of dawn – and spend time with him as soon as you get home. Exercise generates serotonin in the brain and has a calming effect. A dog that has been exercised will be less anxious and more ready for a good nap

4. Leave him in a place of his own where he feels comfortable. If you use a crate, leave the door open, otherwise his favourite dog bed or chair. If possible, leave him in a room with a view of the outside world; this will be more interesting than staring at four blank walls

5. Make sure that it does not get too hot during the day and there are no cold draughts in the place where you leave him

6. Food and drink: Although most Cockapoos love their food, it is still generally a good idea to put food down at specific meal times and remove it after 15 or 20 minutes if uneaten. If food is left out all day, your dog may become a fussy eater or 'punish' you for leaving him alone by refusing to eat. Make sure he has access to water at all times. Dogs cannot cool down by sweating; they do not have many sweat glands (which is why they pant, but this is much less efficient than perspiring) and can die without sufficient water

7. Leave toys available to play with to prevent destructive chewing (a popular occupation of bored Cockapoos or one suffering from separation anxiety). Stuff a Kong toy with treats to keep him occupied for a while. Choose the right size of Kong, you can even smear the inside with peanut butter or another favourite to keep him occupied for longer

8. Consider getting a companion for your Cockapoo. This will involve even more of your time and twice the expense, and if you have not got time for one dog, you have hardly time for

two. A better idea is to find someone you can leave the dog with during the day; there are also dog sitters and doggie day care for those who can afford them

9. Consider leaving a radio or TV on very softly in the background. The 'white noise' can have a soothing effect on some pets. If you do this, select your channel carefully – try and avoid one with lots of bangs and crashes or heavy metal music!

10. Stick to the same routine before you leave your dog home alone. This will help him to feel secure. Before you go to work, get into a daily habit of getting yourself ready, then feeding and exercising your Cockapoo. Dogs love routine. But don't make a huge fuss of him when you leave as this can also stress the dog; just leave the house calmly

Similarly when you come home, your Cockapoo will feel starved of attention and be pleased to see you. Greet him normally, but try not to go overboard by making too much of a fuss as soon as you walk through the door. Give him a pat and a stroke then take off your coat and do a few other things before turning your attention back to him. Lavishing your Cockapoo with too much attention the second you walk through the door may encourage needy behaviour or separation anxiety.

Puppy Stages

It is important to understand how a puppy develops into a fully grown dog. This knowledge will help you to be a good owner. **The first few months and weeks of a puppy's life will have an effect on his behaviour and character for the rest of his life.** This Puppy Schedule will help you to understand the early stages:

Birth to seven weeks	A puppy needs sleep, food and warmth. He needs his mother for security and discipline and littermates for learning and socialisation. The puppy learns to function within a pack and learns the pack order of dominance. He begins to become aware of his environment. During this period, puppies should be left with their mother.
Eight to 12 weeks	A puppy should NOT leave his mother before eight weeks. At this age the brain is fully developed and **he now needs socialising with the outside world**. He needs to change from being part of a canine pack to being part of a human pack. This period is a fear period for the puppy; avoid causing him fright and pain.
13 to 16 weeks	Training and formal obedience should begin. **This is a critical period for socialising with other humans, places and situations.** This period will pass easily if you remember that this is a puppy's change to adolescence. Be firm and fair. His flight instinct may be prominent. Avoid being too strict or too soft with him during this time and praise his good behaviour.
Four to eight months	Another fear period for a puppy is between seven to eight months of age. It passes quickly, but be cautious of fright or pain which may leave the puppy traumatised. The puppy reaches sexual maturity and dominant traits are established. Your Cockapoo should now understand the following commands: 'sit', 'down', 'come' and 'stay'.

Plan Ahead

Most puppies leave the litter for their new homes when they are eight weeks or older. It is important that puppies have time to develop and learn the rules of the pack from their mothers. Some Spaniels take a little longer to develop physically and mentally, and a puppy which leaves the litter too early may suffer with issues, for example a lack of confidence throughout life. Breeders who allow their pups to leave before the correct time may be more interested in a quick buck than a long-term puppy placement. If you want a well-bred Cockapoo puppy, it pays to plan ahead as many good Cockapoo breeders have waiting lists.

Choosing the right breeder is one of the most important decisions you will make. (Pictured is a litter of MoonShine Cockapoos, bred by Rebecca Mae Goins in Indiana).

Like humans, your puppy will be a product of his or her parents and will inherit many of their characteristics. His temperament and how healthy your puppy will be now and throughout his life will largely depend on the genes of his parents.

It is essential that you select a responsible, ethical breeder. They will have checked out the health records and temperament of the parents and will only breed from suitable stock. Good breeding comes at a price and if a puppy is being sold for less, you have to ask why. Some Cockapoo breeders have their own websites and many are trustworthy and conscientious. You have to learn to spot the good ones from the bad ones.

Because of these high prices, unscrupulous breeders with little knowledge of the breed have sprung up, tempted by the prospect of making easy cash. A healthy Cockapoo will be your irreplaceable companion for the next decade or more, so why buy an unseen or imported puppy, or one from a pet shop or general advertisement? Good breeders do not sell their dogs on general purpose websites or in pet shops. Many reputable breeders do not have to advertise, such is the demand for their puppies - so it's up to you to do your research to find a really good breeder.

At the very minimum you MUST visit the breeder personally and follow our **Top 10 Tips for Selecting a Good Breeder** to help you make the right decision. Buying a poorly-bred puppy may save you a few hundred pounds or dollars in the short term, but could cost you thousands in extra veterinary bills in the long run; not to mention the terrible heartache of having a sickly dog. Rescue groups know only too well the dangers of buying a poorly-bred dog; years of problems can arise, usually health-related, but there can also be temperament issues, or bad behaviour due to lack of socialisation at the breeder's.

This is the advice from the British Cockapoo Society:

"So after a lot of thought you have decided to get a Cockapoo puppy and are starting on your search. It is an exciting time and all you want to do is go out and bring home the little bundle of fun. It is important though to stop for a minute and think, because this is a really important decision you are making and you need to do it properly.

"Your puppy will grow into a pooch that could be with you and your family for ten years or more so you want to make sure you choose the right one, and that it has had a good, healthy start in life. Don't just go with the first breeder you find - you need one with a good reputation and who breeds healthy

Cockapoo pups. Unfortunately not all breeders are ethical or good, so you do need to take a bit of time and do your research.

"Starting off on your search can seem a bit daunting - it is a big responsibility after all, but there are some simple things to do to start you off. Talking to other Cockapoo owners is a great way of finding out information and views, not only about the dogs, but where they come from and whether a particular breeder offered a good service. We have an active Facebook chat page where members chat, exchange stories and ask for advice: www.facebook.com/britishcockapoosociety

"Some Cockapoo forums and clubs organise members' walks - ask if you can go along and meet them even if you don't have a dog yet. There is nothing better than seeing a load of Cockapoos running and playing together! Check out the British Cockapoo Society Events page for details of our walks: www.britishcockapoosociety.com

"Search online for Cockapoo breeders' websites but don't take them at face value. The glitzy, smart looking page may not be all it seems, so read what they have to say, but keep an open mind. Look at pet advertising sites like Breeders Online www.breedersonline.co.uk for breeders in your area and to see if they have pups available.

"Don't be fooled by a flashy website and just decide to go with that person - unfortunately there are some unscrupulous people out there and care has to be taken. Have a word with other owners, your local vet, do a search online and join forums and clubs and ask on there too. You can never have too much information.

"Decide if you want to go with a large scale, commercial breeder (breeding more than five litters a year and licensed with the local council) a hobby breeder who breeds less than five litters a year or a person who just breeds a litter now and then, often from their own pet."

In the UK, The Cockapoo Club of Great Britain (CCGB) has a list of approved breeders who have agreed to abide by their Code of Ethics, which strongly promotes animal welfare and breeding from only the best and healthiest dogs: www.cockapooclubgb.co.uk/ccgb-approved-breeders.html Litters from parents with fully accounted pedigrees and health tests are eligible for CCGB Lineage Registration Papers. This is the paperwork which the CCGB says new owners can expect to receive from approved breeders:

> ➢ Vet record of first vaccination
> ➢ CCGB Puppy Care and Training leaflet
> ➢ Worming and flea treatments details
> ➢ Microchip paperwork
> ➢ Health testing on parent(s)
> ➢ Pedigree Certificates from both parents (only applies to F1 puppies)

In the USA a good place to start your search for a breeder is at the American Cockapoo Club (ACC) www.americancockapooclub.com which has a list of breeders who have all agreed to abide by the ACC's Code of Ethics, which states:

ACC Breeder Code of Ethics

We encourage spay and neutering of all Cockapoos not being used in a breeding program and that are not of breeding quality. It is important that only Cockapoos that show breed standard be used in breeding programs.

General:

1. Members of the American Cockapoo Club have an obligation to protect the interest of the breed by conducting themselves with integrity in all manner of business relating to the American Cockapoo Club.

2. Members are expected to observe the highest standards of sportsmanship.

3. Members breeding litters or who allow the use of their stud dog to the same end, shall direct their efforts toward producing Cockapoos of exceptional quality, temperament and condition.

4. Members shall not engage in false or misleading advertising or misrepresentation of the breed, nor shall they malign their competition by making false or misleading statements regarding their competitors' dogs, breeding practice or person.

5. Inappropriate words or photos are not allowed on the American Cockapoo Club website. The American Cockapoo Club reserves the right to, immediately and without notice, remove any and all material posted on this website if it is deemed inappropriate by the owners of the American Cockapoo Club. A violation of this policy may result in immediate termination of membership

Breeders shall:

6. Be familiar with the breed standards for their breeding dogs and strive to breed only those dogs which conform to each breed standard.

7. Be familiar with the Terms of Membership of the American Cockapoo Club and abide by these rules.

8. Use for breeding only those dogs which they believe to be healthy and free from serious congenital and hereditary defects.

9. Produce puppies only when they have the time and facilities to provide adequate attention to physical and emotional development.

10. Retain or house only the number of dogs for which they have adequate facilities.

11. Not knowingly breed a dog that has become affected with or has produced any serious inherited defects.

12. Keep clear records of dogs bred, dates of breedings and whelpings, and number of puppies in each litter.

13. Maintain the best possible standards of health for the animals and care of their kennels. This includes, but is not limited to, keeping all dogs in sanitary conditions, housing appropriate for the climate, adequately sized runs, proper nutrition and veterinary care.

14. Ensure that puppies are never shipped or delivered in dirty, matted condition.

15. Not sell puppies to pet shops, either outright or on consignment, or supply puppies for auctions, raffles or other such enterprises.

16. Take responsibly for any and all Cockapoos that they have bred for the life of that Cockapoo in order to take the burden off rescue groups. Provide written, fully executed guarantee, health records, and American Cockapoo Club registration material to the puppy buyer before or during the delivery of the puppy.

17. Breeders must provide American Cockapoo Registration Numbers of sire and dam on the written guarantee.

18. Remember that a Code of Ethics is more than a set of rules; it is a commitment to a high standard of practice in owning and breeding your dogs.

American Cockapoo Club
American Cockapoo Club
Dedicated to the Preservation of the Cockapoo

Of course, there are no cast iron guarantees that your puppy will be healthy and have a good temperament, but choosing a breeder who conforms to a code of ethics is a very good place to start.

If you've never bought a puppy before, how do you avoid buying one from a 'backstreet breeder' or puppy mill? These are people who just breed puppies for profit and sell them to the first person who turns up with the cash. Unhappily, this can end in heartbreak for a family months or years later when their puppy develops health or temperament problems due to poor breeding.

Price is a good guide, a cheap puppy usually means that corners have been cut somewhere along the line. If a puppy is advertised at a couple of hundred pounds or dollars or so, then you can bet your last penny that the dam and sire are not superb examples of their breed and they haven't been fully health tested, that the puppies are not being fed premium quality food or even kept in the house with the family where the breeder should start to socialise and housetrain them. Here's some advice on what to avoid:

Where NOT to Buy a Cockapoo Puppy

Due to the high cost of Cockapoo puppies – as well as waiting lists for litters - unscrupulous breeders have sprung up to cash in on this hugely popular crossbreed. While new owners might think they have bagged 'a bargain,' this more often than not turns out to be false economy and an emotionally disastrous decision when the puppy develops health problems due to poor breeding, or behavioural problems due to lack of socialisation during the critical early phase of his or her life.

In September 2013 The UK's Kennel Club issued a warning of a puppy welfare crisis, with some truly sickening statistics. The situation is no better in America. The Press release stated:

As the popularity of online pups continues to soar:

> **Almost one in five pups bought (unseen) on websites or social media die within six months**

> One in three buy online, in pet stores and via newspaper adverts - outlets often used by puppy farmers – this is an increase from one in five in the previous year

> The problem is likely to grow as the younger generation favour mail order pups, and breeders of fashionable crossbreeds flout responsible steps

The Kennel Club said: "We are sleepwalking into a dog welfare and consumer crisis as new research shows that more and more people are buying their pups online or through pet shops, outlets often used by cruel puppy farmers, and are paying the price with their pups requiring long-term veterinary treatment or dying before six months old. The increasing popularity of online pups is a particular concern. Of those who source their puppies online, half are going on to buy 'mail order pups' directly over the internet."

The KC research found that:

> One third of people who bought their puppy online, over social media or in pet shops failed to experience 'overall good health'

> Almost one in five puppies bought via social media or the internet die before six months old

> Some 12% of puppies bought online or on social media end up with serious health problems that require expensive on-going veterinary treatment from a young age

Caroline Kisko, Kennel Club Secretary, said: "More and more people are buying puppies from sources such as the internet, which are often used by puppy farmers.

"Whilst there is nothing wrong with initially finding a puppy online, it is essential to then see the breeder and ensure that they are doing all of the right things.

"This research clearly shows that too many people are failing to do this, and the consequences can be seen in the shocking number of puppies that are becoming sick or dying. We have an extremely serious consumer protection and puppy welfare crisis on our hands."

The research revealed that the problem was likely to get worse as mail order pups bought over the internet are the second most common way for the younger generation of 18 to 24-year-olds to buy a puppy (31%).

Marc Abraham, TV vet and founder of Pup Aid, said: "Sadly, if the 'buy it now' culture persists, then this horrific situation will only get worse. There is nothing wrong with sourcing a puppy online, but people need to be aware of what they should then expect from the breeder.

"For example, you should not buy a car without getting its service history and seeing it at its registered address, so you certainly shouldn't buy a puppy without the correct paperwork and health certificates and without seeing where it was bred. However, too many people are opting to buy directly from third parties such as the internet, pet shops, or from puppy dealers, where you cannot possibly know how or where the puppy was raised.

"Not only are people buying sickly puppies, but many people are being scammed into paying money for puppies that don't exist, as the research showed that 7% of those who buy online were scammed in this way".

The Kennel Club has launched an online video and has a Find A Puppy app to show the dos and don'ts of buying a puppy. View the video at www.thekennelclub.org.uk/paw

Caveat Emptor – Buyer Beware

Here are some signs that a puppy may have arrived via a puppy mill, a puppy broker (somebody who makes money from buying and selling puppies) or even an importer. Our strong advice is that if you suspect that this is the case, walk away - unless you want to risk a lot of trouble and heartache in the future. You can't buy a Rolls Royce or a Lamborghini for a couple of thousand pounds or dollars - you'd immediately suspect that the 'bargain' on offer wasn't the real thing. No matter how lovely it looked, you'd be right - and the same applies to Cockapoos. Here are some signs to look out for:

> Websites – buying a puppy from a website does not necessarily mean that the puppy will turn out to have problems. But avoid websites where there are no pictures of the home, environment and owners. If they are only showing close-up photos of cute puppies, click the **X** button

> Don't buy a website puppy with a shopping cart symbol next to his picture

> Don't commit to a website puppy unless you have seen it face-to-face. If this is not possible at the very least you must speak (on the phone) with the breeder and ask questions, don't deal with an intermediary

> At the breeder's you hear: "You can't see the parent dogs because……" ALWAYS ask to see the parents and at a minimum, see the mother and how she looks and behaves

> If the breeder says that the dam and sire are Kennel Club or AKC registered, insist on seeing the registration papers – this only applies to first generation (F1) Cockapoos

> Ignore photographs of so-called 'champion' ancestors (unless you are buying from an approved breeder), in all likelihood these are fiction

- The puppies look small for their stated age. A committed Cockapoo breeder will not let her puppies leave before they are eight weeks old at least

- The person you are buying the puppy from did not breed the dog themselves

- The place you meet the puppy seller is a car park or place other than the puppies' home

- The seller tells you that the puppy comes from top, caring breeders from your or another country. Not true. There are reputable, caring breeders all over the world, but not one of them sells their puppies through brokers

- Ask to see photos of the puppy from birth to present day. If the seller has none, there is a reason – walk away

- Price – if you are offered a cheap Cockapoo, he or she almost certainly comes from dubious stock. Careful breeding, taking good care of mother and puppies and health screening all add up to one big bill for breeders. Anyone selling their puppies at a knock-down price has certainly cut corners – and this involves temperament and health screening and selective breeding

- If you get a rescue Cockapoo, make sure it is from a recognised rescue group and not a 'puppy flipper' who may be posing as a do-gooder but is in fact getting dogs – including stolen ones - from unscrupulous sources

In fact the whole brokering business is just another version of the puppy mill and should be avoided at all costs. Bear in mind that for every cute Cockapoo puppy you see from a puppy mill or broker, other puppies have died.

Good Cockapoo breeders will only breed from dogs which have been carefully selected for health, temperament, physical shape and lineage. There are plenty out there, it's just a question of finding one. The good news is that there are signs to help the savvy buyer spot a good breeder.

Top 10 Tips for Choosing a Good Breeder

1. Good Cockapoo breeders keep the dogs in the home as part of the family - not outside in kennel runs, garages or outbuildings. Check that the area where the puppies are kept is clean and that the puppies themselves look clean. Pictured are a couple of pups making a mess in the home of CCGB-approved breeder Eileen Jackson, of Brimstone Cockapoos, Cambridgeshire, England

2. Their Cockapoos appear happy and healthy. Check that the pup has clean eyes, ears, nose and bum (butt) with no discharge. The pups are alert, excited to meet new people and don't shy away from visitors

3. A good breeder will encourage you to spend time with the puppy's parents - or at least the mother - when you visit. They want your family to meet the puppy and are happy for you to visit more than once

4. They are very familiar with Cockapoos, although they may also breed other breeds and crossbreeds, it is better if these are related types – e.g. Spaniels, or Poodle crosses

5. Cockapoos can have genetic weaknesses. Although not compulsory, good breeders have health certificates at the very least for eyes and possibly hip dysplasia – also the kidney disease FN (affects Cockapoos bred from English Cocker Spaniels), blood disease PFK (American Cockers and their offspring) and von Willebrand's (Miniature Poodles and their offspring)

6. All responsible breeders should provide you with a written contract and health guarantee and allow you plenty of time to read it. They will also show you records of the puppy's visits to the vet, vaccinations, worming medication, etc and explain what other vaccinations your puppy will need

7. They feed their adults and puppies high quality dog food and give you some to take home and guidance on feeding and caring for your puppy. They will also be available for advice after you take your puppy home

8. They don't always have pups available, but keep a list of interested people for the next available litter

9. They don't over-breed, but do limit the number of litters from their dams. Over-breeding or breeding from older females can be detrimental to the female's health

10. If you have selected a breeder and checked if/when she has puppies available, go online to the Cockapoo forums before you visit and ask if anyone out there already has a dog from this breeder. If you are buying from a good breeder, the chances are someone will know her dogs or at least her reputation. If the feedback is negative, cancel your visit and start looking for another breeder

And finally ... good Cockapoo breeders want to know their beloved pups are going to good homes and will ask YOU a lot of questions about your suitability as owners. DON'T buy a puppy from a website or advert where a PayPal or credit card deposit secures you a puppy without any questions.

There's no chance of these puppies getting bored! Picture courtesy of CCGB-approved breeder Karol Watson Todd, of KaroColin Cockapoos, Lincolnshire, England.

Cockapoo puppies should not be regarded as must-have accessories. They are not objects, they are warm-blooded, living, breathing creatures. A good breeder will, if asked, provide references from other people who have bought their puppies; call at least one before you commit. They will also agree to take a puppy back within a certain time frame if it does not work out for you, or if there is a health problem.

Healthy, happy puppies and adult dogs are what everybody wants. Taking the time now to find a responsible and committed breeder with well-bred Cockapoos is time well spent. It could save you a lot of time, money and heartache in the future and help to ensure that you and your chosen puppy are happy together for many years to come.

The Most Important Questions to Ask a Breeder

Many of these points have been covered in the previous section, but here's a reminder and checklist of the questions you should be asking.

Have the parents been health screened? Buy only a pup with DNA-tested parents. Ask to see original copies of health certificates. If no certificates are available, ask what guarantees the breeder or seller is offering in terms of genetic illnesses, and how long these guarantees last – 12 weeks, a year, a lifetime? It will vary from breeder to breeder, but good ones will definitely give you some form of guarantee – always ask for this in writing. They will also want to be informed of any hereditary health problems with your puppy, as they may choose not to breed from the dam or sire (mother or father) again. Some breeders keep a chart documenting the full family health history of the pup – ask if one exists and if you can see it

Can you put me in touch with someone who already has one of your puppies?

Are you a member of one of the Cockapoo clubs or associations? Not all good Cockapoo breeders are members of a club, but clubs are often a good place to start

How long have you been breeding Cockapoos? You are looking for someone who has a track record with the breed

How many litters has the mother had? Female Cockapoos should not have litters until they are two and then only have a few litters in their lifetime, certainly not back-to-back breedings (i.e. every time she comes into season). Also check the age of the mother, too young or too old is not good for her health

What happens to the female once she has finished breeding? Are they kept as part of the family, rehomed in loving homes or sent to animal shelters?

Do you breed any other types of dog? Buy from a Cockapoo specialist

What is so special about this litter? You are looking for a breeder who has used good breeding stock and his or her knowledge to produce healthy, handsome dogs with good temperaments, not just cute dogs in fancy colours. All Cockapoo puppies look cute, don't buy the first one you see – be patient and pick the right one. If you don't get a satisfactory answer, look elsewhere

What do you feed your adults and puppies? A reputable breeder will feed a top quality dog food and advise that you do the same

What special care do you recommend? Your Cockapoo will probably need all or some of the following: regular grooming, trimming and ear cleaning

What is the average lifespan of your dogs? Generally, pups bred from healthy stock live longer

How socialised and housetrained is the puppy? Good breeders will raise their puppies as part of the household and start the socialisation and housetraining process before they leave her

What healthcare have the pups had so far? Ask to see records of flea treatments, wormings and vaccinations

Has the puppy been micro chipped?

Why aren't you asking me any questions? A responsible breeder will be committed to making a good match between the new owners and their puppies. If the breeder spends more time discussing money than the welfare of the puppy and how you will care for him, you can draw your own conclusions as to what his or her priorities are – and they probably don't include improving the breed. Walk away.

TOP TIP: Take your puppy to a vet to have a thorough check-up within 48 hours of purchase. If your vet is not happy with the health of the dog, no matter how painful it may be, return the pup to the breeder. Keeping an unhealthy puppy will only cause more distress and expense in the long run.

Puppy Contracts

Ask if the puppy is being sold with a Puppy Contract. These are recommended by breed clubs around the world and protect both buyer and seller by providing information on diet, worming, vaccination and veterinary visits from the birth of the puppy until it leaves the breeder. You should also have a health guarantee for a specified time period.

The Royal Society for the Prevention of Cruelty to Animals (RSPCA) in the UK has a downloadable puppy contract endorsed by vets and animal welfare organisations – pictured. You can see a copy here and should be looking for something similar from the breeder or seller of the puppy:

http://puppycontract.rspca.org.uk/webContent/staticImages/Microsites/PuppyContract/Downloads/PuppyContractDownload.pdf

A Puppy Contract will answer such questions as:

➢ Is the puppy covered by breeder's insurance and can he be returned if there is a health issue within a certain period of time?
➢ Was he born by Caesarean section?
➢ Has he been micro-chipped and/or vaccinated and details of worming treatments?
➢ Has he been partially or wholly housetrained?
➢ Has he been socialised and where was he kept?
➢ What health issues have the pup and parents have been screened for?
➢ Do you have details of the dam and sire
➢ What is the puppy currently being fed and is any food is being supplied?

It's not easy for caring breeders to part with their puppies after they have lovingly bred and raised them to eight weeks of age or older, and so many supply extensive care notes for new owners. One such breeder is Karol Watson Todd; her Cockapoo Care notes include such information as:

➢ The puppy's daily routine
➢ Feeding schedule
➢ Vet and vaccination schedule
➢ General puppy care
➢ Toilet training
➢ Socialising your dog

➢ Recognising and coping with heatstroke
➢ Lifetime support and guarantee

New owners should do their research before visiting a litter as, once there, the cute Cockapoo puppies will undoubtedly be irresistible and you will buy with your heart rather than your head. If you have any doubts at all about the breeder, seller or the puppy, WALK AWAY.

Spending the time now to get your Cockapoo from a good breeder with a proven track record will help to reduce the chances of health and behaviour problems with your adult dog.

Top 10 Tips for Choosing a Healthy Cockapoo

1. Your puppy should have a well-fed appearance. He or she should not, however, have a distended abdomen (pot belly) as this can be a sign of worms - or other illnesses such as Cushing's disease in adults. The ideal puppy should not be too thin either; you should not be able to see his ribs

2. His nose should be cool, damp and clean with no discharge

3. The pup's eyes should be bright and clear with no discharge or tear stain. Steer clear of a puppy which blinks a lot, this could be the sign of a problem

4. The pup's ears should be clean with no sign of discharge, soreness or redness and no unpleasant smell

5. His gums should be clean and a healthy pink colour

6. Check the puppy's bottom to make sure it is clean and there are no signs of diarrhoea

7. A Cockapoo's coat should be clean with no signs of ticks or fleas. Red or irritated skin or bald spots could be a sign of infestation or a skin condition. Also check between the toes of the paws for signs of redness or swelling

8. Choose a puppy that moves freely without any sign of injury or lameness. It should be a fluid movement, not jerky or stiff, which could be a sign of joint problems

9. When the puppy is distracted, clap or make a noise behind him - not so loud as to frighten him - to make sure he is not deaf

10. One of the Cockapoo's prize attributes is his or her coat; it should look clean, feel soft not matted, and puppies should smell good!

Finally, ask to see veterinary records to confirm your puppy has been wormed and had his first injections. If you are unlucky enough to have a health problem with your pup within the first few months, a reputable breeder will allow you to return the pup. Also, if you get the Cockapoo puppy home and things don't work out for whatever reason, good breeders should also take the puppy back. Make sure this is the case before you commit.

Picking the Right Temperament

You've picked a Cockapoo, presumably, because you love this crossbreed's friendly get-along-with-everybody nature and the way they look. Presumably you're planning to spend a lot of time with your new puppy, as Cockapoos love being with humans. Remember that while different Cockapoos may share many characteristics and temperament traits, each puppy also has his own individual character, just like humans.

The pleasant temperament and highly affectionate nature of the Cockapoo suits most people. Visit the breeder more than once to see how your chosen pup interacts and get an idea of his character in comparison to his littermates. Some puppies will run up to greet you, pull at your shoelaces and playfully bite your fingers. Others will be more content to stay in the basket sleeping. Watch their behaviour and energy levels. Are you an active person who enjoys masses of daily exercise or would a less hyper puppy be more suitable? Choose the puppy which will best fit in with your family and lifestyle.

A submissive dog will by nature be more passive, less energetic and also possibly easier to train. A dominant dog will usually be more energetic and lively. They may also be more stubborn and need a firmer hand when training or socialising with other dogs. If you have a dominant dog you have to be careful about introducing new dogs into the household; two dominant dogs may not live together comfortably.

There is no good or bad, it's a question of which type of character will best suit you and your lifestyle. Here are a couple of quick tests to try and gauge your puppy's temperament; they should be carried out by the breeder in familiar surroundings so the puppy is relaxed. It should be pointed out that there is some controversy over temperament testing, as a dog's personality is formed by a combination of factors, which include inherited temperament, socialisation, training and environment (or how you treat him):

> The breeder puts the pup on his or her back on her lap and gently rests her hand on the pup's chest, or
> She puts her hands under the pup's tummy and gently lifts the pup off the floor for a few seconds, keeping the pup horizontal

A puppy that struggles to get free is less patient than one which makes little effort to get away. A placid, patient dog is likely to fare better in a home with young children than an impatient one.

Useful Tips

Here are some other useful signs to look out for –

> Watch how he interacts with other puppies in the litter. Does he try and dominate them, does he walk away from them or is he happy to play with his littermates? This may give you an idea of how easy it will be to socialise him with other dogs

- After contact, does the pup want to follow you or walk away from you? Not following may mean he has a more independent nature

- If you throw something for the puppy is he happy to retrieve it for you or does he ignore it? This may measure their willingness to work with humans

- If you drop a bunch of keys behind the Cockapoo puppy, does he act normally or does he flinch and jump away? The latter may be an indication of a timid or nervous disposition. Not reacting could also be a sign of deafness

Decide which temperament would fit in with you and your family and the rest is up to you. Whatever hereditary temperament your Cockapoo has, it is true for all dogs that those that have constant positive interactions with people and other animals during the first three to four months of life will be happier and more stable. In contrast, a puppy plucked from its family too early and/or isolated at home alone for long periods will be less happy, less socialised, more needy and may well display behaviour problems later on.

Puppies are like children. Being properly raised contributes to their confidence, sociability, stability and intellectual development. The bottom line is that a pup raised in a warm, loving environment with people is likely to be more tolerant and accepting and less likely to develop behaviour problems.

For those of you who prefer a scientific approach to choosing the right puppy, we are including the full Volhard Puppy Aptitude Test (PAT). This test has been developed by the highly respected Wendy and Jack Volhard who have built up an international reputation over the last 30 years for their invaluable contribution to dog training, health and nutrition. Their philosophy is: "We believe that one of life's great joys is living in harmony with your dog."

They have written several books and the Volhard PAT is regarded as the premier method for evaluating the nature of young puppies. Jack and Wendy have also written the excellent Dog Training for Dummies book. Visit their website at www.volhard.com for details of their upcoming dog training camps, as well as their training and nutrition groups.

The Volhard Puppy Aptitude Test

Here are the ground rules for performing the test:

The testing is done in a location unfamiliar to the puppies. This does not mean they have to be taken away from home. A 10-foot square area is perfectly adequate, such as a room in the house where the puppies have not been.

The puppies are tested one at a time. There are no other dogs or people, except the scorer and the tester, in the testing area.

The puppies do not know the tester. The scorer is a disinterested third party and not the person interested in selling you a puppy.

The scorer is unobtrusive and positions himself so he can observe the puppies' responses without having to move.

The puppies are tested before they are fed. The puppies are tested when they are at their liveliest. Do not try to test a puppy that is not feeling well.

Puppies should not be tested the day of or the day after being vaccinated.

Only the first response counts! Tip: During the test, watch the puppy's tail. It will make a difference in the scoring whether the tail is up or down.

The tests are simple to perform and anyone with some common sense can do them. You can, however, elicit the help of someone who has tested puppies before and knows what they are doing.

Social Attraction - the owner or caretaker of the puppies places it in the test area about four feet from the tester and then leaves the test area. The tester kneels down and coaxes the puppy to come to him or her by encouragingly and gently clapping hands and calling. The tester must coax the puppy in the opposite direction from where it entered the test area. Hint: Lean backward, sitting on your heels instead of leaning forward toward the puppy. Keep your hands close to your body encouraging the puppy to come to you instead of trying to reach for the puppy.

Following - the tester stands up and slowly walks away encouraging the puppy to follow. Hint: Make sure the puppy sees you walk away and get the puppy to focus on you by lightly clapping your hands and using verbal encouragement to get the puppy to follow you. Do not lean over the puppy.

Restraint - the tester crouches down and gently rolls the puppy on its back for 30 seconds. Hint: Hold the puppy down without applying too much pressure. The object is not to keep it on its back but to test its response to being placed in that position.

Social Dominance - let the puppy stand up or sit and gently stroke it from the head to the back while you crouch beside it. See if it will lick your face, an indication of a forgiving nature. Continue stroking until you see a behaviour you can score. Hint: When you crouch next to the puppy avoid leaning or hovering over it. Have the puppy at your side, both of you facing in the same direction.

Tip: During testing maintain a positive, upbeat and friendly attitude toward the puppies. Try to get each puppy to interact with you to bring out the best in him or her. Make the test a pleasant experience for the puppy.

Elevation Dominance - the tester cradles the puppy with both hands, supporting the puppy under its chest and gently lifts it two feet off the ground and holds it there for 30 seconds.

Retrieving - the tester crouches beside the puppy and attracts its attention with a crumpled up piece of paper. When the puppy shows some interest, the tester throws the paper no more than four feet in front of the puppy encouraging it to retrieve the paper.

Touch Sensitivity - the tester locates the webbing of one the puppy's front paws and presses it lightly between his index finger and thumb. The tester gradually increases pressure while counting to ten and stops when the puppy pulls away or shows signs of discomfort.

Sound Sensitivity - the puppy is placed in the centre of the testing area and an assistant stationed at the perimeter makes a sharp noise, such as banging a metal spoon on the bottom of a metal pan.

Sight Sensitivity - the puppy is placed in the centre of the testing area. The tester ties a string around a bath towel and jerks it across the floor, two feet away from the puppy.

Stability - an umbrella is opened about five feet from the puppy and gently placed on the ground.

During the testing, make a note of the heart rate of the pup; this is an indication of how it deals with stress, as well as its energy level.

Puppies come with high, medium or low energy levels. You have to decide for yourself which suits your life style. Dogs with high energy levels need a great deal of exercise, and will get into mischief if this energy is not channelled into the right direction.

Finally, look at the overall structure of the puppy. You see what you get at 49 days age (seven weeks). If the pup has strong and straight front and back legs, with all four feet pointing in the same direction, it will grow up that way, provided you give it the proper diet and environment. If you notice something out of the ordinary at this age, it will stay with puppy for the rest of its life. He will not grow out of it.

Scoring the Results

Following are the responses you will see and the score assigned to each particular response. You will see some variations and will have to make a judgment on what score to give them –

Test	Response	Score
SOCIAL ATTRACTION	Came readily, tail up, jumped, bit at hands	1
	Came readily, tail up, pawed, licked at hands	2
	Came readily, tail up	3
	Came readily, tail down	4
	Came hesitantly, tail down	5
	Didn't come at all	6
FOLLOWING	Followed readily, tail up, got underfoot, bit at feet	1
	Followed readily, tail up, got underfoot	2
	Followed readily, tail up	3
	Followed readily, tail down	4
	Followed hesitantly, tail down	5
	Did not follow or went away	6

RESTRAINT	Struggled fiercely, flailed, bit	1
	Struggled fiercely, flailed	2
	Settled, struggled, settled with some eye contact	3
	Struggled, then settled	4
	No struggle	5
	No struggle, strained to avoid eye contact	6
SOCIAL DOMINANCE	Jumped, pawed, bit, growled	1
	Jumped, pawed	2
	Cuddled up to tester and tried to lick face	3
	Squirmed, licked at hands	4
	Rolled over, licked at hands	5
	Went away and stayed away	6
ELEVATION DOMINANCE	Struggled fiercely, tried to bite	1
	Struggled fiercely	2
	Struggled, settled, struggled, settled	3
	No struggle, relaxed	4
	No struggle, body stiff	5
	No struggle, froze	6
RETRIEVING	Chased object, picked it up and ran away	1
	Chased object, stood over it and did not return	2
	Chased object, picked it up and returned with it to tester	3
	Chased object and returned without it to tester	4
	Started to chase object, lost interest	5
	Does not chase object	6
TOUCH SENSITIVITY	8-10 count before response	1
	6-8 count before response	2
	5-6 count before response	3
	3-5 count before response	4
	2-3 count before response	5
	1-2 count before response	6
SOUND SENSITIVITY	Listened, located sound and ran toward it barking	1
	Listened, located sound and walked slowly toward it	2
	Listened, located sound and showed curiosity	3
	Listened and located sound	4
	Cringed, backed off and hid behind tester	5
	Ignored sound and showed no curiosity	6
SIGHT SENSITIVITY	Looked, attacked and bit object	1
	Looked and put feet on object and put mouth on it	2
	Looked with curiosity and attempted to investigate, tail up	3
	Looked with curiosity, tail down	4
	Ran away or hid behind tester	5
	Hid behind tester	6
STABILITY	Looked and ran to the umbrella, mouthing or biting it	1
	Looked and walked to the umbrella, smelling it cautiously	2
	Looked and went to investigate	3
	Sat and looked, but did not move toward the umbrella	4
	Showed little or no interest	5
	Ran away from the umbrella	6

The scores are interpreted as follows:

Mostly 1s - Strong desire to be pack leader and is not shy about bucking for a promotion. Has a predisposition to be aggressive to people and other dogs and will bite. Should only be placed into a very experienced home where the dog will be trained and worked on a regular basis.

Tip: Stay away from the puppy with a lot of 1s or 2s. It has lots of leadership aspirations and may be difficult to manage. This puppy needs an experienced home. Not good with children.

Mostly 2s - Also has leadership aspirations. May be hard to manage and has the capacity to bite. Has lots of self-confidence. Should not be placed into an inexperienced home. Too unruly to be good with children and elderly people, or other animals. Needs strict schedule, loads of exercise and lots of training. Has the potential to be a great show dog with someone who understands dog behaviour.

Mostly 3s - Can be a high-energy dog and may need lots of exercise. Good with people and other animals. Can be a bit of a handful to live with. Needs training, does very well at it and learns quickly. Great dog for second-time owner.

Mostly 4s - The kind of dog that makes the perfect pet. Best choice for the first time owner. Rarely will buck for a promotion in the family. Easy to train, and rather quiet.

Good with elderly people, children, although may need protection from the children. Choose this pup, take it to obedience classes, and you'll be the star, without having to do too much work!

Pictured is Eileen Jackson's Barney, of Brimstone Cockapoos, Cambridgeshire, UK

Tip: The puppy with mostly 3s and 4s can be quite a handful, but should be good with children and does well with training. Energy needs to be dispersed with plenty of exercise.

Mostly 5s - Fearful, shy and needs special handling. Will run away at the slightest stress in its life. Strange people, strange places, different floor or surfaces may upset it. Often afraid of loud noises and terrified of thunderstorms. When you greet it upon your return, may submissively urinate. Needs a very special home where the environment doesn't change too much and where there are no children. Best for a quiet, elderly couple. If cornered and cannot get away, has a tendency to bite.

Mostly 6s – So independent that he doesn't need you or other people. Doesn't care if he is trained or not - he is his own person. Unlikely to bond to you, since he doesn't need you. A great guard dog for gas stations! Do not take this puppy and think you can change him into a lovable bundle - you can't, so leave well enough alone.

Tip: Avoid the puppy with several 6s. It is so independent it doesn't need you or anyone. He is his own person and unlikely to bond to you.

The Scores - Few puppies will test with all 2s or all 3s, there'll be a mixture of scores. For that first time, wonderfully easy to train, potential star, look for a puppy that scores with mostly 4s and

3s. Don't worry about the score on Touch Sensitivity - you can compensate for that with the right training equipment.

It's hard not to become emotional when picking a puppy - they are all so cute, soft and cuddly. Remind yourself that this dog is going to be with you for eight to 16 years. Don't hesitate to step back a little to contemplate your decision. Sleep on it and review it in the light of day.

Avoid the puppy with a score of 1 on the Restraint and Elevation tests. This puppy will be too much for the first-time owner. It's a lot more fun to have a good dog, one that is easy to train, one you can live with and one you can be proud of, than one that is a constant struggle.

Getting a Dog From a Shelter - Don't overlook an animal shelter as a source for a good dog. Not all dogs wind up in a shelter because they are bad. After that cute puppy stage, when the dog grows up, it may become too much for its owner. Or, there has been a change in the owner's circumstances forcing him or her into having to give up the dog.

Most of the time these dogs are housetrained and already have some training. If the dog has been properly socialised to people, it will be able to adapt to a new environment. Bonding may take a little longer but once accomplished, results in a devoted companion.

So you see, it's not all about the colour or the cutest eyes! When getting a puppy, your thought process should run something like this:

- o Decide to get a Cockapoo
- o Decide which size of Cockapoo would best suit you
- o Decide what generation of Cockapoo to get
- o Find a good breeder
- o Find one with a litter available when you are ready for a puppy – or wait
- o Check on the shedding properties of your chosen breeder's pups - there are no 100% guarantees for allergy sufferers, although **most** do well with Cockapoos
- o Decide on a male or female
- o Pick one with a suitable inherited temperament
- o Once you have decided on all the above factors, choose the colour

Some people pick a puppy based purely on how the dog looks. If coat colour, for example, is very important to you, make sure the other boxes are ticked as well.

---

3. Bringing Your Puppy Home

Before you bring your precious little bundle of joy home, it's a smart idea to prepare the surroundings before he or she arrives while you still have the chance. All puppies are demanding and once they land, they will swallow up most of your time. Here's a list of things you ought to think about getting beforehand:

Puppy Checklist

- ✓ A dog bed or basket
- ✓ Bedding – old towels or a blanket which can easily be washed
- ✓ If possible, a towel or piece of cloth which has been rubbed on the puppy's mother to put in the bed
- ✓ A collar, or harness, and lead
- ✓ An identification tag for the collar or harness
- ✓ Food and water bowls, preferably stainless steel
- ✓ Lots of newspapers for housetraining
- ✓ Poo(p) bags
- ✓ Puppy food – find out what the breeder is feeding and stick with it initially
- ✓ Puppy treats (preferably healthy ones, not rawhide)
- ✓ Toys and chews suitable for puppies
- ✓ A puppy coat if you live in a cool climate
- ✓ A crate if you decide to use one
- ✓ Old towels for cleaning your puppy and covering the crate

AND PLENTY OF TIME!

Later on you'll also need a longer, stronger lead, a grooming brush and comb, dog shampoo, flea and worming products and maybe a travel crate. Pictured is nine-week-old Chummy, bred by Julie Shearman, Crystalwood Cockapoos, Devon, UK.

Puppy Proofing Your Home

Before your puppy arrives at his or her new home, you may have to make a few adjustments to make your home safe and suitable. Young Cockapoo puppies are small bundles of instinct and energy (when they are awake), with little common sense and even less self-control. All young Cockapoos are curious, they love to play and have a great sense of fun. They often have mad bursts of energy before they run out of steam and spend much of the rest of the day sleeping. They are like babies and it's up to you to look after them and set the boundaries – both physically and in terms of behaviour – but one step at a time.

Create an area where the puppy is allowed to go and then keep the rest of the house off-limits until housetraining is complete. This shouldn't take long; Cockapoos are one of the best canines to housetrain, according to the breeders involved in this book. One of the biggest factors influencing the success and speed of housetraining is your commitment - another reason for taking a week or two off work when your puppy arrives home.

Like babies, most puppies are mini chewing machines and so remove anything breakable and/or chewable within the puppy's reach – including wooden furniture. Obviously you cannot remove your kitchen cupboards, doors, skirting boards and other fixtures and fittings, so don't leave him unattended for any length of time where he can chew something which is hard to replace.

A baby gate is a relatively inexpensive method of preventing a puppy from going upstairs and leaving an unwanted gift on your precious bedroom carpets. A puppy's bones are soft and recent studies have shown that if very young pups are allowed to climb or descend stairs regularly, they can develop joint problems later in life. This is worth bearing in mind, especially as some Cockapoos are prone to hip dysplasia. You can also use a baby gate or wire panels, available from pet shops, to keep the puppy enclosed in one room – preferably one with a floor which is easy to wipe clean and not too far away from a door to the garden or yard for housetraining. Many of the breeders we contacted use a puppy pen to contain the pup or pups, while giving them plenty of room to stretch their legs.

In any case, you may also want to remove your expensive oriental rugs to other rooms until he or she is fully housetrained and has stopped chewing everything. Make sure you have some toys soft enough to chew and too big to swallow which are suitable for sharp little teeth. Don't give old socks, shoes or slippers or your pup will regard your footwear as fair game. Avoid rawhide chews as they can get stuck in the dog's throat.

The puppy's designated area or room should be not too hot, cold or damp and free from draughts. Puppies are sensitive to temperature fluctuations and don't do well in very hot or very cold conditions. If you live in a hot climate and it's summer, your new puppy may need air conditioning.

Just as you need a home, your puppy needs a den. This den is a haven where your puppy feels safe for the first few weeks after the traumatic experience of leaving his or her mother and littermates. Young puppies sleep for over 18 hours a day at the beginning; some may sleep for up to 22 hours a day. This is normal. (This handsome chap is an F1b puppy bred by Pat Pollington, Polycinders Cockapoos, Devon, UK).

If you have young children, you must restrict the time they spend with the puppy to a few short sessions a day. Plenty of sleep is **essential** for the normal development of a young dog. You wouldn't wake a baby up every hour or so to play and shouldn't do that with a puppy. Don't invite friends round to see your new puppy for at least a day or two, preferably longer. However excited you are, your new pup needs a few days to get over the stress of leaving his mother and siblings and then to start bonding with you.

You have a couple of options with the den; you can get a dog bed or basket, or you can use a crate. Crates have long been popular in America and are becoming increasingly used in the UK, particularly as it can be quicker to housetrain a puppy using a crate. The idea of keeping a dog in a cage like a rabbit or hamster is abhorrent to many animal-loving Brits; but they can be a useful aid if used properly. Using the crate as a prison to contain the dog for hours on end certainly is cruel, but the crate has its place as a sanctuary for your dog; a place where he or she can go. It is their own space and they know no harm will come to them in there. See **Crate Training** later on in this chapter for getting your Cockapoo used to - and even to enjoy - being in his crate.

Most puppies' natural instinct is NOT to soil the area where they sleep. Put plenty of newspapers down next to the den and your pup should choose to go to the toilet here if you are not quick enough to take him or her outside. Of course, they may also decide to trash their designated area by chewing their blankets and shredding the newspaper – patience is the key in this situation!

If you have a garden or yard that you intend letting your puppy roam in, make sure that every little gap has been plugged. You'd be amazed at the tiny holes puppies can escape through. Also, don't leave your Cockapoo unattended as they can come to harm, and dogs are increasingly being targeted by thieves, who are even stealing from gardens. Make sure there are no poisonous plants which your pup might chew and check there are no low plants with sharp leaves or thorns which could cause eye or other injuries.

In order for puppies to grow into well-adjusted dogs, they have to feel comfortable and relaxed in their new surroundings and they need a great deal of sleep. They are leaving the warmth and protection of their mother and littermates and so for the first few days at least, your puppy will feel very sad. It is important to make the transition from the birth home to your home as easy as possible. Your pup's life is in your hands. How you react and interact with him in the first few days and weeks will shape your relationship and his character for the years ahead.

What the Breeders Say

We asked a number of breeders in the UK and North America what essential advice they would give to new owners of Cockapoo puppies and this is what they said:

Julie Shearman, Crystalwood Cockapoos, Devon, UK: "We vet new owners carefully and tactfully turn away anyone we deem to be an unsuitable owner. However, we stress that bringing a puppy home is like having a toddler in the home! Gardens need to be secure and free from poisonous plants and hazards, as does the house with cleaning products, fires, electrical cords, stairs etc.

"Homes with children are reminded that pups are walking dustbins and any small toys will be in a pup's mouth and swallowed. Keeping puppy in a 'safe zone' with a puppy pen, large crate or the use of baby gates is ideal. Make sure everyone in the household is clear of the puppy's 'house rules' - is the pup allowed on furniture, in bedrooms etc? - or the pup will end up very confused. Equally, everyone in the household should use the same commands for toilet training; 'come' and so on."

Karol Watson Todd, KaroColin Cockapoos, Lincolnshire, UK: "I give my new owners several pages of notes the week before they take their puppy home to read through and ask questions about. I'm very wary of collars being worn in a crate. It's a big issue as collars need to be worn, but I've seen dogs stuck by their collar in a crate and, worse still, two puppies playing and getting hooked onto their collars. Fancy iron dog beds are also an issue for a collar to get hung onto. New owners also need to be aware of any foods and plants poisonous to dogs."

Pat Pollington, Polycinders Cockapoos, Devon, UK: "When bringing a puppy home you need to remember they are just like babies. They will be very scared when they first enter your home. "Dogs go by sense of smell and your home will have a completely different smell to what they are used to. Also, they have just travelled in a car so they are also going to be very stressed, so you need to remember that they will have upset tummies for a few days and this means that they are at higher risk of picking up any bug. Keep the first night calm for the puppy. Although the children will be very excited by the new member of the family, the puppy is going to be very unsure about what's going on.

"You need to do your research into things that are poisonous to dogs. There are a lot of plants and different foods that are very harmful to dogs, especially puppies, so you need to make sure that you and your children know this before the puppy enters the house. Things such as Lego are very dangerous because puppies love to chew and the last thing you want is the puppy being harmed from chewing something like this. Make sure all electric wires are well hidden and if you have an office room, then block that off from the puppy with a stair gate because in that room there will be lots of dangerous electric wires."

Rebecca Mae Goins, MoonShine Cockapoos, Indiana, said: "My advice to new puppy parents when they bring their new puppy home is to stick to your breeder's schedule for feeding and training and do not overwhelm your new puppy with a house full of visitors. Before you bring your little one home, go through your house and puppy proof your home: cabinet locks, puppy gates, etc.

"Make sure you are not using toxic cleaners or air fresheners; make sure you do not have any toxic plants inside or out. Do not take your puppy into public or for walks outside of the safety of your yard until you have completed the puppy shots. Use common sense and watch your new little one close. And most of all enjoy the new little life you have chosen to join your family."

Jackie Stafford, of Dj's Cockapoos, Texas: "The biggest danger to a new puppy is the children of the new puppy owners. It is essential that children are taught good puppy skills and safety. Pups are inquisitive and should be watched closely. Swimming pools are another danger to Cockapoo pups as they love water, but are unable to climb to safety if they fall in."

Jeanne Davis, Wind Horse Offering, Maryland, added: "Don't isolate your puppy, spend time with him. Be consistent with your training so that he knows exactly what to expect from you."

Jessica Sampson, Legacy Cockapoos, Ontario, Canada: "Puppy-proof your home; make sure you pick up and secure any loose wires and small toys. Check your fence perimeter for any spots your puppy could potentially escape through and secure them. Secure stairs with a safety gate until your puppy can competently manage them on his or her own.

"Make sure to get puppy-safe chew toys for the teething stage. Sign up for a puppy obedience class and be consistent; this is the key to successful training."

Pictured is Jessica's standard F2 Cockapoo, Nessa, who was born snow white, but whose wavy fleece coat is now dark apricot.

The First Few Days

Before you collect your puppy, let the breeder know what time you will arrive and ask her not to feed the pup for three or four hours beforehand (unless you have a very long journey, in which case the puppy will need to eat something). He will be less likely to be car sick and should be hungry when he lands in his new home. The same applies to an adult dog moving to a new home. When you arrive, ask the breeder for an old towel which has been with the dam – you can leave one on an earlier visit to collect with the pup. Or take one with you and rub the mother with it to collect her scent and put this with the puppy for the first few days. It may help him to settle in.

Make sure you get copies of any health certificates relating to the parents. A good breeder will also have a Contract of Sale or Puppy Contract – **see Chapter 3. Bringing Your Puppy Home** – which outlines your and their rights and responsibilities. It should also state that you can return the puppy if there are health issues within a certain time frame – although if you have picked your breeder carefully, it should hopefully not come to this. The breeder should also give you details of worming and any vaccinations. Most good breeders supply an information sheet for new owners.

You should also find out exactly what the breeder is feeding and how much. You cannot suddenly switch a dog's diet; their digestive systems cannot cope with a sudden change. In the beginning stick to whatever the puppy is used to initially. (Photo courtesy of Jeanne Davis).

The Journey Home

Bringing a new puppy home in the car can be a traumatic experience. Your puppy will be devastated at leaving his or her mother, brothers and sisters and a familiar environment. Everything will be strange and frightening and he will probably whimper and whine - or even howl or bark - on the way to his or her new home. If you can, take somebody with you to take care of him on that first journey. Under no circumstances have the puppy on your lap while driving. It is simply too dangerous - a little Cockapoo puppy is cute, lively and far too distracting.

The best and safest way to transport the pup is in a crate – either a purpose-made travel crate or a wire crate which he will use at home. Put a comfortable blanket in the bottom - preferably rubbed with the scent of the mother. See if you can get a familiar toy from the breeder as well. Ask your travel companion to sit next to the crate and talk softly to the frightened little bundle of nerves. He or she will almost certainly cry or whimper. If you don't have a crate, your passenger may wish to hold the puppy. If so, have an old towel between the person and the pup as he may quite possibly urinate (the puppy, not the passenger!)

If you have a journey of more than a couple of hours, make sure that you take water and offer the puppy a drink en route. He may need to eliminate or have diarrhoea (hopefully, only due to nerves), but don't let him outside on to the ground in a strange place as he is not yet fully inoculated. If you have a long journey, cover the bottom of the crate with a waterproof material and put newspapers in half of it, so the pup can eliminate without staining the car seats.

Arriving Home

As soon as you arrive home, let your puppy into the garden or yard and when he 'performs,' praise him for his efforts.

These first few days are critical in getting your puppy to feel safe and confident in his new surroundings. Spend time with your new arrival, talk to him often in a reassuring manner. Introduce him to his den and toys, slowly allow him to explore and show him around the house – once you have puppy proofed it. Cockapoo puppies are extremely curious - and amusing, you might be surprised at his reactions to everyday objects. Remember that puppies and babies explore with their mouths, so don't scold for chewing. Instead, remove objects you don't want chewed out of reach and replace them with toys he can chew.

If you have other animals, introduce them slowly and in supervised sessions - preferably once the pup has got used to his new surroundings, not as soon as you walk through the door. Gentleness and patience are the keys to these first few days, so don't over-face your puppy. Have a special, gentle puppy voice with which to talk to him and use his name often in a pleasant, encouraging manner. Never use his name to scold or he will associate it with bad things. The sound of his name should always make him want to pay attention to you as something good is going to happen - praise, food, play time and so on.

Resist the urge to pick the puppy up all the time. Let him explore on his own legs, encouraging a little independence. One of the most important things at this stage is to ensure that your puppy has enough sleep – which is nearly all of the time - no matter how much you want to play with him or watch his antics when awake.

If you haven't decided what to call your Cockapoo yet, 'Shadow' might be a good suggestion, as he or she will follow you everywhere! Many puppies from different breeds do this, but Cockapoos are 'Velcro dogs,' they like to stick close to their owners – both as puppies and adults. Our website receives many emails from worried new owners. Here are some of the most common concerns:

> ➤ My puppy sleeps all the time, is this normal?
> ➤ My puppy won't stop crying or whining
> ➤ My puppy is shivering
> ➤ My puppy won't eat
> ➤ My puppy is very timid
> ➤ My puppy follows me everywhere, she won't let me out of her sight

Most of the above are quite common. They are just a young pup's reaction to leaving his mother and littermates and entering into a strange new world. It is normal for puppies to sleep most of the time, just like babies. It is also normal for some puppies to whine a lot during the first few days.

Make your new pup as comfortable as possible, ensuring he has a warm (but not too hot), quiet den away from draughts, where he is not pestered by children or other pets. Handle him gently, while giving him plenty of time to sleep. During the first few nights your puppy will whine; try your best to ignore the pitiful cries.

Unless they are especially dominant, most puppies will be nervous and timid for the first few days. They will think of you as their new mother and follow you around the house. This is also quite natural, but after a few days start to leave your puppy for a few minutes at a time, gradually building up the time. Cockapoos, like other breeds selectively bred for companionship, can be prone to separation anxiety, particularly if they are used to being with you virtually 24/7. See **Chapter 8. Behaviour** for more information.

If your routine means you are normally out of the house for a few hours during the day, get your puppy on a Friday or Saturday so he has at least a couple of days to adjust to his new surroundings. A far better idea is to book at least a week or two off work to help your puppy settle in. If you don't work, leave your diary free for the first couple of weeks. Helping a new pup to settle in is virtually a full-time job.

This is a frightening time for your puppy. Is your puppy shivering with cold or is it nerves? Avoid placing your puppy under stress by making too many demands on him. Don't allow the kids to pester the pup and, until they have learned how to handle a dog, don't allow them to pick him up unsupervised, as they could inadvertently damage his delicate little body.

If your puppy won't eat, spend time gently coaxing him. If he leaves his food, take it away and try it later. Don't leave it down all of the time or he may get used to turning his nose up at it. The next time you put something down for him, he is more likely to be hungry.

If your puppy is crying, it is probably for one of the following reasons:

> ➢ He is lonely
> ➢ He is hungry
> ➢ He wants attention from you
> ➢ He needs to go to the toilet

If it is none of these, then physically check him over to make sure he hasn't picked up an injury. Try not to fuss over him. If he whimpers, just reassure him with a quiet word. If he cries loudly and tries to get out of his allotted area, he probably needs to go to the toilet. Even if it is the middle of the night, get up (yes, sorry, this is best) and take him outside. Praise him if he goes to the toilet.

The strongest bonding period for a puppy is between eight and 12 weeks of age. The most important factors in bonding with your puppy are TIME spent with him and PATIENCE, even when he or she makes a mess in the house or chews something he shouldn't.

Remember, your Cockapoo pup is just a baby dog and it takes time to learn not to do these things. Spend time with your pup and you will have a loyal friend for life. Cockapoos are very focussed on their humans and that emotional attachment between you and your Cockapoo may grow to become one of the most important aspects of your life – and certainly his.

Where Should the Puppy Sleep?

Where do you want your new puppy to sleep? You cannot simply allow him or her to wander freely around the house. Ideally your puppy will be in a contained area, such as a playpen or a crate, at night. While it is not acceptable to shut a dog in a cage all day, you can keep your puppy in a crate at night until he or she is housetrained. You also have to consider whether you want the pup to sleep in your bedroom or elsewhere. If your puppy is in the bedroom, try to prevent him from jumping on and off beds and/or couches or racing up and down stairs until he has stopped growing, as this can damage his joints.

If he is to sleep outside your bedroom, put him in a comfortable bed of his own, or a crate – and then block your ears for the first couple of nights. He will almost certainly whine and whimper, but this won't last long and he will soon get used to sleeping on his own, without his littermates or you.

We don't recommend letting your new pup sleep on the bed. He will not be housetrained and also a puppy needs to learn his place in the household and have his own den. It's up to you whether you decide to let him on the bed when he's older. Another point to bear in mind is that if your dog is regularly exercised, his paws and coat may pick up mud, grass, brambles and other things you may not want on your bed.

While it is not good to leave a dog alone all day, it is also not healthy to spend 24 hours a day with him. He becomes too reliant on you and this increases the chance of him developing separation anxiety when you do have to leave him. A Cockapoo puppy used to being on his own every night is less likely to develop attachment issues, so consider this when deciding where he should sleep. Our dog sleeps in his own bed in our bedroom and has separation anxiety. Any future dogs will sleep in a separate room from us – no matter how hard that is in the beginning when the puppy is whimpering all night.

Many owners prefer to bite the bullet right from the start by leaving the pup in a safe place downstairs or in a different room to the bedroom, so he gets used to being on his own right from the beginning. If you do this, you might find a set of earplugs very useful for helping (you) to survive the first few nights! In a moment of weakness you might consider letting the puppy sleep in the bedroom for a couple of nights until he gets used to your home, but then it is even harder to turf him out later.

If you decide you definitely do want your Cockapoo to sleep in the bedroom from Day One, initially put him in a crate or similar with a soft blanket covering part of the crate. Put newspapers inside as he will not be able to last the night without urinating.

Once your dog has been housetrained and can access other areas of the house, you may reconsider where he sleeps. Some people will continue to keep him in the place where he started out; others will want the dog to sleep in the bedroom. But before you immediately choose the bedroom, bear in mind that many Cockapoos scratch, snore, fart and wander about in the night!

Vaccinations and Worming

It is **always** a good idea to have your Cockapoo checked out by a vet within a few days of picking him up. Keep him away from other dogs in the waiting room as he will not be fully protected against canine diseases until the vaccination schedule is complete. All puppies need these injections; very occasionally a Cockapoo puppy has a reaction, but this is very rare and the advantages of immunisation far outweigh the disadvantages.

An unimmunised puppy is at risk every time he meets other dogs as he has no protection against potentially fatal diseases – another point is that it is unlikely a pet insurer will cover an unimmunised dog. It should be stressed that vaccinations are generally quite safe and side effects are uncommon. If your Cockapoo is unlucky enough to be one of the very few that suffers an adverse reaction, here are the signs to look out for; a pup may exhibit one or more of these:

MILD REACTION - Sleepiness, irritability and not wanting to be touched. Sore or a small lump at the place where he was injected. Nasal discharge or sneezing. Puffy face and ears.

SEVERE REACTION - Anaphylactic shock. A sudden and quick reaction, usually before leaving the vet's, which causes breathing difficulties. Vomiting, diarrhoea, staggering and seizures.

A severe reaction is extremely rare. There is a far, far greater risk of your Cockapoo either being ill and/or spreading disease if he does not have the injections.

The usual schedule is for the pup to have his first vaccination at six to eight weeks of age. This will protect him from a number of diseases in one shot. In the UK these are Distemper, Canine Parvovirus (Parvo), Infectious Canine Hepatitis (Adenovirus), Leptospirosis and Kennel Cough (Bordetella). In the US this is known as DHPP. Puppies in the US also need vaccinating separately against Rabies. There are optional vaccinations for Coronavirus and - depending on where you live and if your dog is regularly around woods or forests - Lyme Disease.

The puppy requires a second vaccination around four weeks later and then maybe a third to complete his immunity, which is often from 10 to 12 weeks of age. Seven days after that he is safe to mix with other dogs. When you take your Cockapoo for an initial check-up within a few days of bringing him home, check with your vet exactly what shots are needed.

Diseases such as Parvo and Kennel Cough are highly contagious and you should not let your puppy mix with other dogs - unless they are your own and have already been vaccinated - until a week after he has completed his vaccinations, otherwise he will not be fully immunised. Parvovirus can also be transmitted by fox faeces.

You shouldn't take your new puppy to places where unvaccinated dogs might have been, like the local park. This does not mean that your puppy should be isolated - far from it. This is an important time for socialisation. It is OK for the puppy to mix with another dog which you 100% know has been vaccinated and is up to date with its annual boosters. Perhaps invite a friend's dog round to play in your garden to begin the socialisation process.

Once your puppy is fully immunised, you have a window of a few weeks to introduce him to as many new experiences - dogs, people, traffic, noises, other animals, etc. – this critical period before the age of four and a half or five months is when he is at his most receptive. Socialisation should not stop at that age, but continue for the rest of your Cockapoo's life; but it is particularly important to socialise young puppies.

Your dog will need a booster injection every year of his life. The vet should give you a record card or send you a reminder, but it's also a good idea to keep a note of the date in your diary.

All puppies need worming. A good breeder will give the puppies their first dose of worming medication at around two weeks old, then probably again at five and eight weeks before they

leave the litter. Get the details and inform your vet exactly what treatment, if any, your pup has already had. The main types of worms affecting puppies are roundworm and tapeworm. Roundworm can also be transmitted from a puppy to humans – most often children - and can in severe cases cause blindness, or miscarriage in women, so it's important to keep up to date with worming.

Worms in puppies are quite common, they are often picked up through their mother's milk. If you have children, get them into the habit of washing their hands after they have been in contact with the puppy – lack of hygiene is the reason why children are most susceptible. Most vets recommend worming a puppy once a month until he is six months old, and then around every two or three months.

If your Cockapoo, like many, is often out and about running through the woods and fields with his head down, then it is important to stick to a regular worming schedule, as he is more likely to pick up worms than one which spends more time indoors.

Fleas can pass on tapeworms to dogs, but a puppy would not normally be treated unless it is known for certain he has fleas. And then only with caution. You need to know the weight of your pet and then speak to your vet about the safest treatment to rid your puppy of the parasites.

It is not usually worth buying a cheap worming or flea treatment from a supermarket, as they are usually far less effective than more expensive vet-recommended preparations, such as Drontal. Many people living in the US have contacted our website claiming the parasite treatment Trifexis has caused severe side effects and even death to their dogs. Although this evidence is only anecdotal, you might want consider avoiding Trifexis to be on the safe side - even if your vet recommends it.

Photo courtesy of Julie Shearman

4. Cockapoos for Allergy Sufferers

You are either already the proud owner of a Cockapoo or you are thinking about becoming one. Cockapoos make excellent family pets. They have cheerful temperaments, look cute, get on well with children and the elderly and you've heard that they are non-shedding and 'hypoallergenic'.

Some people get a 'hypoallergenic' dog thinking they are guaranteed NOT to have a reaction to the animal. Many allergy sufferers do not have a reaction to their Cockapoo, but it is important to understand that there is no 100% guarantee. Every dog is different; every person is different. This is why some breeders won't let their dogs go to allergy sufferers. They simply don't want to see their beloved puppy out of a home when the sneezing starts.

Allergies are one of the main reasons why Poodle crosses have become so popular – there are now oodles of Doodles and piles of Poos in the dog world! The Poodle, with its tightly curled wool coat is regarded as a minimal shedder and hypoallergenic breed.

Let's look at the hypoallergenic topic more closely. Firstly, the official definition of the word 'hypoallergenic' is 'having a decreased tendency to provoke an allergic reaction'. In other words there is no cast iron guarantee that an allergy or asthma sufferer will not suffer a reaction to a particular individual dog or type of dog. It is true that if you choose a hypoallergenic breed or hybrid such as the Cockapoo, you are **less likely** to have an allergic reaction. But allergies vary from person to person and coats vary from one dog to another. This is particularly true with the Cockapoo, which is not a breed but a crossbreed, and there are even more variables than with a purebred.

A Cockapoo can have one of three types of coat: flatter like the Spaniel, tightly curled more like the Poodle and a looser, wavy fleece. Sometimes the coat will change its characteristics and even colour as the puppy grows, and the type of coat may even vary within pups of the same litter. While a Poodle is regarded as a hypoallergenic breed, a Cocker Spaniel is not. If your pup's coat is more like that of the Spaniel rather than the Poodle, he is more likely to shed some hair and dander. There is, however, plenty of anecdotal evidence that many Cockapoos shed little or no hair and do not trigger a reaction with many allergy sufferers.

However, according to the Kennel Clubs of both the USA and UK, **there is no such thing as a non-shedding dog!** No breeder can guarantee that a specific Cockapoo will be suitable for a specific individual who suffers from allergies to dogs. However, when reputable Cockapoo breeders select their breeding stock, coat is an important factor.

Allergies are on the increase. Amazingly, 50 million Americans are allergy sufferers, according to the Asthma and Allergy Foundation of America. One in five of these (10 million people) is a pet allergy sufferer. In the UK, pets are the second most important cause of allergy in the home, with 40% of asthmatic children reacting to dogs.

It's a common misconception that people are allergic to animal hair, but that's not true. What they are actually allergic to are proteins - or allergens. These are secreted by the animal's oil glands and then shed with the **dander**, which is dead skin cells (like dandruff). They are also found in dog saliva and urine - and if you are allergic to either, you are unlikely ever to be able to successfully share your home with a dog. The good news for dog lovers is that more people are allergic to cats!

Hypoallergenic Breeds

If you have allergies and are determined to go ahead and share your home with Man's Best Friend, then the safest route is to select a non-shedding breed or crossbreed. Actually, there is no such thing as totally non-shedding either. But the American Kennel Club (AKC) and Kennel Club UK both publish lists of **"breeds that generally do well with people with allergies."** For your information only (because you have already set your heart on a Cockapoo), here are the lists.

Kennel Club (UK)

The KC has this to say: "For those owners looking for dogs that don't shed or which are less predisposed to shedding their coat, one of the breeds listed below may be a suitable choice:"

Gundog Group - Lagotto Romagnolo, Irish Water Spaniel, Spanish Water Dog

Working Group - Bouvier des Flandres, Giant Schnauzer, Portuguese Water Dog, Russian Black Terrier

Pastoral Group - Hungarian Puli, Komondor

Toy Group - Bichon Frise, Bolognese, Chinese Crested, Coton de Tulear, Havanese, Maltese, Yorkshire Terrier

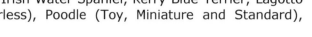

Utility Group - Lhasa Apso, Intermediate Mexican Hairless, Mexican Hairless – all three types (pictured), Miniature Schnauzer, Standard Poodle, Toy Poodle, Miniature Poodle, Shih Tzu, Tibetan Terrier

Terrier Group - Bedlington Terrier, Dandie Dinmont Terrier, Glen of Imaal Terrier, Sealyham Terrier, Soft Coated Wheaten Terrier

"The following Terrier breeds are reported to moult in small amounts: Airedale, Australian, Border, Cairn, Cesky, Fox (Wire), Irish, Kerry Blue, Lakeland, Norfolk, Norwich and Scottish."

The Kennel Club adds: "If you are asthmatic or have an allergy, you should consult your medical advisor before considering obtaining a canine companion, since even dogs that don't shed can cause allergies. Studies have shown that dog hair or dog skin can induce asthma attacks and other related respiratory problems as well as certain allergies, and indeed the advice of Asthma UK is that it is probably better not to have a dog at all."

American Kennel Club

The American Kennel Club says: "While no dog is 100% hypoallergenic, there are a variety of breeds that do well with allergy sufferers. These dogs have a predictable, non-shedding coat which produces less dander. Dander, which is attached to pet hair, is what causes most pet allergies in humans."

Their list of "best breeds for allergy sufferers" is: Afghan Hound, American Hairless Terrier, Bedlington Terrier, Bichon Frise, Chinese Crested, Irish Water Spaniel, Kerry Blue Terrier, Lagotto Romagnolo, Maltese, Peruvian Inca Orchid (Hairless), Poodle (Toy, Miniature and Standard),

Portuguese Water Dog, Schnauzer (Giant, Standard and Miniature), Spanish Water Dog, Soft Coated Wheaten Terrier, Xoloitzcuintli.

Any hybrid dog produced by crossing two of these breeds would also be considered hypoallergenic. The Cockapoo – of whatever generation - is the result of breeding Poodles with Cocker Spaniels. While the Cocker is not regarded as hypoallergenic, many experienced breeders claim that they can produce Cockapoo puppies with consistent low shedding, low dander coats.

The Facts

It is possible for pet allergy sufferers to enjoy living with a dog without spending all of their time sneezing, wheezing, itching or breaking out in rashes. Millions of people are proving the case. As we have seen, some types of dogs are definitely better for allergy sufferers. Any dog can cause an allergic reaction, although you stand a far higher chance of having no reaction to a dog which is a low-shedding, hypoallergenic purebred or hybrid.

You may be fine with a Cockapoo puppy, as tiny puppies often don't shed. But the coat can change in adolescence or adulthood and this could trigger a reaction later on. It would indeed cause distress if you were suddenly allergic to your adult Cockapoo who has become a dearly-loved member of your family. If you have any doubts at all about a puppy - even a tiny reaction - don't get him.

We strongly advise against selecting a Cockapoo solely because you believe the dog will not trigger your allergies. There are no guarantees. For those people with consistent or severe allergies, another option would be to consider a pure bred hypoallergenic breed and then follow certain steps to select a breeder and puppy.

Choosing a suitable dog is not completely straightforward and you do have to put in extra time to make sure that you pick the right dog and maybe make a few adjustments to your home as well. Remember:

No dog is totally non-shedding

No dog is totally hypoallergenic

Two further points to consider are that people's pet allergies vary greatly. Pet allergy sufferers may react differently to different dogs within a breed or crossbreed, or even litter. A sufferer may be fine with one puppy, yet have a reaction to his brother or sister. This is especially true of Cockapoos, where the pups may have different physical characteristics and coats.

All dogs - even so-called 'hairless' dogs - have hair, dander, saliva and urine. Therefore all dogs **can** cause allergic reactions. But not all dogs do. Some hypoallergenic dog breeds and hybrids do not affect pet allergy sufferers as much because of the amount of hair that they shed. If they are not shedding, then the dander remains trapped within the coat. Hypoallergenic dogs virtually do not moult - you might find the *occasional* dog hair or small fur ball around the house - which is why you have to have them clipped.

Choosing a puppy

If you have friends with Cockapoos, spend some time inside their houses with their dogs, stroke the dog, touch your face with the same hand - do you have a reaction? Did you have a reaction the following day? No reaction is a good start, but it doesn't automatically mean that you won't be allergic to a different Cockapoo.

Next step is to find a reputable breeder and ask if you could visit their adult dogs. Make sure there are no cats around which could also trigger allergies. If you are determined to stick with Cockapoos, spend time with both parents of any pup that you are considering buying, if possible – or at least the mother. Also try to spend time with adult dogs or puppies with different coat types to see which, if any, cause a reaction.

Choose a breeder with several years' experience, as he or she will have a better knowledge of how the puppies' coats will develop as the dogs grow up. Then spend some time alone with the specific pup you are thinking of getting to determine whether you have a reaction. This may occur up to two days later. Handle the dog, rub your hands on your face and lick your hands after you have touched the dog in order to absorb as much potential allergen as you can on your short visit.

Go back and visit the breeder at least one or more times before you make that life-changing commitment to buy the puppy. Take an old towel or piece of cloth and rub the puppy with it. Take this home with you and handle it to see if you get a delayed reaction.

Check with the breeder to see if you can return the pup within a certain time period were you to have a reaction back at home. You cannot expect the breeder to take the dog back if the allergies only occur once the dog has reached adulthood.

Here's an interesting fact: everyone with pet allergies can tolerate a certain amount of allergens (things they are allergic to). If that person is just below his or her tolerance, any additional allergen will push him or her over the edge, thus triggering a reaction. So if you reduce the general allergen load in the home, you'll be much more successful when you bring your dog home.

Top Ten Tips for Reducing Pet Allergens

1. Get a HEPA air cleaner in the bedroom and/or main living room. HEPA stands for High Efficiency Particle Air - a type of air filter that removes 99.97% of all particles

2. Use a HEPA vacuum cleaner. Neither the HEPA air nor vacuum cleaner is cheap, but if you suffer allergies and really want to share your life and home with a dog, they are worth considering. Both will dramatically improve the quality of the air you breathe in your home

3. Regardless of what vacuum you use, clean and dust your home regularly

4. Keep the dog out of your bedroom. We spend around a third of our lives here and keeping animals out can greatly reduce allergic reactions

5. Do not allow your dog on the couch, bed or any other furniture. Keep him out of the car, or if this is not possible, use car seat covers or a blanket on the seat

6. Brush your pet regularly - always outdoors - and regularly clean his bedding. Avoid using normal washing powder, as it may trigger a reaction in dogs with sensitive skin

7. Keep your dog's skin healthy by regularly feeding a good multivitamin and a fatty acid supplement, such as Omega 3 fish oil

8. Avoid contact with other dogs and always wash your hands after you have handled any dog, including your own

9. Consider using an allergy-reducing spray such as Allerpet (pictured below), which helps to cleanse the dog's hair of dander, saliva and sebaceous gland secretions. There are also products to reduce allergens from carpets, curtains and furniture

10. There is always the option of consulting your doctor to discuss possible immunotherapy or medication. There are medical advances being made in the treatment of allergies and a range of tablets, sprays and even injections are currently available

Experts aren't sure whether bathing your dog has any effect on allergy symptoms. Some studies have shown that baths reduce the amount of airborne dander, while others haven't found a difference. We wouldn't recommend bathing your dog more than once a month unless he has a skin problem, as this could cause dry skin, which would then be shed.

Of course, the only sure-fire way to GUARANTEE no allergic reaction is not to have a dog, but that's not what you want to hear!

It wasn't what we wanted to hear either when we decided to get a dog nearly 11 years ago, knowing that one of our family members had allergies. We followed the advice given in this chapter before we got our dog and can honestly say that none of us has ever had any reaction to Max. It pays to do your homework.

5. Crate Training and Housetraining

If you are unfamiliar with them, crates may seem like a cruel punishment for a lovable Cockapoo puppy. They are, however, becoming increasingly popular to help with housetraining and to keep the dog safe at night or when you are not there. Many breeders, trainers, behaviourists and people who show dogs use them.

Getting Your Dog Used to a Crate

If you decide to use a crate, then remember that it is not a prison to restrain the dog. It should only be used in a humane manner and time should be spent to make the puppy or adult dog feel like the crate is his own safe little haven. If the door is closed on the crate, your puppy must ALWAYS have access to water while inside. If used correctly and if time is spent getting the puppy used to the crate, it can be a valuable tool.

We tried our dog Max with a crate when he was a young puppy and he howled and whined every time he went in. In the end, we couldn't bear to hear the noise and so we abandoned it. It is now in the porch at our house and makes a very useful storage place for Wellington boots and running shoes. Now, several years later, having heard from so many of our American readers about how much their dogs love their crates, I think perhaps we gave up too easily.

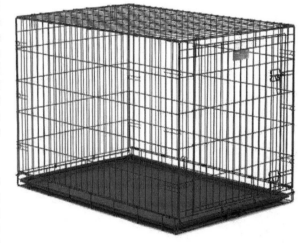

Cockapoos are sensitive dogs and they are also very attached to their humans, and so crates are not suitable for every dog; some may find them distressing. Cockapoos are companion creatures; they are not like hamsters or pet mice which can adapt to life in a cage. They are dogs which thrive on being physically close to their humans – they want to be WITH YOU. Being caged all day is a miserable existence, and a crate should never be used as a means of confinement because you are out of the house all day. If you do decide to use one - perhaps to put your dog in for short periods while you leave the house, or at night - the best place for it is in the corner of a room away from cold draughts or too much heat. Remember, Cockapoos like to be near their family - which is you.

It is only natural for a Cockapoo, or any other dog, to whine in the beginning. He is not crying because he is in a cage. He would cry if he had the freedom of the room and he was alone - he is crying because he is separated from you. However, with patience and the right training he will get used to it and soon come to regard the crate as a favourite place. Leave the crate where the dog can see or hear you. Some owners make the crate their dog's only bed, so he feels comfortable and safe in there.

Dogs with thick coats can overheat easily. When you buy a crate get a wire one (like the one pictured) which allows the air to pass through, not a plastic one which may get very hot. If you cover the crate, don't cover it 100% or you will restrict the flow of air. The crate should be large enough to allow your dog to stretch out flat on his side without being cramped; he should be able to turn round easily and to sit up without hitting his head on the top. Depending on the anticipated adult size of your Cockapoo, you might want to consider a 40" or 42" crate, which will allow your dog plenty of head room and space to move around easily. A 36" crate may be suitable for a Toy Cockapoo. Crates aren't for every owner or every Cockapoo, but used correctly, they can:

- ➢ Create a canine den
- ➢ Be a useful housetraining tool
- ➢ Limit access to the rest of the house while your dog learns the household rules
- ➢ Be a safe way to transport your dog in a car

If you use a crate right from Day One, cover half of it with a blanket to help your puppy regard it as a den. He also needs bedding and it's a good idea to put a chew in as well. A large crate may allow your dog to eliminate at one end and sleep at the other, but this may slow down his housetraining. So, if you are buying a crate which will last for a fully-grown Cockapoo, get adjustable crate dividers – or make them yourself - to block part of it off while he is small so that he feels safe and secure, which he won't do in a very big crate.

Once you've got your crate, you'll need to learn how to use it properly so that it becomes a safe, comfortable den for your dog and not a prison. Here is a tried-and-tested method of getting your dog firstly to accept it, and then to actually want to spend time in there. Initially a pup might not be too happy about going inside, but he will be a lot easier to crate train than an adult dog which has got used to having the run of your house. These are the first steps:

1. Drop a few tasty puppy treats around and then inside the crate

2. Put your puppy's favourite bedding or toy in there

3. Keep the door open

4. Feed your puppy's meals inside the crate. Again, keep the door open

Place a chew or treat INSIDE the crate and close the door while your puppy is OUTSIDE the crate. He will be desperate to get in there! Open the door, let him in and praise him for going in. Fasten a long-lasting chew inside the crate and leave the door open. Let your puppy go inside to spend some time eating the chew.

IMPORTANT: Always remove your dog's collar before leaving him unattended in a crate. A collar can get caught in the wire mesh.

After a while, close the crate door and feed him some treats through the mesh while he is in there. At first just do it for a few seconds at a time, then gradually increase the time. If you do it too fast, he will become distressed. Slowly build up the amount of time he is in the crate. For the first few days, stay in the room, then gradually leave for a short time, first one minute, then three, then 10, 30 and so on.

Next Steps

5. Put your dog in his crate at regular intervals during the day - maximum two hours

6. Don't crate only when you are leaving the house. Place the dog in the crate while you are home as well. Use it as a 'safe' zone

7. By using the crate both when you are home and while you are gone, your dog becomes comfortable there and not worried that you won't come back, or that you are leaving him alone. This helps to prevent separation anxiety later in life

8. Give him a chew and remove his collar, tags and anything else which could become caught in an opening or between the bars

9. Make it very clear to any children that the crate is NOT a playhouse for them, but a 'special room' for the dog

10. Although the crate is your dog's haven and safe place, it must not be off-limits to humans. You should be able to reach inside at any time

The next point is important:

11. Do not let your dog immediately out of the crate if he barks or whines, or he will think that this is the key to opening the door. Wait until the barking or whining has stopped for at least 10 seconds before letting him out

A puppy should not be left in a crate for long periods except at night time, and even then he has to get used to it first. Whether or not you decide to use a crate, the important thing to remember is that those first few days and weeks are a critical time for your puppy. Try and make him feel as safe and comfortable as you can. Bond with him, while at the same time gently and gradually introducing him to new experiences and other animals and humans.

A crate is a good way of transporting your Cockapoo in the car. Put the crate on the shady side of the interior and make sure it can't move around inside the car; put the seatbelt around it if necessary. If it's very sunny and the top of the crate is wire mesh, cover part of it so your dog has some shade and put the windows up and the air conditioning on. Never leave your Cockapoo unattended in a vehicle; he can quickly overheat - or be targeted by thieves.

Allowing your dog to roam freely inside the car is not a safe option, particularly if you - like me – are a bit of a 'leadfoot' on the brake and accelerator! Don't let him put his head out of the window either, he can slip and hurt himself and the wind pressure can cause an ear infection or bits of dust, insects, etc. to fly into your Cockapoo's eyes.

Special travel crates are useful for the car, or for taking your dog to the vet's or a show. Try and pick one with holes or mesh in the side (like the one pictured) to allow free movement of air, rather than a solid plastic one, in which your Cockapoo can become overheated.

Cockapoo Breeders on Crates

Traditionally crates have been more popular in America than in the UK and the rest of Europe, but opinion is slowly changing and more owners are starting to use crates on both sides of the Atlantic. This is perhaps because people's perception of a crate is shifting from regarding it as a prison to thinking of it, if used correctly, as a safe haven as well as a useful tool to help with housetraining and transportation.

Without exception, the breeders we contacted believed that the crate should not be used as a means of imprisoning a dog for hours on end while you are away from the house. This is cruel for any dog, but particularly a Cockapoo, whose greatest desire is to be with his humans. This is what some breeders said – and as you will read, there is a wide variation of opinions:

Julie, of Crystalwood Cockapoos, Devon, UK: "Yes, crates are a good idea if the right-sized crate is used. It should be large enough for dog to stand up and turn around freely. They are ideal for young pups. We sleep our dogs in crates overnight and if out shopping etc, but the maximum time we would leave a dog in a crate is three hours - and then after a good walk. Puppy pens are excellent, but some Cockapoo pups have proved to be very good climbers!"

Karol Watson Todd, KaroColin Cockapoos, Lincolnshire, UK: "Personally I prefer puppy pens, and then no more than a couple of hours, except for overnight. I suggest new owners look at second-hand puppy pens as this stage doesn't last long. I don't like crates or pens as a place of punishment. They should be a sanctuary for the puppy. I recommend feeding in the pen if using one. Crates and pens have become very popular, but they aren't a necessity."

Pat Pollington, of Polycinders Cockapoos, Devon: "We really suggest a crate for a puppy because every puppy needs a safe place where he or she can go when they get tired and need to get away from the children, or when you are trying to cook with hot sauce pans at least you can put them into a crate so you know they are safe. Or when you go out for an hour you know they are not chewing on wires or doing something they shouldn't be because they are safe in their crate.

"No puppy should be left in a crate for longer than a couple of hours, except at night when they are sleeping. During the day they will not want to sleep for more than a couple of hours and then they will be desperate to play and go to the toilet. At night time it is dark so they like to sleep, so they can stay in their crate for longer." Pictured is a handsome trio of four-week-old F1 English Cockapoos bred by Pat and granddaughter Chloe.

Jessica Sampson, Legacy Cockapoos, Ontario, Canada: "I believe crate training is very positive. It creates a safe and familiar environment for your puppy or adult dog. Crating your dog ensures a safe environment for him or her while you are unable to supervise them. It is also a useful tool in potty training as well. You should not leave your dog in a crate longer than three to four hours during the day. They may remain in their crate throughout the night."

Jackie Stafford, Dj's Cockapoo Babies, Texas, USA: "I do believe in crate training and I think that pups should not be left more than two hours at the age of 10 weeks, three hours at 11 weeks and four hours at 12 weeks. As an adult, a dog should not be crated more than eight hours overnight. When a dog is crated, you must ensure they have empty bowels and bladder prior to confinement."

Rebecca Mae Goins, MoonShine Babies Cockapoos, Indiana, USA: "We crate train all our puppies; dogs are den animals and they see their crate as a safe spot that is all theirs. We usually cover the crate to make it dark, which helps to soothe them. We always tell our new puppy parents that if the puppy has to be left in a crate longer than four to five hours, to purchase a round pen and attach it to the crate so the puppy has a place for food and water and a litter pan area."

Jeanne Davis, Wind Horse Offering, Maryland, USA: "We use a crate initially for housebreaking, then for time-out, and for the pet's own protection. Do not leave a puppy unattended in a crate; it isolates them and then they panic."

Top 10 Tips for Housetraining

How easy are Cockapoos to housetrain?

According to our breeders, pretty easy – but the dog is only as good as its owners. In other words, the speed and success of housetraining depends largely on one factor: the time and effort you are prepared to put in. The more vigilant you are during the early days, the quicker your dog will be housetrained. It's as simple as that. Taking the advice in this chapter and being consistent with your routines and repetitions is the quickest way to toilet train (potty train) your Cockapoo.

You have two huge factors in your favour when it comes to housetraining:

1. Cockapoos are desperate to please their owners

2. Most would sell their own mothers for a treat

A further piece of good news is that a puppy's instinct is not to soil his own den. From about the age of three weeks, a pup will leave his sleeping area to go to the toilet. Many good breeders will already have started the housebreaking process with their puppies, so when you pick up your little bundle of joy, all you have to do is ensure that you carry on the good work. Here's what some breeders said:

Rebecca Mae Goins: "The time required to house train a Cockapoo depends on the time devoted to this by the breeder and the new family. As a breeder I start my Cockapoo puppies on housetraining as soon as they are able to toddle around. I will place a potty pad or newspaper in a pan that they can get into that is away from their sleeping and feeding areas. Once they grow, the pan is switched to a deeper walled pan that can hold shredded newspaper or the dog-safe litter of your choice.

"Usually by eight to 10 weeks of age, my puppies are well on their way to being litter box trained, then after they receive their first vaccine, we start to transition them to going outside. This is fairly easy if you scatter some of the same litter they are used to in the spot you want them to go." Pictured is Rebecca's very handsome F2b male Phoenix Rising by the Light of the Red Moon.

Jackie Stafford: "It takes only three weeks to housetrain a puppy on average. The most important thing to do is to make sure that you go to the same place each time. They will soon learn that this place is the place to potty."

Jeanne Davis: "Cockapoos are very quick with housebreaking – they are usually trained about two weeks after they leave me. They are probably one of the quicker breeds to catch onto the whole housebreaking thing."

Jessica Sampson: "Every puppy differs, I have had puppies housetrain in one week and others take four months. I would say the average Cockapoo puppy housetrains in two to four weeks, which is considered quick. The intelligence of the Poodle combined with the eager-to-please mentality of the Cocker make for the ideal combination when training a puppy and, in general, Cockapoos are very easy to train. Consistency is the key when training any dog as well as lots of positive encouragement. Pay less attention to the negatives and reinforce positive behaviour; your puppy will learn quickly this way. I find it is more a matter of training the owner, rather than the dog, with remembering to make regular potty breaks!"

Karol Watson Todd: "Cockapoos are quick to train and I advise new owners to FOCUS on training the puppy completely, i.e. no visitors. My puppies leave me 95% toilet trained. Owners must be aware of the signs of a puppy looking to go to the loo – circling and sniffing - and react calmly and quickly, taking the puppy outside and waiting until they perform. Once accomplished, praise should be lavish. If the neighbours aren't looking over the fence going 'What on Earth?' then you aren't praising enough!"

"Toilet breaks should be on the hour, every hour, when the puppy wakes up, after eating or drinking - and puppies should be carried outside as they simply cannot hold it in on the way out. If an owner focuses on toilet training and watches the puppy for the above signs, then two to three days is all it takes. After that it's just an awareness of toilet breaks. Also think of it like potty training your toddler. Having a puppy is exactly like having a baby."

Julie Shearman: "Cockapoos are very quick to learn. Ours are paper-trained by six weeks and housetrained by four months."

Pat Pollington: "Our Cockapoos are housetrained extremely quickly because we work with the puppies at a young age. We have had puppies that have the odd accident or take a day or two to become housetrained. Occasionally, we have had puppies that take two weeks to housetrain, but it depends how much time you put into the puppy. If the time and effort are put into the puppy, they are fast to housetrain compared with a lot of other breeds."

If you're starting from scratch when you bring your new pup home, your new arrival thinks that the whole house or apartment is his den and doesn't realise it is not the place to eliminate. Therefore you need to gently and persistently teach him that it is unacceptable to make a mess inside the house. Cockapoos, like all dogs, are creatures of routine - not only do they like the same things happening at the same times every day, but establishing a regular routine with your dog also helps to speed up training and housebreaking.

Dogs are also very tactile creatures, so they will pick a toilet area which feels good under their paws. Many dogs like to go on grass - but this will do nothing to improve your lawn, so you should think carefully about what area to encourage your Cockapoo to use. You may want to consider a small patch of gravel crushed into tiny pieces in your garden, or a dog litter tray if you live in an apartment. Some breeders advise against using puppy pads for any length of time as puppies like the softness of the pads, which can encourage them to eliminate on other soft areas - such as your carpets or bed. Follow these tips to speed up housetraining:

1. **Constant supervision** is essential for the first week or two if you are to housetrain your puppy quickly. This is why it is important to book the week or so off work when you bring him home. Make sure you are there to take him outside regularly. If nobody is there, he will learn to urinate or poo(p) inside the house

2. **Take your pup outside at the following times:**
   - As soon as he wakes – every time
   - Shortly after each feed
   - After a drink
   - When he gets excited
   - After exercise or play
   - Last thing at night
   - Initially every hour – whether or not he looks like he wants to go

   You may think that the above list is an exaggeration, but it isn't. Housetraining a pup is almost a full-time job for the first few days. If you are serious about housetraining your puppy quickly, then clear your diary for a few days and keep your eyes firmly glued on your pup…Learn to spot that expression or circling motion just before he makes a puddle - or worse – on your floor

3. Take your Cockapoo to **the same place** every time, you may need to use a lead in the beginning - or tempt him there with a treat if he is not yet lead-trained. Some say it is better to only pick him up and dump him there in an emergency, as it is better if he learns to take himself to the chosen toilet spot. Dogs naturally develop a preference for going in the same place or on the same surface - often grass or dirt. Take him to the same patch every time so he learns this is his bathroom - preferably an area in a corner of your yard or garden

4. **No pressure – be patient.** You must allow your distracted little pup time to wander around and have a good sniff before performing his duties – but do not leave him, stay around a short distance away. Sadly, puppies are not known for their powers of concentration; it may take a while for them to select that perfect restroom!

5. **Housetraining is reward-based.** Praise him or give him a treat immediately when he performs his duties in the chosen spot. Cockapoos love praise, and reward-based training is the most successful method for this sensitive crossbreed

6. **Share the responsibility.** It doesn't have to be the same person that takes the dog outside all the time. In fact it's easier if there are a couple of you, as housetraining is a very time-consuming business. Just make sure you stick to the same principles and patch of ground

7. **Stick to the same routine.** Dogs understand and like routine. Sticking to the same one for mealtimes, short exercise sessions, play time, sleeping and toilet breaks will help not only to housetrain him quicker, but help him settle into his new home

8. **Use your voice if you catch him in the act indoors.** A short sharp negative sound is best - NO! ACK! EH! - it doesn't matter, as long as it is loud enough to make him stop.

Then start running enthusiastically towards your door, calling him into the garden and the chosen place and patiently wait until he has finished what he started indoors. It is no good scolding your dog if you find a puddle or unwanted gift in the house but don't see him do it, he won't know why you are cross with him. Only use the negative sound if you catch him in the act.

9. **No punishment.** Accidents will happen at the beginning, do not punish your Cockapoo for them. He is a baby with a tiny bladder and bowels, and housetraining takes time - it is perfectly natural to have accidents early on. Remain calm and clean up the mess with a good strong-smelling cleaner to remove the odour, so he won't be tempted to use that spot again. Dogs have a very strong sense of smell; use a special spray from your vet or a hot solution of washing powder to completely eliminate the odour. Smacking or rubbing his nose in it can have the opposite effect - he will become afraid to do his business in your presence and may start going behind the couch or under the bed, rather than outside

10. **Look for the signs.** These may be whining, sniffing the floor in a determined manner, circling and looking for a place to go, or walking uncomfortably - particularly at the rear end! Take him outside straight away. If you can help it, don't pick him up. He has to learn to walk to the door himself when he needs to go outside

If you use puppy pads, only do so for a short time or your puppy will get used to them. You can also separate a larger crate into two areas and put a pad in one area to help housetrain your baby Cockapoo. He will eliminate on the pad and keep his bed clean.

If you decide to keep your puppy in a crate overnight and you want him to learn not to soil the crate right from the very beginning, you need to have the crate in the bedroom so you can hear him whine when he needs to go. Initially this might be once or twice a night. By the age of four or five months a Cockapoo pup should be able to last all night without needing the toilet – provided you let him out last thing at night and first thing in the morning.

With a crate, remember that the door should not be closed until your Cockapoo is happy with being inside. He needs to believe that this is a safe place and not a trap or prison. Rather than use a crate, many people prefer to section off an area inside one room or use a puppy pen to confine their pup. Inside this area is a bed and another area with pads or newspapers which the puppy can use as a toilet area.

Apartment Living

Most owners live in houses, but some do live in apartments, particularly those with American Cockapoos which are usually slightly smaller than the English version and often have lower exercise requirements. If you live on the 11th floor of an apartment, housetraining can be a little trickier as you don't have easy access to the outdoors. One suggestion is to indoor housetrain your puppy. Dogs that spend much of their time indoors can be housetrained fairly easily - especially if you start early. Stick to the same principles already outlined - the only difference is that you will be placing your Cockapoo on training pads or newspaper instead of taking him outside.

Start by blocking off a section of the apartment for your new puppy; you can use a baby gate or make your own barrier - pick a chew-proof material - or use a puppy pen. You will be able to keep a better eye on him than if he has free run of the whole place. It will also be easier to monitor his "accidents."

Select a corner away from his eating and sleeping area that will become his permanent bathroom area – carpets are to be avoided if at all possible. At first, cover a larger area than is actually needed - about three to four square feet - with newspaper (or training pads). You can reduce the area as training progresses. Take your puppy there as indicated in our Housetraining Tips.

Praise him enthusiastically when he eliminates on the allotted area. If you catch him doing his business out of the toilet area, pick him up and take him back there. Correct with a firm voice - never a hand. With positive reinforcement and a strict schedule, he will soon be walking to the area on his own.

Owners attempting indoor housetraining should be aware that it will generally take longer than outdoor training; some Cockapoos may resist. Also, once a dog learns to go indoors, it can be difficult to train him to eliminate outdoors. Any laziness on your part by not monitoring your puppy carefully enough - especially in the beginning – will make indoor housetraining a lot longer and more difficult process. The first week is crucial to your puppy learning what is expected of him.

GENERAL HOUSETRAINING TIP: A trigger can be very effective to encourage your dog to perform his duties. Some people use a clicker or a bell - we used a word; well, two actually. Within a week or so I trained our puppy to urinate on the command of "wee wee." Think very carefully before choosing the word or phrase, as I often feel an idiot wandering around our garden last thing at night shouting "Max, WEE WEE!" in an encouraging manner - although I'm not sure that the American expression "GO POTTY" sounds much better!

"How can you tell the dogs need to go out?"

6. Feeding A Cockapoo

To keep your dog's biological machine in good working order, he or she needs the right fuel, just like a finely-tuned sports car.

Feeding the correct diet is an essential part of keeping your Cockapoo fit and healthy.

However, the topic of feeding your dog the right diet is something of a minefield. Owners are bombarded with endless choices as well as countless adverts from dog food companies, all claiming that theirs is best.

There is not one food that will give every single dog the brightest eyes, the shiniest coat, the most energy, the best digestion, the longest life and stop him from scratching or having skin problems. Dogs are individuals, just like people, which means that you could feed a premium food to a group of dogs and find that most of them do great on it, some do not so well, while a few might even get an upset stomach or even an allergic reaction. The question is: "Which food is best for my Cockapoo?"

If you have been given a recommended food from a breeder, rescue centre or previous owner, it is best to stick to this as long as your dog is doing well on it. A good breeder will know which food their dogs thrive on. If you do decide - for whatever reason - to change diet, then this must be done gradually. There are some things to be aware of when it comes to feeding:

1. Most Cockapoos are not fussy eaters and love their food. Add to this their eagerness to please and you have a powerful training tool. You can use feeding time to reinforce a simple command on a daily basis

2. Some dogs do not do well on diets with a high wheat or corn content.

3. Some dogs have food sensitivities or allergies, leading to skin issues and scratching/biting - more on this topic later

4. Controlling your dog's food intake is important, as obesity can trigger or worsen numerous health conditions and shorten lives

5. Sometimes elderly dogs may just get bored with their diet and go off their food. This does not necessarily mean that they are ill, simply that they have lost interest and a new food should be gradually introduced

There are many different options on the market. The most popular manufactured foods include dry complete diets, tinned food (with or without a biscuit mixer), and semi-moist. Some dog foods contain only natural ingredients. Then there is the option of feeding your dog a home-made diet; while other owners feed their dogs vegetarian food.

There are many different qualities of manufactured food. Often, you get what you pay for, so a more expensive food is usually more likely to provide better nutrition for your dog - in terms of minerals, nutrients and high quality meats – rather than a cheap one, which will most likely contain a lot of grain. However, this is not always the case - read the list of ingredients to find out. Dried foods (also called kibble in the US) tend to be less expensive than other foods. They have improved a lot over the last few years and some of the more expensive ones are now a good choice for a healthy, complete diet. Dried foods also contain the least fat and most preservatives.

Our dog Max, who has inhalant allergies, is on a quality dried food made by James Wellbeloved who claims it is 'hypoallergenic,' i.e. good for dogs with allergies. Max seems to do well on it, but not all dogs thrive on dried food. We tried several other foods first; it is a question of each owner finding the best one for their dog. Ask your breeder or vet if you're unsure.

TIP: Beware of buying a food because it is described as 'premium' or 'natural' or both, these terms are meaningless. Many manufacturers blithely use these words, but there are no official guidelines as to what they mean. However **"Complete and balanced"** IS a legal term and has to meet standards laid down by AAFCO (Association of American Feed Control Officials) in the USA.

Always check the ingredients on any food sack, packet or tin to see what is listed first. This is the main ingredient and it should be meat or poultry, not corn or grain. If you are in the US, look for a dog food which has been endorsed by AAFCO. In general, tinned foods are 60-70% water. Often semi-moist foods contain a lot of artificial substances and sugar - which is maybe why dogs love them!

Choosing the right food for your Cockapoo is important; it will certainly influence his health, coat and even temperament. There are also three stages of your dog's life to consider when feeding: Puppy, Adult and Senior (also called Veteran). Some manufacturers also produce a Junior feed for adolescent dogs. Each represents a different physical stage of his life and you need to choose the right food to cope with his body during each particular phase. Also, a pregnant female will require a special diet to cope with the extra demands on her body; this is especially important as she nears the latter stages of pregnancy.

Most owners feed their Cockapoos twice a day; which helps to stop your hungry dog gulping food down in a mad feeding frenzy. Some owners of fussy eaters feed two different meals each day to provide variety. One meal could be dried kibble, while the other might be home-made, with fresh meat, poultry and vegetables, or a moist food. If you do this, speak with your vet to make sure the two separate meals provide a balanced diet and that they are not too rich in protein.

We will not recommend one brand of dog food over another, but do have some general tips to help you choose what to feed. There is also some advice for owners of dogs with food allergies and intolerances. Cockapoos are not particularly prone to them, but they are a growing problem in the canine world generally. Sufferers may itch, lick or chew their paws and/or legs, or rub their face. They may also get frequent ear infections as well as redness and swelling on their face.

Switching to a grain-free diet can help to alleviate the symptoms, as your dog's digestive system does not have to work as hard. In the wild, a dog or wolf's staple diet would be meat with some vegetable matter from the stomach and intestines of the herbivores (plant eating animals) he ate – but no grains. Dogs do not digest corn or wheat (which are often staples of cheap commercial dog food) very efficiently. Grain-free diets still provide carbohydrates through fruits and vegetables, so your dog still gets all his nutrients.

15 Top Tips for Feeding your Cockapoo

1. If you choose a manufactured food, **don't pick one where meat or poultry content is NOT the first item listed on the bag.** Foods with lots of cheap cereals or sugar are not the best choice

2. Some Cockapoos suffer from sensitive skin, 'hot spots' or allergies. A cheap dog food, often bulked up with grain, will only make this worse. If this is the case, bite the bullet and **choose a high quality – usually more expensive – food, or consider a raw diet.** You'll probably save money in vets' bills in the long run and your dog will be happier. A food described as 'hypoallergenic' on the sack means 'less likely to cause allergies' and is a good place to start

3. **Feed your Cockapoo twice a day**, rather than once. Smaller feeds are easier to digest, and reduce flatulence and the risk of bloat from gulping food. Puppies need to be fed more often; discuss exactly how often with your breeder

4. **Establish a feeding regime and stick to it**. Dogs like routine. If you are feeding twice a day, feed once in the morning and then again at tea-time. Stick to the same times of day. Do not give the last feed too late, or your dog's body will not have chance to process or burn off the food before sleeping. He will also need a walk or letting out in the garden or yard after his second feed to allow him to empty his bowels. Feeding at the same times each day helps your dog establish a toilet regime

5. **Take away any uneaten food between meals.** Most Cockapoos are good eaters, but any dog can become fussy if food is available all day. Imagine if your dinner was left on the table for hours until you finished it. Returning to the table two or three hours later would not be such a tempting prospect, but coming back for a fresh meal would be far more appetising. Also, when food is left down all day, some dogs seem to take the food for granted and lose their appetite. Then they begin to leave the food and you are at your wits' end trying to find something they will actually eat. Put the food bowl down twice a day and then take it up after 20 minutes – even if he has left some. If he is healthy and hungry, he will look forward to his next meal and soon stop leaving food. If your dog does not eat anything for a couple of days, it could well be a sign that he is not well

6. **Do not feed too many titbits and treats between meals.** Extra weight will place extra strain on your dog's joints and organs, have a detrimental effect on his health and even his lifespan. It also throws his balanced diet out of the window. Try to avoid feeding your dog from the table or your plate, as this encourages attention-seeking behaviour and drooling

7. **Never give your dog cooked bones,** as these can splinter and cause him to choke or suffer intestinal problems. If your dog is a gulper, it's a good idea to avoid giving rawhide, as dogs who rush their food have a tendency to quickly chew and swallow rawhide without first bothering to nibble it down into smaller pieces

8. **NEVER feed the following items to your dog**: grapes, raisins, chocolate, onions, Macadamia nuts, any fruits with seeds or stones, tomatoes, avocadoes, rhubarb, tea, coffee or alcohol. ALL of these are poisonous to dogs

9. **If you switch to a new food, do the transition gradually.** Unlike humans, dogs' digestive systems cannot handle sudden changes in diet. Begin by gradually mixing some of the new food in with the old and increase the proportion so that after seven to eight days, all the food is the new one. The following ratios are recommended by Doctors Foster & Smith Inc: Days 1-3 add 25% of the new food, Days 4-6 add 50%, Days 7-9 add 75%, Day 10 feed 100% of the new food. By the way, if you stick to the identical brand, you can change flavours in one go

10. **Check your dog's faeces** (aka stools, poo or poop!) If his diet is suitable, the food should be easily digested and produce dark brown, firm stools. If your dog produces soft or light stools, or has a lot of gas or diarrhoea, then the diet may not suit him, so consult your vet or breeder for advice

11. **Feed your dog in stainless steel or ceramic dishes.** Plastic bowls don't last as long and can also trigger an allergic reaction in some sensitive dogs. Ceramic bowls are best for keeping water cold

12. **If you have more than one dog, consider feeding them separately**. Cockapoos usually get on fine with other pets, especially if introduced at an early age. But feeding dogs together can sometimes lead to dog food aggression from your Cockapoo either protecting his own food or trying to eat the food designated for another pet

13. **If you do feed leftovers, feed them INSTEAD of a balanced meal,** not as well as (unless you are feeding a raw diet). High quality dog foods already provide all the nutrients, vitamins, minerals and calories that your dog needs. Feeding titbits or leftovers may be too rich for your Cockapoo in addition to his regular diet and cause him to scratch or have other problems, as well as get fat. You can feed your dog vegetables, such as carrots, as a healthy low-calorie treat; most dogs love 'em. (Picture of Bea courtesy of Judy and Greg Moorhouse)

14. **Keep your dog's weight in check.** Obesity can lead to the development of serious health issues, such as diabetes, high blood pressure and heart disease. Although the weight varies from dog to dog, a good rule of thumb is that your Cockapoo's tummy

should be higher than or, at worst, level with his rib cage. If his belly hangs down below it, he is overweight

15. And finally, **always make sure that your Cockapoo has access to clean, fresh water.** Change the water and clean the bowl regularly – it gets slimy!

Types of Dog Food

We are what we eat. The right food is a very important part of a healthy lifestyle for dogs as well as humans. Here are the main options explained:

Dry dog food - also called kibble, this is a popular and relatively inexpensive way of providing a balanced diet. It comes in a variety of flavours and with differing ingredients to suit the different stages of a dog's life. Cheap foods are often false economy, particularly if your Cockapoo does not tolerate grain/cereal very well, as they often contain a lot of grain. You may also have to feed larger quantities to ensure he gets sufficient nutrients.

Canned food - another popular choice – and it's often very popular with dogs too. They love the taste and it generally comes in a variety of flavours. Canned food is often mixed with dry kibble, and a small amount may be added to a dog on a dry food diet if he has lost interest in food. It tends to be more expensive than dried food and many owners don't like the mess. These days there are hundreds of options, some are very high quality and made from natural, organic ingredients and containing herbs and other beneficial ingredients. A part-opened tin can sometimes smell when you open the fridge door. As with dry food, read the label closely. Generally, you get what you pay for and the origins of cheap canned dog food are often somewhat dubious.

Semi-Moist - These are commercial dog foods shaped like pork chops, salamis, bacon, burgers or other meaty foods and they are the least nutritional of all dog foods. They are full of sugars, artificial flavourings and colourings to help make them visually appealing. Cockapoos don't care what their food looks like, they only care how it smells and tastes; the shapes are designed to appeal to us humans. While you may give your dog one as an occasional treat, they are not a diet in themselves and do not provide the nutrition that your dog needs. Steer clear of them for regular feeding.

Freeze-Dried - This is made by frozen food manufacturers for owners who like the convenience – this type of food keeps for six months to a year - or for those going on a trip with their dog. It says 'freeze-dried' on the packet and is highly palatable, but the freeze-drying process bumps up the cost.

Home-Cooked - Some dog owners want the ability to be in complete control of their dog's diet, know exactly what their dog is eating and to be absolutely sure that his nutritional needs are being met. Feeding your dog a home-cooked diet is time consuming and expensive, and the difficult thing – as with the raw diet - is sticking to it once you have started out with the best of intentions. But many owners think the extra effort is worth the peace of mind. If you decide to go ahead, you should spend the time to become proficient and learn about canine nutrition to ensure your dog gets all his vital nutrients.

What the Breeders Feed

We asked a number of Cockapoo breeders what they fed their dogs. We are not recommending one brand over another, but the breeders' answers give a good insight as to what issues are important when considering food and why a particular brand has been chosen.

Jeanne Davis, Wind Horse Offering, Maryland, USA, said: "Feeding is slightly complex. For me there is no simple answer. I feed the moms a dry kibble that is no less than 28% protein and about two weeks before they whelp, I start feeding them a bit of canned food. Any dry or canned food that I feed HAS to be devoid of wheat, corn, soy, gluten (and of course any kind of sugars/corn syrup). These days there are many manufacturers who are catching up with that nutritional preference.

"To my thinking, the reason why so many dogs develop allergies is that many of the foods have been corn-based (supposedly to make the coat shiny), but dogs are not grain eaters, so it messes with their pH, and slowly they 'get sick'.

"I feed the moms a really good vitamin during gestation and throughout the time that they have their puppies. When the puppies are about a month old, they will start getting into mom's food. Since their teeth are only just coming through, 'eating' kibble doesn't really happen, but they do get a certain amount of the canned/wet food." Pictured is one of Jeanne's handsome puppies.

"I continue the puppies on the 28% kibble with some canned food; and send them home with a bag of what they have been eating and a small can of wet food. I tell the new puppy owners to put a dollop of wet food on the puppy's food for a while to keep him or her eating during the transition to their new home, but they need not stay on the canned food.

"At eight weeks, they are fully eating kibble anyway. I also suggest that if the puppy is fussy, to pour some (organic) chicken or beef broth over the kibble for a while to keep the puppy hydrated and eating. I also provide new owners with literature about, and a sample of, the vitamins (from NuVet) that the moms have been eating."

Jessica Sampson, Legacy Cockapoos, Ontario, Canada: "We feed a high quality commercial diet - Dick Van Patten's Natural Balance. We love this food as it is made from high quality ingredients and has no fillers (corn, wheat, rice, etc). and is packed full of vitamins and minerals. We have had great success with this food over the years. It is an all-stages diet, which means we feed the same food to all our dogs and puppies. We do not feed our puppies a food formulated specifically for puppies as our vet years ago advised us against it. The reasoning was that when you feed puppy food it causes puppies to grow too quickly and can give a higher rate of joint issues (hip dysplasia, luxating patella etc). The bone and muscle development have trouble keeping up with each other which can lead to issues.

"When you feed an all-stages diet to puppies they grow at a slower rate, which allows their bone and muscle development to keep up with one another. They still reach the same finished size and weight as they would if they ate puppy food. They just get there slower, which is better for their development."

Linda Zarro, of Sugar and Spice Cockapoos, South Carolina, added: "We use Kirkland brand dog/puppy food from Costco. We used to give raw chicken legs and thighs to our dogs when we only had about six dogs, but we don't see any difference in their health, so give them the Costco food, which has a very high rating for dog foods. We also give our dogs and puppies (starting at six weeks of age) a nutritional supplement called NuVet Plus. This supplement helps to boost the immune system of dogs and puppies. It is full of herbs, vitamins and minerals to help keep them in the best of health. We believe that giving it to our dogs and puppies reduces the risk of many potential health issues."

In the UK, Karol Watson Todd, of KaroColin Cockapoos, Lincolnshire said: "I feed Royal Canin dried food and go right through all the stages, so HT42 (a special food formulated to meet the nutritional needs of breeding females) from first day of season to day 42 of pregnancy, then we go to starter food for mum and it's also the weaning food - I purée it down to gruel consistency. Then at eight weeks the puppies go on to Junior and mum goes onto the Cocker Maintenance Food.

"I like Royal Canin because it's a well-known food and an easy-to-buy brand for the new owners. The nutrition is good; I have tried all sorts of other foods and found them to be too rich and not enough quantity (like Eden). All my girls look fantastic after having a litter of puppies on the Royal Canin and I have never had a bitch that is thin or in poor condition after a litter. That speaks volumes as puppies take a lot out of the bitch, but she can only give it if she has it there to give.

"I also feed chicken, which I cook in the slow cooker, to all my dogs and add it to the dry food. The mums can get several breasts a day in addition to the huge amounts of Royal Canin. Further, I always have puppy formula in, and I give this to mum during the birthing process to keep her energy levels up, and I feed it slightly warm. It's called Nutrola: http://animal-health.co.uk/nutrolac.html. I like the formula for mums and puppies that have feeding problems and also as it is goat's milk-based. It is also very easy to mix up and I make up baby bottles and keep in fridge for 24 hours if I have a puppy that needs extra feeding. I use the sponge feeding method for any puppies that need supplementary feeding, as tubing a puppy will stop the sucking reflex and they will then miss out on an important part of their babyhood."

Another UK breeder who is a fan of Royal Canin is Pat Pollington, of Polycinders Cockapoos, Devon: "I feed my dogs on Royal Canin Adult. I feed my puppies on Royal Canin Mini Starter, they also have some Royal Canin Starter Mousse mixed in and I give them a bowl of Royal Canin Starter Milk to drink during weaning time. I feed my pregnant bitches a mixture of Royal Canin Mini Starter and Royal Canin Adult. A week before the end of their pregnancy, they have all Royal Canin Mini Starter and a bowl of Royal Canin Starter Milk.

"I feed Royal Canin because I feel it is a brilliant food. It keeps my dogs on tip top form. I don't need to feed them very much of it. I have tried lots of different food brands for both my dogs and puppies, but nothing compares to it. I have really fussy typical Poodles and the only food I can get them to eat is Royal Canin. All my puppies have a fantastic coat on them and they are always very healthy. The food you feed puppies is important because they need so many different things in their food to help them grow - and Royal Canin has it all. I never have a skinny bitch after pregnancy - they all hold their weight and, if anything, sometimes a bit too much weight."

Julie Shearman, of Crystalwood Cockapoos, Devon, added: "We fed Burns Natural dog and puppy food. It's made with natural quality ingredients and we find that both the pups and all our adult dogs thrive on it. A dry dog food gives the dogs something to crunch, which slows down their eating (Cockers are pigs!) and it is also good for teeth and gums.

The Raw Diet

There is a quiet revolution going on in the world of dog food. After years of feeding dry or tinned dog food, increasing numbers of owners are now feeding a raw diet to their beloved pets. There is anecdotal evidence that many dogs thrive on a raw diet, although scientific proof is lagging behind. There are a number of claims made by fans of the raw diet, including:

➢ Reduced symptoms of - or less likelihood of – allergies, and less scratching

➢ Better skin and coats

➢ Easier weight management

➢ Improved digestion

➢ Less doggie odour and flatulence

➢ Fresher breath and improved dental health

➢ Helps fussy eaters

➢ Drier and less smelly stools, more like pellets

➢ Reduced risk of bloat

➢ Overall improvement in general health and less disease

➢ Higher energy levels

➢ Most dogs love a raw diet

It's fair to say that most breeders and owners we contacted has generally found there was no need to feed a raw diet to Cockapoos, as their dogs thrived on commercially-prepared food, or a mixture of manufactured and home-prepared food. A raw diet is expensive and involves more effort on the part of the owner.

However, food intolerances and allergies, as well as other types of allergies, are on the increase and if you find your Cockapoo is unlucky enough to be a sufferer, you might want to consider a raw diet. Jessica Sampson is one breeder who has found it beneficial: "I am pro raw diet if it is manageable for you, but only if it is done under the guidance of a canine nutritionist and quality human grade products are used. I have in the past had great success with the raw diet.

"What first made me try it was I had a dog that suffered from chronic colitis. I did all the vet's recommendations and did a year of veterinary diets and expensive medications every month. My dog was not improving; in fact she was getting worse and was a shadow of her former self (basically a walking skeleton). At my wits' end and desperate and frightened that I would lose her,

I tried the raw diet. Within one day her colitis completely disappeared. She quickly began putting weight back on and in about two months she was as healthy as can be again.

"The other positive outcome of the raw diet was the amount of waste pick up. I went from picking up after her three times a day to once a day, and it was so small it was barely worth the effort! Everything she was eating she was using and there was no extra undigested filler, like in commercial food, to come back out. Her coat was shiny and glossy and her teeth whiter. She also had bundles more of energy. All around she was a much healthier dog and she lived to the ripe old age of 17." Pictured are two of Jessica's beautiful puppies.

Rebecca Mae Goins, MoonShine Babies Cockapoos, Indiana, adds: "I have seen many Cockapoos that have wheat and other food allergies benefit from raw diets, but unless your Cockapoo has this issue, I see no reason to feed a raw diet unless it is your choice."

Karol Watson Todd says: "I'm very interested in a raw diet and have dabbled in it a little. Puppies love to gnaw on a frozen raw chicken wing. Feeding is a huge issue and, in general, the bigger the price tag, the better the food."

Pat Pollington is another UK breeder who has given it a go: "Raw diets are very good because the dog is going back to natural instincts. We don't believe that puppies should have a raw diet because puppies need certain things to help with their bones, their coats and growth. Puppy biscuits contain everything a puppy needs. If you want to feed raw diet, we suggest that you introduce this when the puppy hits 12 months old. Raw diet is very good for dogs. The only problem with it is in the summer it can cause flies around the bowl during feeding. Also it is not good for dog's teeth. If you are going to feed a raw diet, we suggest you brush your dog's teeth at least every day."

If your dog is not doing well on a commercially-prepared dog food, it's certainly worth considering a raw diet, which emulates the way dogs used to eat. Commercial foods may contain artificial preservatives and excessive protein and fillers – causing a reaction in some dogs. Dry, canned and other styles of processed food were mainly created as a means of convenience, but unfortunately this convenience sometimes can affect a dog's health.

Some nutritionists believe that dogs fed raw whole foods tend to be healthier than those on other diets, claiming there are inherent beneficial enzymes, vitamins, minerals and other qualities in meats, fruits, vegetables and grains in their natural forms that are denatured or destroyed when cooked. Many also believe dogs are less likely to have allergic reactions to the ingredients on this diet. But unsurprisingly, the topic is not without controversy.

Critics say that the risks of nutritional imbalance, intestinal problems and food-borne illnesses caused by handling and feeding raw meat outweigh any benefits. It's true that owners must pay strict attention to hygiene when preparing a raw diet and it may not be suitable if there are children in the household. A dog may also be more likely to ingest bacteria or parasites such as Salmonella, E.coli and Ecchinococcus.

Frozen food can be a valuable aid to the raw diet. The food is highly palatable, made from high quality ingredients and dogs usually wolf it down. The downsides are that not all pet food stores stock it and it is expensive. There are two main types of raw diet, one involves feeding raw, meaty bones and the other is known as the BARF diet (*Biologically Appropriate Raw Food* or *Bones And Raw Food),* created by Dr Ian Billinghurst.

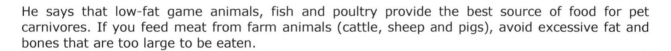

Raw Meaty Bones

This diet is:

> ➢ Raw meaty bones or carcasses, if available, should form the bulk of the diet
> ➢ Table scraps both cooked and raw, such as vegetables, can be fed
> ➢ As with any diet, fresh water should be constantly available. **NOTE: Do NOT feed cooked bones, they can splinter**

Australian veterinarian Dr Tom Lonsdale is a leading proponent of the raw meaty bones diet. He believes the following foods are suitable:

> ➢ Chicken and turkey carcasses, after the meat has been removed for human consumption
> ➢ Poultry by-products, including heads, feet, necks and wings
> ➢ Whole fish and fish heads
> ➢ Sheep, calf, goat, and deer carcasses sawn into large pieces of meat and bone
> ➢ Other by-products, e.g. pigs' trotters, pigs' heads, sheep heads, brisket, tail and rib bones
> ➢ A certain amount of offal can be included in the diet, e.g. liver, lungs, trachea, hearts, tripe

He says that low-fat game animals, fish and poultry provide the best source of food for pet carnivores. If you feed meat from farm animals (cattle, sheep and pigs), avoid excessive fat and bones that are too large to be eaten.

Some of it will depend on what's available locally and how expensive it is. If you shop around you should be able to source a regular supply of suitable raw meaty bones at a reasonable price. Start with your local butcher or farm shop. When deciding what type of bones to feed your Cockapoo, one point to bear in mind is that dogs are more likely to break their teeth when eating large knuckle bones and bones sawn lengthwise than when eating meat and bone together.

You'll also need to think about WHERE you are going to feed your dog. A dog takes some time to eat a raw bone and will push it around the floor, so the kitchen may not be the most suitable or hygienic place. Outside is one option, but what do you do when it's raining?

Establishing the right quantity to feed is a matter of trial and error. You will reach a decision based on your dog's activity levels, appetite and body condition. High activity and a big appetite show a need for increased food, and vice versa. A very approximate guide, based on raw meaty bones, for the average dog is 15%-20% of body weight in one week, or 2%-3% a day. Table scraps should be fed as an extra component of the diet. These figures are only a rough guide and relate to adult pets in a domestic environment. Pregnant or lactating females and growing puppies may need much more food than adult animals of similar body weight.

Dr Lonsdale says: "Wherever possible, feed the meat and bone ration in one large piece requiring much ripping, tearing and gnawing. This makes for contented pets with clean teeth. Wild carnivores feed at irregular intervals. In a domestic setting, regularity works best and accordingly I suggest that you feed adult dogs and cats once daily. If you live in a hot climate, I recommend that you feed pets in the evening to avoid attracting flies.

"I suggest that on one or two days each week your dog may be fasted — just like animals in the wild. On occasions you may run out of natural food. Don't be tempted to buy artificial food, fast your dog and stock up with natural food the next day. Puppies...sick or underweight dogs should not be fasted (unless on veterinary advice)."

Table scraps and some fruit and vegetable peelings can also be fed, but should not make up more than one-third of the diet. Liquidising cooked and uncooked scraps in a food mixer can make them easier to digest.

Things to Avoid

➤ Excessive meat off the bone — not balanced
➤ Excessive vegetables — not balanced
➤ Small pieces of bone — can be swallowed whole and get stuck
➤ Cooked bones — get stuck
➤ Mineral and vitamin additives — create imbalance
➤ Processed food — leads to dental and other diseases
➤ Excessive starchy food — associated with bloat
➤ Onions, garlic and chocolate, grapes, raisins, sultanas, currants — toxic to pets
➤ Fruit stones (pips) and corn cobs — get stuck
➤ Milk — associated with diarrhoea. Animals drink it whether thirsty or not and consequently get fat

Points of Concern

➤ Old dogs accustomed to processed food may experience initial difficulty when changed to a natural diet. Discuss the change with your vet first and then, if he or she agrees, switch your dog's diet over a period of a week to 10 days

➤ Raw meaty bones are not suitable for dogs with dental or jaw problems

➤ This diet may not be suitable if your dog gulps his food, as the bones can become lodged inside him; larger bones may prevent gulping

➤ The diet should be varied, any nutrients fed to excess can be harmful

➤ Liver is an excellent foodstuff, but should not be fed more than once weekly

➤ Other offal, e.g. ox stomachs, should not make up more than half of the diet

➤ Whole fish are an excellent source of food, but avoid feeding one species of fish constantly. Some species, e.g. carp, contain an enzyme which destroys thiamine (vitamin B1)

➤ If you have more than one dog, do not allow them to fight over the food; feed them separately if necessary

➤ Be prepared to monitor your dog while he eats the bones, especially in the beginning, and do not feed bones with sharp points. Take the bone off your dog before it becomes small enough to swallow

➤ Make sure that children do not disturb the dog when he is feeding or try to take the bone away

➤ Hygiene: Make sure the raw meaty bones are kept separate from human food and clean thoroughly any surface the uncooked meat or bones have touched. This is especially important if you have children. Feeding bowls are unnecessary. Your dog will drag the bones across the floor, so feed them outside if you can, or on a floor which is easy to clean

➤ Puppies can and do eat diets of raw meaty bones, but you should consult the breeder or a vet before embarking on this diet with a young dog

You will need a regular supply of meaty bones – either locally or online - and you should buy in bulk to ensure a consistency of supply. For this you will need a large freezer. You can then parcel up the bones into daily portions. You can also feed frozen bones; some dogs will gnaw them straight away, others will wait for them to thaw.

More information is available from the website www.rawmeatybones.com and I would strongly recommend discussing the matter with your breeder or vet first before switching to raw meaty bones.

The BARF Diet

A variation of the raw meaty bones diet is the BARF created by Dr Ian Billinghurst, who owns the registered trademark 'Barf Diet'. A typical BARF diet is made up of 60%-75% of raw meaty bones (bones with about 50% meat, such as chicken neck, back and wings) and 25%-40% of fruit and vegetables, offal, meat, eggs or dairy foods. Bones must not be cooked or they can splinter inside the dog. There is a great deal of information on the BARF diet on the internet.

One point to consider is that a raw diet is not suitable for every dog. You could consider a gradual shift and see how your Cockapoo copes with the raw bones. You might also consider feeding two different daily meals to your dog - one dry kibble and one raw diet, for example. If you do, then research the subject, and consult your vet to make sure that the two combined meals provide a balanced diet.

NOTE: Only start a raw diet if you have done your research and are sure you have the time and money to keep it going. There are numerous websites and canine forums with information on switching to a raw diet and everything it involves.

Food Allergies

Symptoms

Dog food allergies affect about one in 10 dogs. They are the third most common canine allergy for dogs after atopy (inhaled or contact allergies) and flea bite allergies. While there's no scientific evidence of links between specific breeds/crossbreeds and food allergies, there is anecdotal evidence from owners that some bloodlines do suffer from food allergies or intolerances. Cockapoos are not regarded as particularly susceptible, but any individual dog of whatever type can suffer from them.

Food allergies affect males and females in equal measures as well as neutered and intact pets. They can start when your dog is five months or 12 years old - although the vast majority start when the dog is between two and six years old. It is not uncommon for dogs with food allergies to also have other types of allergies. If your Cockapoo is not well, how do you know if the problem lies with his food or not? Here are some common symptoms of food allergies to look out for:

 ➢ Itchy skin (this is the most common). Your Cockapoo may lick or chew his paws or legs and rub his face with his paws or on the furniture, carpet, etc.
 ➢ Excessive scratching
 ➢ Ear infections
 ➢ Hot patches of skin
 ➢ Hair loss
 ➢ Redness and inflammation on the chin and face
 ➢ Recurring skin infections
 ➢ Increased bowel movements (maybe twice as often as usual)
 ➢ Skin infections that clear up with antibiotics but recur when the antibiotics run out

Allergies or Intolerance?

There's a difference between dog food *allergies* and dog food *intolerance*:

Typical reactions to allergies are skin problems and/or itching

Typical reactions to intolerance are diarrhoea and/or vomiting

Dog food intolerance can be compared to people who get diarrhoea or an upset stomach from eating spicy food. Both can be cured by a change to a diet specifically suited to your dog, although a food allergy may be harder to get to the root cause of. As they say in the canine world: "One dog's meat is another dog's poison".

With dogs, certain ingredients are more likely to cause allergies than others. In order of the most common triggers they are: **Beef, dairy products, chicken, wheat, eggs, corn, soya (soy).** Unfortunately, these most common offenders are also the most common ingredients in dog foods! By the way, don't think if you put your dog on a rice and lamb kibble diet that it will automatically cure the problem. It might, but then again there's a fair chance it won't. The reason lamb and rice were thought to be less likely to cause allergies is simply because they have not traditionally been included in dog food recipes - therefore fewer dogs had reactions to them.

It is also worth noting that a dog is allergic or sensitive to an **ingredient**, not to a particular brand of dog food, so it is very important to read the label on the sack or tin. If your Cockapoo has a reaction to beef, for example, he will react to any food containing beef, regardless of how expensive it is or how well it has been prepared.

Symptoms of food allergies are well documented. Unfortunately, the problem is that these conditions may also be symptoms of other issues such as environmental or flea bite allergies, intestinal problems, mange and yeast or bacterial infections. If your Cockapoo suffers from ear infections, there could be a number of different causes. It is more likely to be a bacterial or yeast infection due to the lack of air circulation under the hairy ear flap, but a reaction to a certain type of food should also be considered. You can have a blood test on your dog for food allergies, but many vets now believe that this is not accurate enough.

The only way to completely cure a food allergy or intolerance is complete avoidance. This is not as easy as it sounds. First you have to be sure that your dog does have a food allergy, and then you have to discover which food is causing the reaction.

Blood tests are not thought to be reliable and, as far as I am aware, the only true way to determine exactly what your dog is allergic to is to start a food trial. If you don't or can't do this for the whole 12 weeks, then you could try a more amateurish approach, which is eliminating ingredients from your dog's diet one at a time by switching diets – remember to do this over a period of a week to 10 days.

A food trial is usually the option of last resort, due to the amount of time and attention that it requires. It is also called '*an exclusion diet*' and is the only truly accurate way of finding out if your dog has a food allergy and what is causing it. Before embarking on one, try switching dog food. A hypoallergenic dog food, either commercial or home-made, is a good place to start. There are a number of these on the market and they all have the word '*hypoallergenic*' in the name.

Although usually more expensive, hypoallergenic dog food ingredients do not include common allergens such as wheat protein or soya, thereby minimising the risk of an allergic reaction. Many may have less common ingredients, such as venison, duck or types of fish. Here are some things to look for in a high quality food: meat or poultry as the first ingredient, vegetables, natural herbs such as rosemary or parsley, oils such as rapeseed (canola) or salmon.

Here's what to avoid: corn, corn meal, corn gluten meal, meat or poultry by-products (as you don't know exactly what these are or how they have been handled), artificial preservatives (including BHA, BHT, Propyl Gallate, Ethoxyquin, Sodium Nitrite/Nitrate and TBHQBHA), artificial colours, sugars and sweeteners like corn syrup, sucrose and ammoniated glycyrrhizin, powdered cellulose, propylene glycol. If you can rule out all of the above, and you have tried switching diet without much success, then a food trial may be the only option left.

Food Trials

Before you embark on one of these, you need to know that they are a real pain-in-the-you-know-what to monitor. You have to be incredibly vigilant and determined, so only start one if you 100% know you can see it through to the end, or you are wasting your time. It is important to keep a diary during a food trial to record any changes in your dog's symptoms, behaviour or habits.

A food trial involves feeding one specific food for 12 weeks, something the dog has never eaten before, such as rabbit and rice or venison and potato. Surprisingly, dogs are typically NOT allergic to foods they have never eaten before. The food should contain no added colouring, preservatives or flavourings. There are a number of these commercial diets on the market, as well as specialised diets that have proteins and carbohydrates broken down into such small molecular sizes that they no longer trigger an allergic reaction. These are called **'limited antigen'** or **'hydrolysed protein'** diets.

Home-made diets are another option as you can strictly control the ingredients. The difficult thing is that this must be the **only thing** the dog eats during the trial. Any treats or snacks make the whole thing a waste of time. During the trial, you shouldn't allow your dog to roam freely, as you cannot control what he is eating or drinking when he is out of sight outdoors. Only the recommended diet must be fed. Do NOT give:

- ➢ Treats
- ➢ Rawhide (you shouldn't feed these to a Cockapoo, anyway)
- ➢ Pigs' ears
- ➢ Cows' hooves
- ➢ Flavoured medications (including heartworm treatments) or supplements
- ➢ Flavoured toothpastes
- ➢ Flavoured plastic toys

If you want to give a treat, use the recommended diet. (Tinned diets can be frozen in chunks or baked and then used as treats). If you have other dogs, either feed them all on the trial diet or feed the others in an entirely different location. If you have a cat, don't let the dog near the cat litter tray. And keep your pet out of the room when you are eating. Even small amounts of food dropped on the floor or licked off of a plate can ruin an elimination trial, meaning you'll have to start all over again.

Grain

Although beef is the food most likely to cause allergies in the general dog population, there is evidence to suggest that the ingredient most likely to cause a problem in many dogs of all types is grain. Grain is wheat or any other cultivated cereal crop. Foods that are high in grains and sugar can cause an increase in unhealthy bacteria and yeast in the stomach. This crowds out the good bacteria in the stomach and can cause toxins to occur that affect the immune system.

When the immune system is not functioning properly, the itchiness related to food allergies can cause secondary bacterial and yeast infections. These often show as ear infections, skin disorders, bladder infections and reddish or dark brown tear stains. Symptoms of a yeast infection also include:

- ➢ Itchiness
- ➢ A musty smell
- ➢ Skin lesions or redness on the underside of the neck, the belly or paws

Although drugs such as antihistamines and steroids will temporarily help, they do not address the cause. Long term use of steroids is definitely not recommended as it can lead to organ problems.

Switching to a grain-free diet may help your dog get rid of the yeast and toxins. Some owners also feed their Cockapoos a daily spoonful of natural or live yoghurt, as this contains healthy bacteria and helps to balance the bacteria in your dog's digestive system (by the way, it works for humans too!) Others have switched their dogs to a raw diet. Switching to a grain-free diet may help to get rid of yeast and bad bacteria in the digestive system. Introduce the new food over a week to 10 days and be patient, it may take two to three months for symptoms to subside – but you will definitely know if it has worked after 12 weeks.

Wheat products are known to produce flatulence in some dogs, while corn products and feed fillers may cause skin rashes or irritations. It is also worth noting that some of the symptoms of food allergies - particularly the scratching, licking, chewing and redness - can also be a sign of inhalant or contact (environmental) allergies, which are caused by a reaction to such triggers as pollen, grass or dust. Some dogs are also allergic to flea bites. See **Chapter 10. Skin and Allergies** for more details.

If you suspect your Cockapoo has a food allergy, the first port of call should be to the vet to discuss the best course of action. Many vets' practices promote specific brands of dog food, which may or may not be the best for your dog. Don't buy anything without first checking every ingredient on the label.

How Much Food?

This is another question I am often asked. The answer is … there is no easy answer! The correct amount of food for your dog depends on a number of factors:

> Breed/crossbreed
> Gender
> Age
> Energy levels
> Amount of daily exercise
> Health
> Environment
> Number of dogs in house
> Quality of the food

Some breeds have a higher metabolic rate than others. Cockapoos are generally regarded as dogs with medium to high activity levels – although this depends on the breed of the parents. Very broadly, dogs bred from English Working Cockers have the highest energy levels, followed by English Show Cockers and American Cockers - but this is misleading, as energy levels vary tremendously from individual dog to dog. (Pictured is Nigel and Julie Houston's lively six-year-old, Lincoln).

Generally smaller dogs have faster metabolisms so require a higher amount of food per pound of body weight. Female dogs can be slightly more prone to putting on weight than male dogs. Some people say that dogs which have been spayed or neutered are more likely to put on weight, although this is disputed by others. Growing puppies and young dogs need more food than senior dogs with a slower lifestyle.

Every dog is different. You can have two Cockapoos from the same litter with different temperaments and energy levels; the energetic dog will burn off more calories. Maintaining a healthy body weight for dogs – and humans – is all about balancing what you take in with how much you burn off.

If your dog is exercised for a couple of hours a day and has play sessions with humans or other dogs, he will need more calories than, for example, an American Cockapoo who spends most of his time in an apartment. And certain health conditions, such as an underactive thyroid, diabetes, arthritis or heart disease, can lead to dogs putting on weight, so their food has to be adjusted accordingly.

Just like us, a dog kept in a very cold environment will need more calories to keep warm than a dog in a warm climate. They burn extra calories in keeping themselves warm. (Pictured are Jeanne Davis's Shine and Muffin enjoying a romp in the snow). Here's an interesting fact: a dog kept on his own is more likely to be overweight than a dog kept with other dogs. This is because he receives all of the food-based attention.

Manufacturers of cheaper foods usually recommend feeding more to your dog, as much of the food is made up of cereals, which are not doing much except bulking up the weight of the food – and possibly triggering allergies in your Cockapoo.

The daily recommended amount listed on food sacks or tins is generally too high – after all, the more your dog eats, the more they sell! Because there are so many factors involved, there is no simple answer. However, below we have listed a broad guideline of the average number of **calories** a Cockapoo with medium energy and activity levels needs.

We feed our dog a dried hypoallergenic dog food made by James Wellbeloved in England. Max has seasonal allergies which make him scratch, but he seems to do pretty well on this food. Here we list James Wellbeloved's recommended feeding amounts for dogs, listed in kilograms and grams. (28.3 grams=1 ounce. 1kg=2.2 pounds).

The number on the left is the dog's **adult weight** in kilograms. The numbers on the right are the amount of daily food in grams that an average dog with average energy levels requires, measured in grams (divide this by 28.3 to get the amount in ounces). For example, a three-month-old Cockapoo puppy which will grow into a 10kg (22lb) adult would require around 190 grams of food per day (6.73 ounces).

NOTE: These are only very general guidelines; your dog may need more or less than this. Use the chart as a guideline only and if your dog appears to lose or gain weight, adjust his or her feeds accordingly.

Canine Feeding Chart

PUPPY

Size type	Expected adult body weight (kg)	Daily serving (g)					
		2 mths	3 mths	4 mths	5 mths	6 mths	> 6 mths
Toy	2	50	60	60	60	55	
	5	95	110	115	115	110	Change to Adult or Small Breed Adult
Small	10	155	185	195	190	185	
Medium	17	215	265	285	285	280	Change to Junior
	25	270	350	375	375	370	
	32	300	400	445	450	450	
	40	355	475	525	530	530	
	50	405	545	610	625		
	60	450	605	685			
	70	485	670				
Large	90	580					Change to Large Breed Junior

JUNIOR

Size type	Expected adult body weight (kg)	Daily serving (g)						
		6 mths	7 mths	8 mths	10 mths	12 mths	14 mths	16 mths
	10	195	185	175	160			
Medium	17	290	285	270	245	Change to Adult		
	25	390	380	365	330	320		
	32	445	435	415	380	365		Change to Large Breed Adult
Large	40	555	545	530	500	460	460	

ADULT

Size type	Bodyweight (kg)	Daily serving (g)		
		High activity	Normal activity	Low activity
Toy	2-5	60-115	55-100	45-85
Small	5-10	115-190	100-170	85-145
Medium	10-15	190-255	170-225	145-195
	15-25	255-380	225-330	195-285
	25-40	380-535	330-475	285-410
	40-55	535-680	475-600	410-520
	55-70	680-820	600-720	520-620
Large	70-90	820-985	720-870	620-750

SENIOR

Size type	Bodyweight (kg)	Daily serving (g)	
		Active	Normal
Toy	2-5	50-105	45-90
Small	5-10	105-175	90-150
Medium	10-15	175-235	150-205
	15-25	235-345	205-300
	25-40	345-495	300-425
	40-55	495-625	425-540
	55-70	625-750	540-650
Large	70-90	750-905	650-780

Overweight Dogs

It is far easier to regulate your Cockapoo's weight and keep it at a healthy level than to try and slim down a voraciously hungry dog when he becomes overweight. Overweight and obese dogs are susceptible to a range of illnesses. According to James Howie, Veterinary Advisor to Lintbells, some of the main ones are:

Joint disease – excessive body weight may increase joint stress which is a risk factor in joint degeneration (arthrosis), as is cruciate disease (knee ligament rupture). Joint disease tends to lead to a reduction in exercise which then increases the likelihood of weight gain, which reduces exercise further. A vicious cycle is created. Overfeeding Cockapoos while they are growing can lead to various problems, including the worsening of hip dysplasia. Weight management may be the only measure required to control clinical signs in some cases.

Heart and lung problems – fatty deposits within the chest cavity and excessive circulating fat play important roles in the development of cardio-respiratory and cardiovascular disease.

Diabetes – resistance to insulin has been shown to occur in overweight dogs, leading to a greater risk of diabetes mellitus.

Tumours – obesity increases the risk of mammary tumours in female dogs.

Liver disease – fat degeneration may result in liver insufficiency.

Reduced lifespan - one of the most serious proven findings in obesity studies is that obesity in both humans and dogs reduces lifespan.

Exercise intolerance – this is also a common finding with overweight dogs, which can compound an obesity problem as fewer calories are burned off and are therefore stored, leading to further weight gain.

Most Cockapoos are very attached to their humans. However, beware of going too far in regarding your dog as a member of the family. **You have to resist those beautiful big, pleading eyes!** It has been shown that dogs regarded as 'family members' (i.e. anthropomorphosis) by the owner are at greater risk of becoming overweight. This is because attention given to the dog often results in food being given as well.

The important thing to remember is that many of the problems associated with being overweight are reversible. Increasing exercise increases the calories burned, which in turn reduces weight. If you do put your dog on a diet, the reduced amount of food will also mean reduced nutrients, so he may need a supplement during this time.

Feeding Puppies

Puppy foods

Feeding your Cockapoo puppy the right diet is important to help his young body and bones grow strong and healthy. Puppyhood is a time of rapid growth and development, and puppies require different levels of nutrients to adult dogs.

For the first six weeks, puppies need milk about five to seven times a day, which they take from their mother. Generally they make some sound if they want to feed. The frequency is reduced when the pup reaches six to eight weeks old.

Cockapoo puppies should stay with their mothers and littermates until **at least** eight weeks old. During this time, the mother is still teaching her offspring some important rules about life. Good breeders will tell you in detail what your puppy is being fed and often provide you with a sample of the food to take home. Leaving the litter is a very stressful time for puppies and a change of diet is the last thing they need. You should continue feeding the same puppy food and at the same times as the breeder at least for the first few days or weeks at home. Dogs do not adapt to changes in their diet or feeding habits as easily as humans.

You can then slowly change the food based on information from the breeder and your vet. This should be done very gradually by mixing in a little more of the new food each day over a period of seven to 10 days. If at any time your puppy starts being sick, has loose stools or is constipated, slow the rate at which you are switching him over. If he continues vomiting, seek veterinary advice as he may have a problem with the food you have chosen. Puppies who are vomiting or who have diarrhoea quickly dehydrate.

Because of their special nutritional needs, you should only give your puppy a food that is approved either just for puppies or for all life stages. If a feed is recommended for adult dogs only, it won't have enough protein, and the balance of calcium and other nutrients will not be right for a pup. Puppy food is very high in calories and nutritional supplements, so you want to switch to a junior or adult food once he leaves puppyhood. Feeding puppy food too long can result in obesity and orthopaedic problems – check with your vet on the right time to switch.

Getting the amount and type of food right for your pup is important. Feeding too much will cause him to put on excess pounds, and overweight puppies are more likely to grow into overweight adults. As a very broad guideline, dogs normally mature into fully developed adults at around two years old, although some Cocker Spaniels - and therefore Cockapoos bred from Cockers – may develop a little more slowly.

DON'T:

> Feed table scraps from the table. Your Cockapoo will get used to begging for food; it will also affect a puppy's carefully balanced diet

> Feed food or uncooked meat which has gone off. Puppies have sensitive stomachs, stick to a prepared puppy food suitable for Cockapoo, preferably one recommended by your breeder

DO:

> Regularly check the weight of your growing puppy to make sure he is within normal limits for his age. There are charts available on numerous websites, just type "puppy weight chart" into Google – you'll need to know the exact age and current weight of your puppy

> Take your puppy to the vet if he has diarrhoea or is vomiting for two days

> Remove his food after it has been down for 15 to 20 minutes. Food available 24/7 encourages fussiness

How Often?

Puppies have small stomachs but big appetites, so feed them small amounts on a frequent basis. Establishing a regular feeding routine with your puppy will also help with toilet training. Get him used to regular mealtimes and then let him outside to do his business as soon as he has finished. Puppies have fast metabolisms, so the results may be pretty quick!

Don't leave food out for the puppy so that he can eat it whenever he wants. You need to be there for the feeds because you want him and his body on a set schedule. Smaller meals are easier for him to digest and energy levels don't peak and fall so much with frequent feeds. There is some variation between recommendations, but as a general rule of thumb:

> ➢ Up to the age of three or four months, feed your puppy four times a day
> ➢ Feed him three times a day until he is six months old
> ➢ Then twice a day for the rest of his life

It's up to you to control your dog's intake and manage his or her diet. Stick to the correct amount; you're doing your pup no favours by overfeeding. Unless your puppy is particularly thin (which is highly unlikely), don't give in - no matter how much your cute Cockapoo pleads with his big brown eyes. You must be firm and resist the temptation to give him extra food or treats.

A very broad rule of thumb is to feed puppy food for a year, but some owners start earlier on adult food, while others delay switching until their Cockapoo is 18 months or even two years old. If you are not sure, consult your breeder or your vet.

TIP: Cockapoos are very loving companions. If your dog is not responding well to a particular family member, a useful tactic is to get that person to feed the dog every day. The way to a dog's heart is often through his or her stomach!

Feeding Seniors

Once your adolescent dog has switched to an adult diet he will be on this for several years. As a dog moves towards old age, his body has different requirements to those of a young dog. This is the time to consider switching to a senior diet. Dogs are living much longer than they did 30 years ago. There are many factors contributing to this, including better vaccines and veterinary care, but one of the most important factors is better nutrition. Generally a dog is considered to be 'older' or senior if he is in the last third of his normal life expectancy.

Some owners of large breeds - such as Great Danes with a lifespan of nine years - switch their dogs from an adult to a senior diet when they are only six or seven years old. Cockapoos are known for having a long lifespan, often to the mid to late teens. Some have even been known to live to 20 years old. When you change to a senior food depends on your individual Cockapoo, his or her size, energy levels and general health. Look for signs of your dog slowing down or having joint problems. That may be the time to talk to your vet about switching. You can describe any changes at your dog's annual vaccination appointment, rather than having the expense of a separate consultation.

As a dog grows older, his metabolism slows down, his joints may stiffen, his energy levels decrease and he needs less exercise, just like with humans. You may notice in middle or old age that your dog starts to put weight on. The adult diet he is on may be too rich and have too many calories, this would be the time to consider switching.

Even though he is older, keep his weight in check, as obesity in old age only puts more strain on his body - especially joints and organs - and makes any health problems even worse. Because of lower activity levels, many older dogs will gain weight and getting an older dog to slim down can be very difficult. It is much better not to let your Cockapoo get too chunky than to put him on a diet. But if he is overweight, put in the effort to shed the extra pounds. This is one of the single most important things you can do to increase your Cockapoo's quality AND length of life.

Other changes in canines are again similar to those in older humans and as well as stiff joints or arthritis, they might move more slowly and sleep more. Hearing and vision may not be so sharp and organs don't all work as efficiently as they used to, and his teeth may have become worn down. You may also notice that your old Cockapoo isn't quite as tolerant as he used to be – particularly with boisterous puppies – they can become grumpy old men and women too!

Specially formulated senior diets are lower in protein and calories but help to create a feeling of fullness. Older dogs are more prone to develop constipation, so senior diets are often higher in fibre - at around 3% to 5%. Wheat bran can also be added to regular dog food to increase the amount of fibre - but do not try this if your Cockapoo has a low tolerance or intolerance to grain. If your dog has poor kidney function, then a low phosphorus diet will help to lower the workload for the kidneys.

Aging dogs have special dietary needs, some of which can be provided in the form of supplements, such as glucosamine and chondroitin, which help joints. If your dog is not eating a complete balanced diet, then a vitamin/mineral supplement is recommended to prevent any deficiencies. Some owners also feed extra antioxidants to an older dog – ask your vet's advice on your next visit. Antioxidants are also found naturally in fruit and vegetables.

While some older dogs put on weight more easily, others have the opposite problem – they lose weight and are disinterested in food. If your old dog is losing weight and not eating well, firstly get him checked out by the vet to rule out any possible disease problems. If he gets the all-clear, your next challenge is to tempt him to eat. He may be having trouble with his teeth, so if he's on a dry food, try smaller kibble or moistening it with water.

Our dog loved his twice daily feeds until he recently got to the age of 10 when he suddenly lost interest in his daily food, a hypoallergenic kibble. We tried switching flavours within the same brand, but that didn't work. After a short while we mixed his daily feeds with a little gravy and a spoonful of tinned dog food – Bingo! He's wolfing it down again and lively as ever.

Some dogs can tolerate a small amount of milk or eggs added to their food, and home-made diets of boiled rice, potatoes, vegetables and chicken or meat with the right vitamin and mineral supplements can also work well. See **Chapter 14. Caring for Older Dogs** for more information on looking after a senior.

Reading Dog Food Labels

A NASA scientist would have a hard job understanding some dog food manufacturers' labels, so it's no easy task for us lowly dog owners. Here are some things to look out for on the manufacturers' labels:

> The ingredients are listed by weight and the top one should always be the main content, such as chicken or lamb. Don't pick one where grain is the first ingredient, it is a poor quality feed and some Cockapoos can develop grain intolerances or allergies - often it is specifically wheat they have a reaction to

Ingredients: Chicken, Chicken By-Product Meal, Corn Meal, Ground Whole Grain Sorghum, Brewers Rice, Ground Whole Grain Barley, Dried Beet Pulp, Chicken Fat (preserved with mixed Tocopherols, a source of Vitamin E), Chicken Flavor, Dried Egg Product, Fish Oil (preserved with mixed Tocopherols, a source of Vitamin E), Potassium Chloride, Salt, Flax Meal, Sodium Hexametaphosphate, Fructooligosaccharides, Choline Chloride, Minerals (Ferrous Sulfate, Zinc Oxide, Manganese Sulfate, Copper Sulfate, Manganous Oxide, Potassium Iodide, Cobalt Carbonate), DL-Methionine, Vitamins (Ascorbic Acid, Vitamin A Acetate, Calcium Pantothenate, Biotin, Thiamine Mononitrate (source of vitamin B1), Vitamin B12 Supplement, Niacin, Riboflavin Supplement (source of vitamin B2), Inositol, Pyridoxine Hydrochloride (source of vitamin B6), Vitamin D3 Supplement, Folic Acid), Calcium Carbonate, Vitamin E Supplement, Brewers Dried Yeast, Beta-Carotene, Rosemary Extract.

> High up the list should be meat or poultry by-products, these are clean parts of slaughtered animals, not including meat. They include organs, blood and bone, but not hair, horns, teeth or hooves

> Guaranteed Analysis (pictured below) – This guarantees that your dog's food contains the labelled percentages of crude protein, fat, fibre and moisture. Keep in mind that wet and dry dog foods use different standards. (It does not list the digestibility of protein and fat and this can vary widely depending on their sources). While the guaranteed analysis is a start in understanding the food quality, be wary about relying on it too much. One pet food manufacturer made a mock product with a Guaranteed Analysis of 10% protein, 6.5% fat, 2.4% fibre, and 68% moisture (not unlike what's on many canned pet food labels) – the only problem was that the ingredients were old leather boots, used motor oil, crushed coal and water!

> Chicken meal (dehydrated chicken) has more protein than fresh chicken, which is 80% water. The same goes for beef, fish and lamb. So, if any of these meals are number one on the ingredient list, the food should contain enough protein

Crude Protein (min)	32.25%
Lysine (min)	0.43%
Methionine (min)	0.49%
Crude Fat (min)	10.67%
Crude Fiber (max)	7.3%
Calcium (min)	0.50%
Calcium (max)	1.00%
Phosphorus (min)	0.44%
Salt (min)	0.01%
Salt (max)	0.51%

> A certain amount of flavourings can make a food more appetising for your dog. Chose a food with a specific flavouring, like **'beef flavouring'** rather than a general **'meat flavouring',** where the origins are not so clear

> Find a food that fits your dog's age and size. Talk to your vet or visit an online Cockapoo forum and ask other owners what they are feeding their dogs

> If your Cockapoo has a food allergy or intolerance to wheat, check whether the food is gluten free. All wheat contains gluten

> The USA's FDA says: "The term **'natural'** is often used on pet food labels, although that term does not have an official definition either. AAFCO has developed a feed term definition for what types of ingredients can be considered 'natural' and "Guidelines for Natural Claims" for pet foods. For the most part, 'natural' can be construed as equivalent to a lack

of artificial flavors, artificial colors, or artificial preservatives in the product." However, as artificial flavours and colours are not used in many foods, the word 'natural' on dog food does not mean a lot, neither are there legal guidelines regarding use of the word 'organic'

➢ In the USA, dog food that meets minimum nutrition requirements has a label that confirms this. It states: "*[food name] is formulated to meet the nutritional levels established by the AAFCO Dog Food Nutrient Profiles for [life stage(s)]*"

➢ **'Complete and balanced'** DO have a legal meaning'; these are the words to look for on a packet or tin. The FDA states: "This means the product contains the proper amount of all recognized essential nutrients needed to meet the needs of the healthy animal."

Vitamin E		Min.	425 IU/kg
Ascorbic Acid* (Vitamin C)		Min.	95 mg/kg
Docosahexaenoic Acid* (DHA)		Min.	0.1 %
Eicosapentaenoic Acid* (EPA)		Min.	0.15 %
Omega-3 Fatty Acids*		Min.	0.5 %

* Not recognized as an essential nutrient by the AAFCO Dog Food Nutrient Profiles.

AAFCO Statement: Animal feeding tests using AAFCO procedures substantiate that Science Diet® Puppy Healthy Development Small Bites provides complete and balanced nutrition for growing puppies and gestating or lactating adult female dogs.

Protect from moisture. Store in a cool, dry place.

Even better, look for a food that meets the minimum nutritional requirements **'as fed'** to real pets in an AAFCO-defined feeding trial, then you know the food really delivers the nutrients it claims to. AAFCO feeding trials on real dogs are the gold standard. Brands that do costly feeding trials (including Nestlé and Hill's, pictured) indicate so on the package.

NOTE: Dog food labelled '*supplemental*' isn't complete and balanced. Unless you have a specific, vet-approved need for it, it's not something you want to feed your dog for an extended period of time. Check with your vet if in doubt. If it all still looks a bit baffling, you might find the following websites very useful; I have no vested interest in either website, but have found them to be a good source of independent advice.

www.dogfoodadvisor.com provides useful information with star ratings for grain-free and hypoallergenic dogs foods for USA brands. It is run by Mike Sagman who has a medical background and analyses and rates hundreds of brands of dog food based on the listed ingredients and meat content. You might be surprised at some of his findings.

In the UK there is www.allaboutdogfood.co.uk by David Jackson, who used to be employed in the dog food industry.

To recap: no one food is right for every dog; you must decide on the best for yours. If you have a puppy, initially stick to the same food that the breeder has been feeding the litter, and only change diet later and gradually. Once you have decided on a food, monitor your puppy or adult. The best test of a food is how well your dog is doing on it.

If your Cockapoo is happy and healthy, interested in life, has plenty energy, is not too fat and not too thin, doesn't scratch a lot and has healthy-looking stools, then...

Congratulations, you've got it right!

7. Exercise and Training

One thing all dogs have in common – including every Cockapoo ever born - is that they need daily exercise, and the best way to give them this is by regular walks. Here is what daily exercise does for your dog - and you:

> It strengthens respiratory and circulatory systems
> Helps get oxygen to tissue cells
> Wards off obesity
> Keeps muscles toned and joints flexible
> Aids digestion
> Releases endorphins which trigger positive feelings
> Helps to keep dogs mentally stimulated and socialised

Whether you live in a small house, an apartment or on a farm, start regular exercise patterns early so your dog gets used to his daily routine and gets chance to blow off steam and excess energy. Daily exercise helps to keep your dog content, healthy and free from disease.

How Much Exercise?

Most Cockapoos will take as much exercise as you are prepared to give them. They are generally regarded as having medium to high exercise requirements, but there is no one-rule-fits-all solution. The amount of exercise that each individual dog needs varies tremendously. It depends on a number of issues, including size, temperament, natural energy levels, your living conditions, whether your dog is kept with other dogs and, importantly, what he gets used to.

Another major factor is your Cockapoo's ancestry – particularly on the Cocker Spaniel side. Was he bred from an English working or show Cocker, or an American Cocker? While there are, of course, variations within the breeds, many breeders feel that Cockapoos from working Spaniels need more exercise. After all, it makes sense. (With thanks to Nigel Houston and Lincoln for modelling for the training photos).

A Cockapoo whose parent was bred to run all day and be on the lookout for game is likely to have higher energy demands than one bred to have a calmer nature for the show ring. And don't forget that the Poodle was also originally bred as a working dog to retrieve water fowl. Working dogs have high energy drives; they are not usually couch potatoes. That's not so say Cockapoos don't love snuggling up on the couch with you; they most certainly do. They just need their exercise as well.

Ideally you should have the time to exercise your Cockapoo for a minimum of an hour a day – even longer is better. (A minimum of 30 minutes for Toy Cockapoos). You can hike with a Cockapoo bred from working parents all day long and still not tire him out. A fenced garden or yard where he can burn off energy between walks is an advantage, but should never be seen as a replacement for daily exercise away from the home. While Toy Cockapoos require less exercise than their larger cousins, you shouldn't think about getting a Cockapoo if you cannot commit to at least one walk every day. If you don't think you have the time or the energy levels for this, then look at getting a dog which requires less exercise and mental stimulation. Your Cockapoo will enjoy going for walks on the lead (leash), but will enjoy it far more when he is allowed to run free. A Cockapoo is never happier than when running around with his nose to the ground following a scent or chasing an old stick or ball. Cockapoos excel at Fly Ball, agility events and other canine activities which involve lots of energy and mental challenges.

Make sure it is safe to let your dog off the lead, away from traffic and other hazards. And do not let him run free until he has learned the recall. There is also growing concern in both North America and the UK about attacks from loose dogs in public parks and dog parks. If you are at all worried about this, avoid public areas and find woodlands, fields, a beach or open countryside where your dog can exercise safely.

Establish a Routine

Establish an exercise regime early in the dog's life. Dogs like routine. If possible, get him used to walks at the same time every day, at a time that fits in with your daily routine. For example, take your dog out after his morning feed, then perhaps for a longer walk in the afternoon or when you come home from work, and a short toilet trip last thing at night.

Daily exercise could mean a walk, a jog, playing fetch or swimming - an activity loved by most Cockapoos. Swimming is a great way for dogs to exercise; so much so that many veterinary practices are now incorporating small water tanks - not only for remedial therapy - but also for canine recreation! Cockapoos will dash in and out of the water all day if you'll let them, but remember that swimming is a lot more strenuous for a dog than walking or even running. Don't constantly throw that stick or ball into the water - your Cockapoo will fetch it back until he drops; the same is true if he is following you on your cycle. Overstretching him could place a strain on his heart. He should exercise within his limits.

Whatever routine you decide on, your Cockapoo should be getting walked at least once or twice a day and you should stick to it. If you begin by taking your dog out three times a day and then suddenly stop, he will become restless and attention-seeking because he has been used to having more exercise. Conversely, don't expect a dog used to very little exercise to suddenly go on day-long hikes; he will probably struggle. Mini and Standard Cockapoos may make suitable hiking or jogging companions, but they need to build up to that amount of exercise gradually - and such strenuous activity is not suitable for puppies.

To those owners who say their dog is happy and getting enough exercise playing in the yard or garden, just show him his lead (leash) and see how he reacts. Do you think he is excited at the prospect of leaving the property and going for a walk? Of course he is. Nothing can compensate for interesting new scents, meeting other dogs, playing games, frolicking in the snow or going swimming. Cockapoos are extremely playful with a great sense of fun and love all these activities.

Exercising a dog requires a big commitment from owners – you are looking at daily walks for perhaps 15 or more years when you get a Cockapoo. Don't think that as your dog gets older, he won't need exercising. Older dogs need exercise to keep their body, joints and systems functioning properly. They need a less strenuous regime, but still enough to keep them physically and mentally active. Regular exercise can add months or even years to a dog's life. Look on the bright side, a brisk walk is a great way of keeping both you and your dog fit – even when it's raining or snowing. Most Cockapoos love snow, but it can present problems for their long, soft, wavy hair. This is what the British Cockapoo Society (BCS) says: "Because of their fur type, snow sticks, leading to clumps of snow and ice building up on their paws, legs and tummy. It can build up quickly and heavily, until it looks like we are walking a Yeti, not a Cockapoo.

"An added problem is when the local council uses salt or de-icing products on roads and pathways. Some of them contain ingredients which are poisonous to dogs and have been thought to cause illness, and even death, on some occasions. As the snow builds up on our dogs' fur, so do the levels of these toxins. And as your dog licks or chews at its fur to remove some of the ice balls, it can ingest a dangerous quantity of these chemicals and become ill. This does not mean that you should not take your dog out in the snow; with a bit of thought both you and your dog can enjoy the Winter Wonderland."

The BCS has some suggestions: "Use a dog jumper or coat to cut down on the amount of snow that your dog will get covered with. Spray the dog with coconut oil, which is natural, non-sticky and good for the skin and coat. It acts as a repellent for the ice and stops it sticking to your dog's fur. Spray it on paws, legs and tummy to cut down on ice balls forming. When you get home, bathe your dog's paws in some warm (NOT HOT) water to defrost and remove the ice.

"You may need to pop them in a warm bath if they have a lot of ice balls sticking to their tummy and sides etc. When drying them, just check their feet and pads to make sure that there are no lumps of ice stuck between their pads and toes and that their paws are not getting sore from the combination of snow, ice and rock salt on pavements."

There are also special dog boots (pictured), which are highly effective in preventing ice balls from forming on your dog's paws – provided you can get the boots to stay on.

Mental Stimulation

Cockapoos are highly intelligent. They inherit their brains from their Poodle parents and grandparents. This is good news when it comes to training, as Cockapoos learn very quickly. But the downside is that this intelligence needs to be fed. Without mental challenges, a dog can become bored, unresponsive, destructive attention-seeking and/or needy. You should factor in play time with your Cockapoo – even for old dogs.

If your Cockapoo's behaviour deteriorates or he suddenly starts chewing things he's not supposed to or barking a lot, the first question you should ask yourself is: "Is he getting enough exercise?" Boredom through lack of exercise or mental stimulation (such as being alone and staring at four walls a lot) leads to bad behaviour and it's why some Cockapoos end up in rescue centres, through no fault of their own. On the other hand, a Cockapoo at the heart of the family getting plenty of daily exercise and play time is a happy Cockapoo and a companion second to none.

Exercising Puppies

There are strict guidelines to stick to with puppies, as it is important not to over-exercise young pups. Their bones and joints are developing and cannot tolerate a great deal of stress, so playing fetch for hours on end with your adolescent or baby Cockapoo is not a good option. You'll end up with an injured dog and a pile of vet's bills.

We are often asked how much to exercise a pup. It does, of course, vary depending on whether you have a Toy, Mini or Standard Cockapoo as well as the dog's natural energy level. Cockapoo puppies, like babies, have different temperaments and some will be livelier and need more exercise than others. The golden rule is to start slowly and build it up. The worst danger is a combination of over exercise and overweight when the puppy is growing. Do not take him out of the yard or garden until he has completed his vaccinations and it is safe to do so – unless you carry him around to start the socialisation process. Then start with short walks on the lead every day. A good guideline is:

Five minutes of on-lead exercise per month of age

until the puppy is fully grown. That means a total of 15 minutes when he is three months (13 weeks old), 20 minutes when four months (17 weeks) old, and so on. Slowly increase the time as he gets used to being exercised on the lead and this will gradually build up his muscles and stamina. Too much walking on pavements early on places stress on young joints. It's OK, however, for your young pup to have free run of your garden or yard (once you have plugged any gaps in the fence), provided it has a soft surface such as grass, not concrete. He will take things at his own pace and stop to sniff or rest. Once he is fully grown, your dog can go out for much longer walks on the lead. And when your little pup has grown into an adorable adult with a skeleton capable of carrying him through a long and healthy life, it will have been worth all the effort.

A long, healthy life is best started slowly

Puppies have enquiring minds. Get your pup used to being outside the home environment and experiencing new situations as soon as he is clear after vaccinations. Start to train your puppy to come back to you so that you are soon confident enough to let him roam off the lead. Under no circumstances leave a puppy imprisoned in a crate for hours on end. Cockapoos are extremely sociable; they love being physically close to their humans and definitely do not like being left alone for long periods.

If you are considering getting two puppies, you might consider waiting until the first pup is older so he can teach the new arrival some good habits. Some say that if you keep two puppies from the same litter, their first loyalty may be to each other, rather than to you as their owner. (Others say this is simply untrue!)

As already outlined, your Cockapoo will get used to an exercise routine. If you over-stimulate and constantly exercise him as a puppy, he will think this is the norm. This is fine with your playful little pup, but may not be such an attractive prospect when your fully-grown Cockapoo constantly needs and demands your attention and exercise a year or two later, or your work patterns change and you have not so much time to devote to him. The key is to start a routine that you can stick to.

Exercise Tips

➢ Cockapoos are intelligent and playful with a great sense of fun. They need to use their brains. Make time to play indoor and outdoor games, such as Fetch or Hide-The-Toy, regularly with your dog - even elderly Cockapoos like to play

➢ If you want your Cockapoo to fetch a ball, don't fetch it back yourself or he will never learn to retrieve. Train him when he's young by giving him praise or a treat when he brings the ball or toy back to your feet

➢ Don't strenuously exercise your dog straight after or within an hour of a meal as this can cause bloat, particularly in larger dogs. Canine bloat causes gases to build up quickly in the stomach, blowing it up like a balloon, which cuts off normal blood circulation to and from the heart. The dog can go into shock and then cardiac arrest within hours. If you suspect this is happening, get him to a vet immediately

➢ Do not throw a ball or toy repeatedly for a dog; he will do it to please you and because it's great fun. Stop the activity after a while - no matter how much he begs you to throw it again. He may become over-tired, damage his joints, pull a muscle, strain his heart or otherwise injure himself. Keep an eye out for heavy panting and other signs of over-exertion or overheating

➢ The same goes for swimming, which is an exhausting exercise for a dog. Repeatedly retrieving from water may cause him to overstretch himself and get into difficulties. Gentle swimming is a good low-impact activity for older Cockapoos

➢ Follow the tips earlier in this chapter and/or invest in a set of doggie boots if your Cockapoo spends a lot of time in snow. It can actually be quite painful for your dog when his legs and face become covered in snowballs. Bathe your dog's legs in lukewarm water - **never** hot – at home afterwards to wash off snowballs and salt

➢ Some dogs, particularly adolescent ones, may try to push the boundaries when out walking on the lead. If your Cockapoo stares at you and tries to pull you in another direction, ignore him. Do not return his stare, just continue along the way you want to go, not him!

➢ Start exercise slowly and gently with older dogs - especially in cold weather when it is harder to get their bodies moving. Have a cool-down period at the end of the exercise to reduce stiffness and soreness; it helps to remove lactic acids from the dog's body

➢ Vary your exercise route – it will be more interesting for both of you

➢ If exercising off-lead at night, buy a battery-operated flashing collar for your dog

➢ Make sure your dog has constant access to fresh water. Dogs can't sweat and many Cockapoos don't shed much either. They need to drink water to cool down

Admittedly, when it is pouring down with rain, freezing cold (or scorching hot), the last thing you want to do is to venture outdoors with your dog. But the lows are more than compensated for by the highs. Exercise helps you to bond with your dog, keeps you both fit; you see different places and meet new companions - both canine and human. In short, it enhances both your lives.

Socialisation

Your adult Cockapoo's character will depend largely on two things. The first is his temperament, which he is born with, and presumably one of the reasons you have chosen a Cockapoo. (The importance of picking a good breeder who selects breeding stock based on temperament, physical characteristics and health cannot be over-emphasised). The second factor is environment – or how you bring him up and treat him. In other words, it's a combination of **nature and nurture**. These two factors will form his character. And one absolutely essential aspect of nurture is socialisation.

Scientists have come to realise the importance that socialisation plays in a dog's life. We also now know that there is a fairly small window which is the optimum time for socialisation – up to the age of up to around four months (14 to 16 weeks) - depending on which study you read.

Most young animals, including dogs, are naturally able to get used to their everyday environment - until they reach a certain age. When they reach this age they become much more suspicious of things they haven't yet experienced. This is why it often takes longer to train an older dog.

The age-specific natural development allows a puppy to get comfortable with the normal sights, sounds, people and animals that will be a part of his life. It ensures that he doesn't spend his life jumping in fright or growling at every blowing leaf or bird in song. The suspicion that dogs develop in later puppyhood – after the critical window - also ensures that they do react with a healthy dose of caution to new things that could really be dangerous - Mother Nature is clever!

Socialisation means learning to be part of society, or integration. When we talk about socialising puppies, it means helping them learn to be comfortable within a human society that includes many different types of people, environments, buildings, sights, noises, smells, animals and other dogs. Your Cockapoo may already have a wonderful temperament, but he still needs socialising to avoid him thinking that the world is tiny and it revolves around him, which leads to unwanted adult behaviour traits.

The ultimate goal of socialisation is to have a happy, well-adjusted dog that you can take anywhere. Socialisation will give your dog confidence and teach him not to be afraid of new experiences. Ever seen a therapy or service Cockapoo in action and noticed how incredibly well-adjusted to life they are? This is no coincidence. These dogs have been extensively socialised and are ready and able to deal in a calm manner with whatever situation they come to encounter. They are relaxed and comfortable in their own skin - just like you want your own dog to be.

You have to start socialising your puppy as soon as you bring him home - waiting until he has had all his vaccinations is leaving it too late. Start by socialising him around the house and garden and, if it is safe, carry him out of the home environment (but do not put him on the floor or allow him to sniff other dogs until he's got the all-clear after his shots). Regular socialisation should continue until your dog is around 18 months of age. After that, don't just forget about it. Socialisation isn't only for puppies; it should continue throughout your dog's life. As with any skill, if it is not practised, your dog will become less proficient at interacting with other people, animals, and environments.

Developing the Well-Rounded Adult Dog

Well-socialised puppies usually develop into safer, more relaxed and enjoyable adult dogs. This is because they're more comfortable in a wider variety of situations than poorly socialised canines. Dogs which have not been properly integrated are much more likely to react with fear or aggression to unfamiliar people, dogs and experiences.

 Cockapoos which are relaxed about other dogs, honking horns, cats, cyclists, veterinary examinations, crowds and noise are easier to live with than dogs who find these situations challenging or frightening. Well socialised dogs also live more relaxed, peaceful and happy lives than dogs which are constantly stressed by their environment. Socialisation isn't an "all or nothing" project. You can socialise a puppy a bit, a lot, or a whole lot. The wider the range of experiences you expose him to, the better his chances are of becoming a more relaxed adult.

Don't over-face your little puppy. Socialisation should never be forced, but approached systematically and in a manner that builds confidence and curious interaction. If your pup finds a new experience frightening, take a step back, introduce him to the scary situation much more gradually, and make a big effort to do something he loves during the situation or right afterwards.

For example, if your puppy seems to be frightened by noise and vehicles at a busy junction, a good method would be to go to a quiet road, sit with dog away from - but within sight of - the traffic. Every time he looks towards the traffic say "YES" and reward him with a treat. Keep each session down to a couple of minutes initially. If dog doesn't take food or snatches it, this is sign of stress, so you are too near traffic and need to move further away. When your dog takes the food in a calm manner, he is becoming more relaxed and getting used to traffic sounds, so you can edge a bit nearer - but still just for short periods until he becomes totally relaxed.

Meeting Other Dogs

When you take your gorgeous and vulnerable little pup out with other dogs for the first few times, you are bound to be a little nervous. To start with, introduce your puppy to just one other dog – one which you know to be friendly, rather than taking him straight to the park where there are lots of dogs of all sizes racing around, which might frighten the life out of your timid little darling. Always make the initial introductions on neutral ground, so as not to trigger territorial behaviour. You want your Cockapoo to approach other dogs with confidence, not fear.

From the first meeting, help both dogs experience good things when they're in each other's presence. Let them sniff each other briefly, which is normal canine greeting behaviour. As they do, talk to them in a happy, friendly tone of voice; never use a threatening tone. Don't allow them to sniff each other for too long as this may escalate to an aggressive response. After a short time, get the attention of both dogs and give each a treat in return for obeying a simple command, such as "sit" or "stay." Continue with the "happy talk," food rewards, and simple commands. Here are some signs of fear to look out for when your dog interacts with other canines.

 - ➢ Running away
 - ➢ Freezing on the spot
 - ➢ Frantic/nervous behaviour, such as excessive sniffing, drinking or playing with a toy frenetically

- ➤ A lowered body stance or crouching
- ➤ Lying on his back with his paws in the air – this is a submissive gesture
- ➤ Lowering of the head, or turning the head away
- ➤ Lips pulled back baring teeth and/or growling
- ➤ Hair raised on his back (hackles)
- ➤ Tail lifted in the air
- ➤ Ears high on the head

Some of these responses are normal. A pup may well crouch on the ground or roll on to his back to show other dogs he is not a threat. Try not to be over-protective, your Cockapoo has to learn how to interact with other dogs, but if the situation looks like escalating into something more aggressive, calmly distract the dogs or remove your puppy – don't shout or shriek. The dogs will pick up on your fear and this in itself could trigger an unpleasant situation.

Another sign to look out for is eyeballing. In the canine world, staring a dog in the eyes is a challenge and may trigger an aggressive response. This is more relevant to adult dogs, as a young pup will soon be put in his place by bigger or older dogs; it is how they learn. The rule of thumb with puppy socialisation is to keep a close eye on your pup's reaction to whatever you expose him to so that you can tone things down if he seems at all frightened. Always follow up a socialisation experience with praise, petting, a fun game or a special treat. One positive sign from a dog is the play bow, when he goes down on to his front elbows but keeps his backside up in the air. This is a sign that he is feeling friendly towards the other dog and wants to play.

Although Cockapoos are not naturally aggressive dogs, aggression is often grounded in fear, and a dog which mixes easily is less likely to be aggressive. Similarly, without frequent and new experiences, some dogs can become timid and nervous when introduced to new experiences. Take your new dog everywhere you can. You want him to feel relaxed and calm in any situation, even noisy and crowded ones. Take treats with you and praise him when he reacts calmly to new situations. Once he has settled into your home, introduce him to your friends and teach him not to jump up. If you have young children, it is not only the dog that needs socialising! Youngsters also need training on how to act around dogs, so both parties learn to respect the other.

Once excellent way of getting your new puppy to meet other dogs in a safe environment is at a puppy or kindergarten class. Ask around locally if any classes are being run. Some vets and dog trainers run puppy classes for very junior pups who have had all their vaccinations. These help pups get used to other dogs of similar age.

Obedience Training

Training a young dog is like bringing up a child. Put in the effort early on to teach them the guidelines and you will be rewarded with a well-adjusted, sociable individual who will be a joy to live with. Cockapoos are intelligent, incredibly eager to please and love being with their humans. All of this adds up to one of the easiest breeds of all to train - but only if you are prepared to put in the time too.

Cockapoos make wonderful companions for us humans, but let yours behave exactly how he wants, and you may well finish up with a wilful, attention-seeking adult. Cockapoos make such natural companion for humans - after all, that is what they are bred for – that it becomes all too easy to treat them like a human and spoil them. The secret of training Cockapoos can be summed up quite simply:

Praise, Patience, Consistency and Plenty of Rewards.

Praise and treats are the two prime motivators; training should ALWAYS be reward-based, never punishment-based. Cockapoos are sensitive critters. Many owners would say they have empathy (the ability to understand the feelings of others) and they do not respond well to heavy-handed training methods. They are also highly intelligent, making it easy for them to pick up commands - provided you make it clear exactly what you want them to do; don't give conflicting signals.

Psychologist and canine expert Dr Stanley Coren has written a book called **"The Intelligence of Dogs"** in which he ranks 140 breeds. He used "understanding of new commands" and "obey first command" as his standards of intelligence, surveying dog trainers to compile the list. He says there are three types of dog intelligence:

- ➤ Adaptive Intelligence (learning and problem-solving ability). This is specific to the individual animal and is measured by canine IQ tests
- ➤ Instinctive Intelligence. This is specific to the individual animal and is measured by canine IQ tests
- ➤ Working/Obedience Intelligence. This is breed-dependent

The brainboxes of the canine world are the 10 breeds ranked in the 'Brightest Dogs' section of his list. All dogs in this class:

- ➤ Understand New Commands with Fewer than Five Repetitions
- ➤ Obey a First Command 95% of the Time or Better

It will come as no surprise to anyone who has even been into the countryside and seen sheep being worked by a farmer and his right-hand man (his dog) to learn that the Border Collie is the most intelligent of all dogs. The second smartest dog is the Poodle, parent or grandparent(s) of the Cockapoo. The second group is called 'Excellent Working Dogs' and in the middle of this group, at Number 18 is the English Cocker Spaniel and at Number 20 is the (presumably American) Cocker Spaniel. These dogs understand new commands with five to 15 repetitions and obey a first command 85% of the time or better.

By the author's own admission, the drawback of this rating scale is that it is heavily weighted towards obedience-related behavioural traits, which are often found in working dogs, rather than understanding or creativity (found in hunting dogs). As a result, some breeds, such as the Bully breeds (Bulldogs, Mastiffs, Bull Terriers, Pug, Rottweiler, etc)., are ranked quite low on the list, due to their stubborn or independent nature.

But as far as Cockapoos are concerned, given their ancestry, it's true to say that you are starting out with a puppy that not only has the intelligence to pick up new commands very quickly, but he also really wants to learn and please you. Three golden rules when training a Cockapoo are:

1. Training must be reward-based, not punishment based
2. Keep sessions short or your dog will get bored
3. Keep sessions fun, give your Cockapoo a challenge and a chance to shine

You might also consider enlisting the help of a professional trainer – although that option may not be within the budget of many new owners. If it is, then choose a trainer registered with the Association of Professional Dog Trainers (APDT); you can find a list for all countries here: https://apdt.com. Make sure the one you choose uses positive reward-based training methods, as the old alpha-dominance theories have been discredited.

When you train your dog, it should never be a battle of wills between you and him; it should be a positive learning experience for you both. Bawling at the top of your voice or smacking should play no part in training. If you have a high spirited, high energy Cockapoo, you have to use your brain to think of ways which will make training challenging for your dog and to persuade him that what you want him to do is actually what **he** wants to do. He will come to realise that when he does something you ask of him, something good is going to happen – verbal praise, pats, treats, play time, etc.

Establishing the natural order of things is not something forced on a dog through shouting or violence; it is brought about by mutual consent and good training. Like most dogs, Cockapoos are happiest and behave best when they know and are comfortable with their place in the household. They may push the boundaries, especially as adolescents, but stick to your rules and everything will run much smoother. All of this is done with positive techniques.

Sometimes your dog's concentration will lapse, particularly with a pup or adolescent dog. Keep training short and fun. If you have adopted an older dog, you can still train him, but it will take a little longer to get rid of bad habits and instil good manners. Patience and persistence are the keys here.

Common Training Questions

1. **At what age can I start training my puppy?** As soon as he arrives home. Begin with a few minutes a day

2. **How important is socialisation for Cockapoos?** Extremely; this can't be emphasised enough. Your puppy's breeder should have already begun this process with the litter and then it's up to you to keep it going when the pup arrives home. Up to 16 weeks' old puppies can absorb a great deal of information, but they are also vulnerable to bad experiences. Pups who are not properly exposed to different people and other animals can find them very frightening when they do finally encounter them when older

They may react by cowering, barking, growling, or biting. Food possession can also become an issue with some Cockapoos. But if they have positive experiences with people and animals before they turn 16 weeks of age, they are less likely to be afraid or try to push the boundaries later.

Don't just leave your dog at home in the early days, take him out and about with you, get him used to new people, places and noises. Cockapoos that miss out on being socialised can develop behavioural issues as adults

3. **What challenges does training involve?** Chewing is an issue with most puppies. Train your young Cockapoo only to chew the things you give him – so don't give him your footwear, an old piece of carpet or anything that resembles anything you don't want him to chew. Buy purpose-made long-lasting chew toys

Jumping up is a common issue with Cockapoos. They love everybody and are so enthusiastic about life, so it's often a natural reaction when they see somebody. You don't, however, want your fully grown dog to jump up on grandma when he has just come back from a romp through the muddy woods. Teach him not to jump up while he is still small

13 Tips for Training Your Cockapoo

1. **Start training and socialising early.** Like babies, puppies learn quickly and it's this learned behaviour which stays with them through adult life. Old dogs can be taught new tricks, but it's a lot harder to unlearn bad habits. It's best to start training with a clean slate. Puppy training should start with a few minutes a day from Day One when you bring him home, even if he's only a few weeks old

2. **Your voice is a very important training tool.** Your dog has to learn to understand your language and you have to understand him. Commands should be issued in a calm, authoritative voice - not shouted. Praise should be given in a happy, encouraging voice, accompanied by stroking or patting. If your dog has done something wrong, use a stern voice, not a harsh shriek. This applies even if your Cockapoo is unresponsive at the beginning

3. **Avoid giving your dog commands you know you can't enforce.** Every time you give a command that you don't enforce, he learns that commands are optional

4. **Train your dog gently and humanely.** Cockapoos do not respond well to being shouted at or hit. Keep training sessions short and upbeat so the whole experience is enjoyable for

you and him. If obedience training is a bit of a bore, pep things up a bit by 'play training'. Use constructive, non-adversarial games such as Go Find, Hide and Seek, or Fetch

5. **Begin your training around the house and garden or yard**. How well your dog responds to you at home affects his behaviour away from the home as well. If he doesn't respond well at home, he certainly won't respond any better when he's out and about where there are 101 distractions, such as food scraps, other dogs, people, cats, interesting scents, etc.

6. **Mealtimes are a great time to start training your dog.** Teach him to sit and stay at dinnertime and breakfast, rather than simply putting the dish down and allowing him to dash over immediately. He might not know what you mean in the beginning, so gently place him into the sitting position while you say "Sit." Then place a hand on his chest during the "Stay" command - gradually letting go – and then give him the command to eat his dinner, followed by encouraging praise - he'll soon get the idea

7. **One command equals one response.** Give your dog only one command - twice maximum - then gently enforce it. Repeating commands or nagging will make your Cockapoo tune out. They also teach him that the first few commands are a bluff. Telling your dog to **"SIT, SIT, SIT, SIT!!!"** is neither efficient nor effective. Give your dog a single "SIT" command, gently place him in the sitting position and then praise him

8. **Use your dog's name often and in a positive manner.** When you bring your pup or new dog home, start using his name often so he gets used to the sound of it. He won't know what it means in the beginning, but it won't take him long to realise you're talking to him. DON'T use his name when reprimanding, warning or punishing. He should trust that when he hears his name, good things happen.

    His name should always be a word he responds to with enthusiasm, never hesitancy or fear. Use the words "No" or "Bad Boy/Girl" in a stern - not shouted - voice instead. Some parents prefer not to use the word "No" with their dog, as they use it often around the human youngsters and it is likely to confuse the young canine! You can make a sound like "ACK!" instead. Say it sharply and the dog should stop whatever it is he is doing wrong – it works for us

9. **Have a "No" sound.** When a puppy is corrected by his mother – for example if he bites her with his sharp baby teeth – she growls at him to warn him not to do it again. When your puppy makes a mistake, make a short sharp sound like "Ack!" to tell the puppy not to do that again. This works surprisingly well

10. **Don't give your dog lots of attention (even negative attention) when he misbehaves.** Cockapoos love their owners' attention. If he gets lots of attention when he jumps up on you, his bad behaviour is being reinforced. If he jumps up, push him away, use the command "No" or "Down" and then ignore him

11. **Timing is critical to successful training.** When your puppy does something right, praise him immediately. If you wait a while he will have no idea what he has done right. Similarly, when he does something wrong, correct him straight away. For example, if he eliminates in the house, don't shout and certainly don't rub his nose in it; this will only make things

worse. If you catch him in the act, use your "No" or "Ack" sound and immediately carry him out of the house. Then use the toilet command (whichever word you have chosen) and praise your pup or give him a treat when he performs. If your pup is constantly eliminating indoors, you are not keeping a close enough eye on him

12. **Give your dog attention when YOU want to** – not when he wants it. When you are training, give your puppy lots of positive attention when he is good. But if he starts jumping up, nudging you constantly or barking to demand your attention, ignore him. Don't give in to his demands. Wait a while and pat him when you want and after he has stopped demanding your attention

13. **Start as you mean to go on.** In other words, in terms of rules and training, treat your cute little Cockapoo as though he were fully grown; introduce the rules you want him to live by as an adult. If you don't want your dog to take over your couch or bed or jump up at people when he is an adult, don't allow him to do it when he is small. You can't have one set of rules for a pup and one set for a fully grown dog; he won't understand. Also make sure that everybody in the household sticks to the same set of rules. Your dog will never learn if one person lets him jump on the couch and another person doesn't

Remember this simple phrase: **TREATS, NOT THREATS.**

Teaching Basic Commands

Sit - Teaching the Sit command to your Cockapoo is relatively easy. Teaching a young pup to sit still is a bit more difficult! In the beginning you may want to put your protégé on a lead to hold his attention.

1. Stand facing each other and hold a treat between your thumb and fingers just an inch or so above his head. Don't let your fingers and the treat get any further away or you might have trouble getting him to move his body into a sitting position. In fact, if your dog jumps up when you try to guide him into the Sit, you're probably holding your hand too far away from his nose. If your dog backs up, you can practice with a wall behind him.

   NOTE: It's rather pointless paying for a high quality, possibly hypoallergenic dog food and then filling him with trashy treats. Buy premium treats with natural ingredients which won't cause allergies, or use natural meat, fish or poultry titbits.

2. As he reaches up to sniff it, move the treat upwards and back over the dog towards his tail at the same time as saying "Sit". Most dogs will track the treat with their eyes and follow it with their noses, causing their snouts to point straight up.

3. As his head moves up toward the treat, his rear end should automatically go down towards the floor. TaDa! (drum roll!)

4. As soon as he sits, say "Yes!" give him the treat and tell your dog (s)he's a good boy or girl. Stroke and praise him for as long as he stays in the sitting position. If he jumps up on his back legs and paws you while you are moving the treat, be patient and start all over again. Another method is to put one hand on his chest and with your other hand, gently push down on his rear end until he is sitting, while saying "Sit". Give him a treat and praise, even though you have made him do it, he will eventually associate the position with the word 'sit'.

5. Once your dog catches on, leave the treat in your pocket (or have it in your other hand). Repeat the sequence, but this time your dog will just follow your empty hand. Say "Sit" and bring your empty hand in front of your dog's nose, holding your fingers as if you had a treat. Move your hand exactly as you did when you held the treat.

6. When your dog sits, say "Yes!" and then give him a treat from your other hand or your pocket.

7. Gradually lessen the amount of movement with your hand. First, say "Sit" then hold your hand eight to 10 inches above your dog's face and wait a moment. Most likely, he will sit. If he doesn't, help him by moving your hand back over his head, like you did before, but make a smaller movement this time. Then try again. Your goal is to eventually just say "Sit" without having to move or extend your hand at all.

Once your dog reliably sits on cue, you can ask him to sit whenever you meet and talk to people (admittedly, it may not work, but it might calm him down a bit). The key is anticipation. Give your Cockapoo the cue before he gets too excited to hear you and before he starts jumping up on the person just arrived. Generously reward your dog the instant he sits. Say "Yes" and give him treats every few seconds while he holds the Sit.

Whenever possible, ask the person you're greeting to help you out by walking away if your dog gets up from the sit and lunges or jumps towards him or her. With many consistent repetitions of this exercise, your dog will learn that lunging or jumping makes people go away, and polite sitting makes them stay and give him attention.

'Sit' is a useful command and can be used in a number of different situations. For example, when you are putting his lead on, while you are preparing his meal, when he returned the ball you have just thrown, when he is jumping up, demanding attention or getting over-excited.

Come - This is another basic command which you can teach right from the beginning. Teaching your dog to come to you when you call (also known as the recall) is an important lesson. A dog who responds quickly and consistently can enjoy freedoms that other dogs cannot. Although you might spend more time teaching this command to your Cockapoo than any other, the benefits make it well worth the investment. By the way, "Come" or a similar word is better than "Here" if you intend using the "Heel" command, as these words sound too similar.

No matter how much effort you put into training, no dog is ever going to be 100% reliable at coming when called and especially not an independent-minded Cockapoo. Dogs are not machines.

They're like people in that they have their good days and their bad days. Sometimes they don't hear you call, sometimes they're paying attention to something else, sometimes they misunderstand what you want, and sometimes a Cockapoo simply decides that he would rather do something else.

Whether you're teaching a young puppy or an older Cockapoo, the first step is always to establish that coming to you is the best thing he can do. Any time your dog comes to you whether you've called him or not, acknowledge that you appreciate it. You can do this with smiles, praise, affection, play or treats. This consistent reinforcement ensures that your dog will continue to "check in" with you frequently.

1. Say your dog's name followed by the command **"Come!"** in an enthusiastic voice. You'll usually be more successful if you walk or run away from him while you call. Dogs find it hard to resist chasing after a running person, especially their owner.

2. He should run towards you. NOTE: Dogs tend to tune us out if we talk to them all the time. Whether you're training or out for an off-lead walk, refrain from constantly chattering to your dog - no matter how much of a brilliant conversationalist you are! If you're quiet much of the time, he is more likely to pay attention when you call him. When he does, praise him and give him a treat.

3. Often, especially outdoors, a dog will start off running towards you but then get distracted and head off in another direction. Pre-empt this situation by praising your dog and cheering him on when he starts to come to you and before he has a chance to get distracted.

   Your praise will keep him focused so that he'll be more likely to come all the way to you. If he stops or turns away, you can give him feedback by saying "Uh-uh!" or "Hey!" in a different tone of voice (displeased or unpleasantly surprised). When he looks at you again, smile, call him and praise him as he approaches you.

Progress your dog's training in baby steps. If he's learned to come when called in your kitchen, you can't expect him to be able to do it straight away at the park or on the beach when he's surrounded by distractions. When you first try this outdoors, make sure there's no one around to distract your dog. It's a good idea to consider using a long training lead - or to do the training within a safe, fenced area. Only when your dog has mastered the recall in a number of locations and in the face of various distractions can you expect him to come to you regularly.

Down - There are a number of different ways to teach this command. It is one which does not come naturally to a young pup, so it may take a little while for him to master. Don't make it a battle of wills and, although you may gently push him down, don't physically force him down against his will. This will be seen as you asserting dominance in an aggressive manner and your Cockapoo will not respond well.

1. Give the **Sit** command.

2. When your dog sits, don't give him the treat immediately, but keep it in your closed hand. Slowly move your hand straight down toward the floor, between his front legs. As your dog's nose follows the treat, just like a magnet, his head will bend all the way down to the floor.

3. When the treat is on the floor between your dog's paws, start to move it away from him, like you're drawing a line along the floor. (The entire luring motion forms an L-shape).

4. At the same time say "Down" in a firm manner.

5. To continue to follow the treat, your dog will probably ease himself into the Down position. The instant his elbows touch the floor, say "Yes!" and immediately let him eat the treat. If your dog doesn't automatically stand up after eating the treat, just move a step or two away to encourage him to move out of the Down position. Then repeat the sequence above several times. Aim for two short sessions of five minutes or so per day.

If it doesn't work, try using a different treat. And if your dog's back end pops up when you try to lure him into a Down, quickly snatch the treat away. Then immediately ask your dog to sit and try again. It may help to let your dog nibble on the treat as you move it toward the floor. If you've tried to lure your dog into a Down but he still seems confused or reluctant, try this trick:

➢ Sit down on the floor with your legs straight out in front of you. Your dog should be at your side. Keeping your legs together and your feet on the floor, bend your knees to make a "tent" shape

➢ Hold a treat right in front of your dog's nose. As he licks and sniffs the treat, slowly move it down to the floor and then underneath your legs. Continue to lure him until he has to crouch down to keep following the treat

➢ The instant his belly touches the floor, say "Yes!" and let him eat the treat. If your dog seems nervous about following the treat under your legs, make a trail of treats for him to eat along the way

Some dogs find it easier to follow a treat into the Down from a standing position.

➢ Hold the treat right in front of your dog's nose, and then slowly move it straight down to the floor, right between his front paws. His nose will follow the treat

➢ If you let him lick the treat as you continue to hold it still on the floor, your dog will probably plop into the Down position

➢ The moment he does, say "Yes!" and let him eat the treat

Many dogs are reluctant to lie on a cold floor. It may be easier to teach yours to lie down on a carpet. The next step is to introduce a hand signal. You'll still reward him with treats, though, so keep them nearby or hidden behind your back.

➢ Start with your dog in a Sit

➢ Say "Down"

➢ Without a treat in your fingers, use the same hand motion you did before

➢ As soon as your dog's elbows touch the floor, say "Yes!" and immediately get a treat to give him. Important: Even though you're not using a treat to lure your dog into position, you must still give him a reward when he lies down. You want your dog to learn that he doesn't have to see a treat to get one.

Clap your hands or take a few steps away to encourage him to stand up. Then repeat the sequence from the beginning several times for a week or two. When your dog readily lies down as soon as you say the cue and then use your new hand signal, you're ready for the next step.

You probably don't want to keep bending all the way down to the floor to make your Cockapoo lie down. To make things more convenient, you can gradually shrink the signal so that it becomes a smaller movement. To make sure your dog continues to understand what you want him to do, you'll need to progress slowly.

Repeat the hand signal, but instead of guiding your dog into the Down by moving your hand all the way to the floor, move it almost all the way down. Stop moving your hand when it's an inch or two above the floor. Practice the Down exercise for a day or two, using this slightly smaller hand signal. Then you can make your movement an inch or two smaller, stopping your hand three or four inches above the floor.

After practising for another couple of days, you can shrink the signal again. As you continue to gradually stop your hand signal farther and farther from the floor, you'll bend over less and less. Eventually, you won't have to bend over at all. You'll be able to stand up straight, say "Down," and then just point to the floor.

Your next job is a bit harder - it's to practise your dog's new skill in many different situations and locations so that he can lie down whenever and wherever you ask him to. Slowly increase the level of distraction, for example, first practise in calm places, like different rooms in your house or in your garden, when there's no one else around. Then increase the distractions, practise at home when family members are moving around, on walks and then at friends' houses, too.

Stay - This is a very useful command, but it's not so easy to teach a lively and distracted young Cockapoo pup to stay still for any length of time. Here is a simple method to get your dog to stay; if you are training a young dog, don't ask him to stay for more than a few seconds at the beginning.

1. This requires some concentration from your dog, so pick a time when he's relaxed and well exercised or just after a game or mealtimes, especially if training a youngster.. Start with your dog in the position you want him to hold, either the Sit or Down position.

2. Command your dog to sit or lie down, but instead of giving a treat as soon as he hits the floor, hold off for one second. Then say "Yes!" in an enthusiastic voice and give him a treat. If your dog tends to bounce up again instantly, have two treats ready. Feed one right away, before he has time to move; then say "Yes!" and feed the second treat.

3. You need a release word or phrase. It might be "Free!" or "Here!" or a word which you only use to release your dog from this command. Once you've given the treat, immediately give your release cue and encourage your dog to get up. Then repeat the exercise, perhaps up to a dozen times in one training session, gradually wait a tiny bit longer before releasing the treat. (You can delay the first treat for a moment if your dog bounces up).

4. A common mistake is to hold the treat high and then give the reward slowly. As your dog doesn't know the command yet, he sees the treat coming and gets up to meet the food. Instead, bring the treat toward your dog quickly - the best place to deliver it is right between his front paws. If you're working on a Sit-Stay, give the treat at chest height.

5. When your dog can stay for several seconds, start to add a little distance. At first, you'll walk backwards, because your Cockapoo is more likely to get up to follow you if you turn away from him. Take one single step away, then step back towards your dog and say "Yes!" and give the treat. Give him the signal to get up immediately, even if five seconds haven't passed. The stay gets harder for your dog depending on how long it is, how far away you are, and what else is going on around him.

   Trainer shorthand is **"distance, duration, distraction."** For best success in teaching a stay, work on one factor at a time. Whenever you make one factor more difficult, such as distance, ease up on the others at first, then build them back up. That's why, when you take that first step back from your dog, adding **distance,** you should cut the **duration** of the stay.

6. Now your dog has mastered the Stay with you alone, move the training on so that he learns to do the same with distractions. Have someone walk into the room, or squeak a toy or bounce a ball once. A rock-solid stay is mostly a matter of working slowly and patiently to start with. Don't go too fast, the ideal scenario is that your Cockapoo never breaks out of the Stay position until you release him.

   If he does get up, take a breather and then give him a short refresher, starting at a point easier than whatever you were working on when he cracked. If you think he's tired or had enough, leave it for the day and come back later – just finish off on a positive note by giving one very easy command you know he will obey, followed by a treat reward.

Don't use the "Stay" command in situations where it is unpleasant for your Cockapoo. For instance, avoid telling him to stay as you close the door behind you on your way to work. Finally, don't use Stay to keep a dog in a scary situation.

Clicker Training

Clicker training is a method of training that uses a sound - a click - to tell an animal when he does something right. The clicker is a tiny plastic box held in the palm of your hand, with a metal tongue that you push quickly to make the sound.

The clicker creates an efficient language between a human trainer and a trainee. First, a trainer teaches a dog that every time he hears the clicking sound, he gets a treat. Once the dog understands that clicks are always followed by treats, the click becomes a powerful reward.

When this happens, the trainer can use the click to mark the instant the animal performs the right behaviour. For example, if a trainer wants to teach a dog to sit, she'll click the instant his rump hits the floor and then deliver a tasty treat. With repetition, the dog learns that sitting earns rewards.

So the 'click' takes on huge meaning. To the animal it means: "What I was doing the moment my trainer clicked, **that's** what she wants me to do." The clicker in animal training is like the winning buzzer on a game show that tells a contestant he's just won the money! Through the clicker, the trainer communicates precisely with the dog, and that speeds up training.

Although the clicker is ideal because it makes a unique, consistent sound, you do need a spare hand to hold it. For that reason, some trainers prefer to keep both hands free and instead use a one-syllable word like "Yes!" or "Good!" to mark the desired behaviour. In the steps below, you can substitute the word in place of the click to teach your pet what the sound means. It's easy to introduce the clicker to your Cockapoo. Spend half an hour or so teaching him that the sound of the click means "Treat!" Here's how:

1. Sit and watch TV or read a book with your dog in the room. Have a container of treats within reach.

2. Place one treat in your hand and the clicker in the other. (If your dog smells the treat and tries to get it by pawing, sniffing, mouthing or barking at you, just close your hand around the treat and wait until he gives up and leaves you alone).

3. Click once and immediately open your hand to give your dog the treat. Put another treat in your closed hand and resume watching TV or reading. Ignore your dog.

4. Several minutes later, click again and offer another treat.

5. Continue to repeat the click-and-treat combination at varying intervals, sometimes after one minute, sometimes after five minutes. Make sure you vary the time so that your dog doesn't know exactly when the next click is coming. Eventually, he'll start to turn toward you and look expectantly when he hears the click—which means he understands that the sound of the clicker means a treat is coming his way.

If your dog runs away when he hears the click, you can make the sound softer by putting it in your pocket or wrapping a towel around your hand that's holding the clicker. You can also try using a different sound, like the click of a retractable pen or the word "Yes."

Clicker Training Basics

Once your dog seems to understand the connection between the click and the treat, you're ready to get started.

1. Click just once, right when your pet does what you want him to do. Think of it like pressing the shutter of a camera to take a picture of the behaviour.

2. Remember to follow every click with a treat. After you click, deliver the treat to your pet's mouth **as quickly as possible.**

3. It's fine to switch between practising two or three behaviours within a session, but work on one command at a time. For example, say you're teaching your Cockapoo to sit, lie down and raise his paw. You can do 10 repetitions of sit and take a quick play break. Then do 10

repetitions of down, and take another quick break. Then do 10 repetitions of stay, and so on. Keep training sessions short and stop before you or your dog gets tired of the game.

4. End training sessions on a good note, when your dog has succeeded with what you're working on. If necessary, ask him to do something you know he can do well at the end of a session.

Collar and Lead Training

You have to train your Cockapoo to get used to a collar or harness and lead (leash), and then he has to learn to walk nicely on the lead. Teaching these manners can be challenging because many young Cockapoos are very lively and don't necessarily want to walk at the same pace as you. All dogs will pull on a lead initially. This isn't because they want to show you who is boss, it's simply that they are excited to be outdoors and are forging ahead.

If you are worried about pulling on your Cockapoo's collar, you might prefer to use a body harness instead. Harnesses work well with many Cockapoos as they are not a breed noted for dragging their owners around on a walk. A harness takes the pressure away from a dog's sensitive neck area and distributes it more evenly around the body. Those with a chest ring for the lead can be effective for training. When your dog pulls, the harness turns him around.

Another option is to start your dog on a padded collar and then change to a harness once he has learned some lead etiquette – although padded collars can be quite heavy. Some dogs don't mind collars; some will try to fight them, while others will slump to the floor like you have hung a two-ton weight around their necks! You need to be patient and calm and proceed at a pace comfortable to him; don't fight your dog and don't force the collar on.

1. The secret to getting a collar is to buy one that fits your puppy now - not one he is going to grow into - so choose a small lightweight one that he will hardly notice. A big collar may be too heavy and frightening. You can buy one with clips to start with, just put it on and clip it together, rather than fiddling with buckles, which can be scary when he's wearing a collar for the first time. Stick to the principle of positive reward-based training and give him a treat once the collar is on, not after you have taken it off. Then gradually increase the length of time you leave the collar on.

IMPORTANT: If you leave your dog in a crate, or leave him alone in the house, take off the collar. He is not used to it and it may get caught on something, causing panic or injury to your dog.

So put the collar on when there are other things that will occupy him, like when he is going outside to be with you, or in the home when you are interacting with him. Or put it on at mealtimes or when you are doing some basic training. Don't put the collar on too tight, you want him to forget it's there. If he scratches the collar, get his attention by encouraging him to follow you or play with a toy so he forgets the irritation.

2. Once your puppy is happy wearing the collar, introduce the lead. An extending or retractable one is not particularly suitable for starting off with, as they are not very strong and no good for training him to walk close. Buy a fixed-length lead. Start off in the house; don't try to go out and about straight away. Think of the lead as a safety device to stop him running off, not something to drag him around with. You want a Cockapoo that doesn't pull, so don't start by pulling him around. You definitely don't want to get into a tug-of-war contest.

3. Attach the lead to the collar and give him a treat while you put it on. The minute it is attached, use the treats (instead of pulling on the lead) to lure him beside you, so that he gets used to walking with the collar and lead. As well as using treats you can also make good use of toys to do exactly the same thing - especially if your dog has a favourite. Walk around the house with the lead on and lure him forwards with the toy.

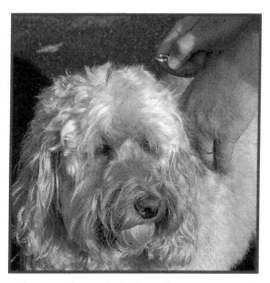

It might feel a bit odd but it's a good way for your pup to develop a positive relationship with the collar and lead with the minimum of fuss. Act as though it's the most natural thing in the world for you to walk around the house or apartment with your dog on a lead – and just hope that the neighbours aren't watching! Some dogs react the moment you attach the lead and they feel some tension on it – a bit like when a horse is being broken in for the first time.

Drop the lead and allow him to run round the house or yard, dragging it after him, but be careful he doesn't get tangled and hurt himself. Try to make him forget about it by playing or starting a short fun training routine with treats. Treats are a huge distraction for most Cockapoos. While he is concentrating on the new task, occasionally pick up the lead and call him to you. Do it gently and in an encouraging tone.

4. The most important thing is not to yank on the lead. If it gets tight, just lure him back beside you with a treat or a toy while walking. All you're doing is getting him to move around beside you. Remember to keep your hand down (the one holding the treat or toy) so your dog doesn't get the habit of jumping up at you. If you feel he is getting stressed when walking outside on a lead, try putting treats along the route you'll be taking to turn this into a rewarding game: good times are ahead... That way he learns to focus on what's ahead of him with curiosity and not fear.

Take collar and lead training slowly, give your Cockapoo time to process all this new information about what the lead is and does. Let him gain confidence in you, and then in the lead and himself. Some dogs can sit and decide not to move. If this happens, walk a few steps away, go down on one knee and encourage him to come to you using a treat, then walk off again.

For some pups, the collar and lead can be restricting and they will react with resistance. Some dogs are perfectly happy to walk alongside you off-lead, but behave differently when they have one on. Proceed in tiny steps if that is what your puppy is happy with, don't over face him, but stick at it if you are met with resistance. With training, your puppy **will** learn to walk nicely on a lead; it is just a question of when, not if.

Walking on a Lead

There are different methods, but we have found the following one to be successful for quick results. Initially, the lead should be kept fairly loose. Have a treat in your hand as you walk, it will encourage your dog to sniff the treat as he walks alongside. He will not pull ahead, as he will want to remain near the treat.

Give him the command **Walk** or **Heel** and then proceed with the treat in your hand, keep giving him a treat every few steps initially, then gradually extend the time between treats. Eventually, you should be able to walk with your hand comfortably at your side, periodically (every minute or so) reaching into your pocket to grab a treat to reward your dog.

If your dog starts pulling ahead, first give him a warning, by saying **No** or **Easy,** or a similar command. If he slows down, give him a treat. But if he continues to pull ahead so that your arm becomes fully extended, stop walking and ignore your dog. Wait for him to stop pulling and to look up at you. At this point reward him for good behaviour before carrying on your walk.

Be sure to quickly reward him with treats and praise any time he doesn't pull and walks with you with the lead slack. If you have a lively young pup who is dashing all over the place on the lead, try starting training when he is already a little tired - after a play or exercise session – (but not exhausted).

Another way is what dog trainer Victoria Stillwell describes as the Reverse Direction Technique. When your dog pulls, say "Let's Go!" in an encouraging manner, then turn away from him and walk off in the other direction, without jerking on the lead. When he is following you and the lead is slack, turn back and continue on your original way. It may take a few repetitions, but your words and body language will make it clear that pulling will not get your dog anywhere, whereas walking calmly by your side - or even slightly in front of you - on a loose lead will get him where he wants to go.

There is an excellent video (in front of a beautiful house!) which shows Victoria demonstrating this technique and highlights just how easy it is with a dog that's easy to please. It only lasts three minutes and is well worth watching: https://positively.com/dog-behavior/basic-cues/loose-leash-walking.

Puppy Biting

All puppies spend a great deal of time chewing, playing, and investigating objects. All of these normal activities involve them using their mouths and their needle-sharp teeth. Like babies, this is how they investigate the world. When puppies play with people, they often bite, chew and mouth on people's hands, limbs and clothing.

Play biting is normal for puppies, they do it all the time with their littermates. They bite moving targets with their sharp teeth; it's a great game. But when they arrive in your home, they have to be taught that human skin is sensitive and body parts are not suitable material for biting. Biting is never acceptable, not even from a small dog or puppy.

As a puppy grows and feels more confident in his surroundings, he may become bolder and his bites may hurt someone – especially if you have children or elderly people at home. Make sure every time you have a play session, you have a soft toy nearby and when he starts to chew your hand or feet, clench your fingers (or toes!) to make it more difficult and distract him with a soft toy in your other hand. Keep the game interesting by moving the toy around or rolling it around in front of him. (He may be too young to fetch it back if you throw it). He may continue to chew you, but will eventually realise that the toy is far more interesting and lively than your boring hand.

Do not play too aggressively with your dog; keep playtimes fun - they should not be a battle of wills. If your dog becomes over-excited and too aggressive with a toy, if he growls a lot, stop playing with him and **walk away**. Although it might be quite cute and funny now, you don't want your Cockapoo doing this as an adult. Remember, if not checked, any unwanted behaviour traits will continue into adulthood, when you certainly don't want him to bite a child's hand or face – even accidentally.

When you walk away, don't say anything or make eye or physical contact with your puppy. Simply ignore him; this is extremely effective and often works within a few days. If your pup is more persistent and tries to bite your legs as you walk away, thinking this is another fantastic game, stand still and ignore him. If he still persists, tell him **"No!"** in a very stern voice, then praise him when he lets go. If you have to physically remove him from your trouser leg or shoe, leave him alone in the room for a while and ignore his demands for attention if he starts barking.

Many Cockapoos are very sensitive and another method which can be very successful is to make a sharp cry of **"Ouch!"** when your pup bites your hand – even when it doesn't hurt. This worked very well for us. Your pup may well jump back in amazement, surprised that he has hurt you.

Divert your attention from your puppy to your hand. He will probably try to get your attention or lick you as a way of saying sorry. Praise him for stopping biting and continue with the game. If he

bites you again, repeat the process. A sensitive Cockapoo will soon stop biting you. You may also think about keeping the toys you use to play with your puppy separate from other toys. That way he will associate certain toys with having fun with you and will work harder to please you.

Cockapoos love playing and you can use this to your advantage by teaching your dog how to play nicely with you and the toy and then by using play time as a reward for good behaviour. NOTE: If your puppy is either in a hyperactive mood or is exhausted, he is not likely to be very receptive to training.

CREDIT: With thanks to the American Society for the Prevention of Cruelty to Animals for assistance with parts of this chapter. The ASPCA has a great deal of good advice and training tips on its website at: http://www.aspca.org/pet-care/virtual-pet- behaviourist/dog- behaviour/training-your-dog

---

What Breeders and Owners Say

We asked some Cockapoo breeders and owners how much exercise they gave their dogs and how easy they thought Cockapoos were to train. Here is what they said, starting in the UK:

Breeder Karol Watson Todd says that she finds Cockapoos "excellent" to train. Pictured, wearing her harness for a romp in the fields, is Amber, bred by Karol and owned by Christine Grey, who says:

"One thing that we have discovered is how much exercise Amber needs. We give her at least two hours a day (two or three walks) and she seems to have a never-ending supply of energy! Not a problem for us as we love walking, but anyone unable or unprepared for this commitment should probably think twice before parenting a Cockapoo!"

Keith and Diane Raymond own Zippy, also bred by Karol. They added: "To any potential owners of Cockapoos, you need to think very hard about why you want one. They are not dogs for just sitting at your feet all day long. They need plenty of exercise. Our Zippy has up to two or three hours a day and she always wants more."

Breeder Pat Pollington says: "Our dogs have their own field they run in and a concrete yard. They then go for a walk twice a day. We believe every dog needs at least one good walk a day. They also need time off-lead in an area where they can run and use their natural instincts. If your dog is unable to go off-lead, there are places that have fully secure fields for dogs to just run and they will need this a good once a week. If they can go off-lead in the playing field and play with other dogs, all the better.

"If you put the work into a Cockapoo, they are very easy to train. They are very loyal dogs, so they always want to please their owner. There are a lot of training classes for puppies and it is always a good idea to book into one of these. A lot of our puppies have learnt sit, paw and stay in just a couple of days of being in their new home. The best time to use is feed time. Make them ask for their food, i.e. sit and paw. Never let a Cockapoo get away with anything just because they are a puppy. If you allow this, then they will want the same when they are adults, and it is a lot harder to train an older dog."

Julie Shearman: "We exercise our Cockapoos for a minimum of an hour 'off-lead' each day. Although, if there's a foot of snow, you're ill, etc. and can't walk the dog, Cockapoos are calm indoors and quite happy to cuddle up with their owner. They are the fastest breed we have ever trained! Reports from new owners confirm this, stating that they are top of the obedience class and often picked out to use as demonstration dogs."

Eileen Jackson: "My Cockapoos are from both show and working stock. The difference is in the size; the temperament is much the same. They all need stimulation i.e. games, or hiding toys either in the garden or in the house. They make ideal dogs for Fly Ball and love their walks."

This is what the North American breeders said, starting with Jeanne Davis: "I exercise my Cockapoos regularly and daily; they do not need to be worn-out like some high performance/high energy dogs. They are extremely easy to obedience train."

Jessica Sampson: "My Cockapoos get one or two good 20 to 30-minute walks each day; also they get lots of play time in the yard to chase balls and just be dogs! They are also adept swimmers and enjoy spending lots of time in the water."

Jackie Stafford: "Cockapoos are easy apartment dwellers as they conform to the regimen of their owners. They should be allowed to exercise at least 30 minutes a day. Cockapoos are usually very easy to obedience train by repetition. They can be taught to sit in just a few minutes with treats and repetitive commands."

Rebecca Mae Goins: "Exercising your Cockapoo is fairly simple; you can get your Cockapoo a few interactive toys that can help occupy them if you are busy or away. If you have a fenced-in yard, take your Cockapoo out for a game of fetch that lasts around 15 to 20 minutes. If you do not have a fenced yard, take your Cockapoo for walks."

Pictured, one with a collar and the other with a harness, are Josie (left), owned by Deanna Sargent of Deaz Cockapoos, and Scarlett, owned by Rebecca Goins of MoonShine Babies Cockapoos. Both are F3s bred by Deanna, mentored by Rebecca.

She added: "I have found that Cockapoos are very intelligent and are very fast learners, but the time required to obedience train a Cockapoo depends on the time devoted to this by the breeder and the new family. As a breeder, I start my puppies on manners and basic obedience training as soon as they are up walking around. The sooner you teach them to accept a human handling them, the sooner they will start learning what you are trying to teach them."

8. Behaviour

Just as with humans, a Cockapoo's personality is made up of a combination of temperament and character.

Temperament is the nature – or inherited traits - a dog is born with; a predisposition to act or react in a certain way. This is why getting your puppy from a good breeder is so important. Not only will a responsible breeder produce puppies from physically healthy dams and sires, but she will also look at the temperament of her dogs and breed from those with good traits.

Character is what develops through the dog's life and is formed by a combination of temperament and environment. How you treat your Cockapoo will have a huge effect on his or her

personality and behaviour. Starting off on the right foot with good routines for your puppy is very important; so treat your dog well, spend time with him and give him plenty of socialisation and exercise. All dogs need different environments, scents and experiences to keep them stimulated and well-balanced.

Praise good behaviour, use positive methods and keep training short and fun. At the same time, be consistent so your dog learns the guidelines quickly. All of these measures will help your Cockapoo grow into a happy, well-adjusted and well-behaved adult dog that is a delight to be with.

If you adopt a Cockapoo from a rescue centre, you may need a little extra patience. These eager-to-please people-loving dogs may also arrive with some baggage. They have been abandoned by their previous owners for a variety of reasons - or perhaps forced to produce puppies in a puppy mill - and may very well still carry the scars of that trauma. They may feel nervous and insecure or they may not know how to properly interact with a loving owner. Your time and patience is needed to teach these poor animals to trust again and to become happy in their new forever homes.

Understanding Canine Emotions

As pet lovers, we are all too keen to ascribe human traits to our dogs; this is called **anthropomorphism** – "the attribution of human characteristics to anything other than a human being." Most of us dog lovers are guilty of that, as we come to regard our pets as members of the family - and Cockapoos certainly regard themselves as members of the family. In fact some are convinced that they are the centre of it and we belong to them!

An example of anthropomorphism might be that the owner of a male dog might not want to have him neutered because he will "miss sex," as a human might if he or she were no longer able to have sex. This is simply not true. A male dog's impulse to mate is entirely governed by his hormones, not emotions. If he gets the scent of a bitch on heat, his hormones (which are just chemicals) tell him he has to mate with her. He does not stop to consider how attractive she is or whether she is '**the one**' to produce his puppies. No, his reaction is entirely physical, he just wants to dive in there and get on with it!

It's the same with females. When they are on heat, a chemical impulse is triggered in their brain making them want to mate – with any male, they aren't at all fussy. So don't expect your little princess to be all coy when she is on heat, she is not waiting for Prince Charming to come along - the tramp down the road or any other scruffy pooch will do! It is entirely physical, not emotional. Food is another issue. A dog will not stop to count the calories of that lovely treat (you have to do that). No, he or she is driven by food and just thinks about getting the treat. Most will eat as long as you will feed them.

Cockapoos are very loving and extremely eager to please you, and if yours doesn't make you laugh from time to time, you must have had a humour by-pass. They also want to spend all of their time with their owners. All of these characteristics add up to one thing: an extremely endearing and loving family member that it's all too easy to reward - or spoil. Treating a Cockapoo like a child is all too easy, but it is to be avoided.

It's fine to treat your Cockapoo like a member of the family - as long as you keep in mind that he is a canine and not a human. Understand his mind, patiently train him to learn his place in the household and that there are household rules he needs to learn – like not jumping on the couch when he's covered in mud - and you will be rewarded with a companion who is second to none and fits in beautifully with your family and lifestyle.

Dr Stanley Coren is a psychologist well known for his work on canine psychology and behaviour. He and other researchers believe that in many ways a dog's emotional development is equivalent to that of a young child. Dr Coren says: "Researchers have now come to believe that the mind of a dog is roughly equivalent to that of a human who is two to two-and-a-half years old. This conclusion holds for most mental abilities as well as emotions.

"Thus, we can look to the human research to see what we might expect of our dogs. Just like a two-year-old child, our dogs clearly have emotions, but many fewer kinds of emotions than found in adult humans. At birth, a human infant only has an emotion that we might call excitement. This indicates how excited he is, ranging from very calm up to a state of frenzy. Within the first weeks of life the excitement state comes to take on a varying positive or a negative flavour, so we can now detect the general emotions of contentment and distress.

"In the next couple of months, disgust, fear, and anger become detectable in the infant. Joy often does not appear until the infant is nearly six months of age and it is followed by the emergence of shyness or suspicion. True affection, the sort that it makes sense to use the label "love" for, does not fully emerge until nine or ten months of age."

So, our Cockapoos can truly love us – but we knew that already!

According to Dr Coren, dogs can't feel shame, so if you are housetraining your puppy, don't expect him to be ashamed if he makes a mess in the house, he can't; he simply isn't capable of feeling shame. But he will not like it when you ignore him when he's behaving badly, and he will love it when you praise him for eliminating outdoors. He is simply responding to your reaction with his simplified range of emotions.

Dr Coren also believes that dogs cannot experience guilt, contempt or pride. I'm not sure I agree. Take a Cockapoo to a local dog show or agility class, watch him perform and then maybe win a rosette - surely the dog's delight is something akin to pride? And Cockapoos can certainly experience joy.

They love your attention, and when they are showing off and lapping up your attention, their reaction can only be described as a mixture of pure joy and pride. What about when they run through the muddy woods and come back with a wonderful present for you in the form of a small, deceased furry mammal - isn't there a hint of pride then? Pictured looking very pleased with herself after winning a rosette is Mabel, bred by Eileen Jackson, of Brimstone Cockapoos, Cambridgeshire, England.

Cockapoos can certainly show empathy - "the ability to understand and share the feelings of another" - and this is one reason why they make such excellent therapy and service dogs. Like many companion breeds, after a while they get into tune with the rhythms of the household and pick up on the mood and emotions of the owner. Both parent breeds - Poodles and Cocker Spaniels – are sensitive breeds, and Poodles in particular are known for being intuitive and having the ability to pick up on their owners' moods.

One emotion which all dogs can experience is jealousy – with Cockapoos this may be displayed when you give your precious attention to animals other than themselves. Or they may guard their food. An interesting article was published in the PLOS (Public Library of Science) Journal in summer 2014 following an experiment into whether dogs get jealous. Building on research that shows that six-month old infants display jealousy, the scientists studied 36 dogs in their homes and video recorded their actions when their owners displayed affection to a realistic-looking stuffed canine.

Over three-quarters of the dogs were likely to push or touch the owner when they interacted with the decoy (pictured, right). The envious mutts were more than three times as likely to do this for interactions with the stuffed dog compared to when their owners gave their attention to other objects, including a book. Around a third tried to get between the owner and the plush toy, while a quarter of the put-upon pooches snapped at the dummy dog!

"Our study suggests not only that dogs do engage in what appear to be jealous behaviours, but also that they were seeking to break up the connection between the owner and a seeming rival," said Professor Christine Harris from University of California in San Diego.

The researchers believe that the dogs understood that the stuffed dog was real. The authors cite the fact that 86% of the dogs sniffed the toy's rear end during and after the experiment!

"We can't really speak of the dogs' subjective experiences, of course, but it looks as though they were motivated to protect an important social relationship. Many people have assumed that jealousy is a social construction of human beings - or that it's an emotion specifically tied to sexual and romantic relationships," said Professor Harris.

"Our results challenge these ideas, showing that animals besides ourselves display strong distress whenever a rival usurps a loved one's affection."

Typical Cockapoo Traits

1. Cockapoos are bred as companions with a naturally sweet and happy temperament. They make wonderful companions and family dogs and are known for being good with children

2. One thing which surprises many new Cockapoo owners is the amount of exercise they need. It does, of course, depend on factors such as whether your dog was bred from working or show Spaniels, but two or three hours of exercise a day is not unusual for some dogs

3. They love running off the lead, they are good swimmers and most love snow. Cockapoos' parents and grandparents were working breeds

4. They also love chilling out and snuggling up with their owners, provided they have had enough exercise

5. An under-exercised, under-stimulated Cockapoo will display poor behaviour, as any dog would

6. Cockapoos have been described as "Velcro dogs"; they want to be with you 24/7 and will often follow you from room to room. Spend some time apart to avoid separation anxiety - which Cockapoos are prone to - and which is stressful for both dog and owner

7. They do not like being left alone for long. If you are away from the home a lot, consider another type of dog not so dependent on humans for happiness

8. Cockapoos are highly intelligent and need mental as well as physical stimulation. They love to play both indoor and outdoor games and enjoy activities which make them think

9. Provided you put the time in, Cockapoos are among the easiest of all types of dog to train - and they can be trained to a very high level. They also excel in canine competitions, such as Fly Ball and Agility, where physical and mental agility is required. Their intelligence and eagerness to please are powerful training aids

10. The same goes for housetraining; a Cockapoo can pick it up in a few days, as long as you are extremely vigilant in the beginning

11. They are not aggressive dogs and generally get on well with other dogs, provided they have been properly socialised

12. Some Cockapoos can suffer from submissive urination, especially if they are under-socialised, insecure or over-excited. Proper socialisation and plenty of exercise can help to combat this issue

13. Cockapoos will steal your heart. OK, so that's not very scientific - but ask anyone who owns one, like Jackie Stafford, of Dj's Cockapoos, who bred this cute and curious little puppy.

Cause and Effect

Treated well, socialised and trained, Cockapoos make incomparable canine companions. They are extremely affectionate and sociable, they love being around people, form close bonds and entertain their humans - which is why once you've had one, no other dog seems quite the same. But sometimes Cockapoos, just like other breeds and crossbreeds, can develop behaviour problems. There are numerous reasons for this; every dog is an individual with his or her own temperament and environment, both of which influence the way he or she interacts with you and the world. Poor behaviour may result from a number of factors, including:

➢ Poor breeding
➢ Lack of socialisation
➢ Boredom, due to lack of exercise or mental challenges
➢ Being badly treated
➢ Being left alone too long
➢ A change in living conditions
➢ Anxiety or insecurity
➢ Fear
➢ Being spoiled

Bad behaviour may show itself in a number of different ways, such as:

➢ Constantly demanding attention
➢ Chewing or destructive behaviour
➢ Jumping up
➢ Excessive barking
➢ Nipping or biting
➢ Soiling or urinating inside the house
➢ Aggression towards other dogs
➢ Growling

This chapter looks at some familiar behaviour problems. Although every dog is different, some common causes of unwanted behaviour are covered, along with tips to help improve the situation. The best way to avoid poor behaviour is to put in the time early on to socialise and train your dog, and nip any potential problems in the bud. If you are rehoming a dog, you'll need extra time and patience to help your new arrival unlearn some bad habits.

Ten Ways to Avoid Bad Behaviour

Different dogs have different reasons for exhibiting bad behaviour. There is no simple cure for everything. Your best chance of ensuring your Cockapoo does not become badly behaved is to start out on the right foot and follow these simple guidelines:

1. **Buy from a good breeder**. They use their expertise to match suitable breeding couples, taking into account factors such as good temperament and health

2. **Start training early -** you can't start too soon. Like babies, Cockapoo puppies have incredibly enquiring minds which can quickly absorb a lot of new information. You can start teaching your puppy to learn his own name as well as some simple commands as soon as you bring him home

3. **Basic training should cover several areas:** housetraining, chew prevention, puppy biting, simple commands like 'sit', 'come', 'stay' and familiarising him with a collar or harness and lead. Adopt a gentle approach and keep training sessions short. Cockapoos are sensitive to you and your mood and do not respond well to harsh words or treatment. Start with five or 10 minutes a day and build up. Often the way a dog responds to his or her environment is a result of owner training and management – or lack of it. Puppy classes or adult dog obedience classes are a great way to start, but make sure you do your homework afterwards. Spend a few minutes each day reinforcing what you have both learned in class - owners need training as well as Cockapoos!

4. **Start socialisation right away -** we are beginning to realise the vital role that early socialisation plays in developing a well-rounded adult dog. It is essential to expose your dog to other people, places, animals and experiences as soon as possible. Give him a few days to settle in and then start – even if this means carrying him places until his vaccination schedule is complete. Lack of socialisation is one of the major causes of unwanted behaviour traits. Exposing your Cockapoo to as many different things as possible goes a long way in helping a dog become a more stable, happy and trustworthy companion

IMPORTANT: Socialisation does not end at puppyhood. Dogs are social creatures that thrive on seeing, smelling and even licking. While the foundation for good behaviour is laid down during the first few months, good owners will reinforce social skills and training throughout a dog's life. Cockapoos love to be the centre of attention and it is important that they learn when young that they are not the centre of the universe. Socialisation helps them to learn their place in that universe and to become comfortable with it

5. **Reward your dog for good behaviour.** All behaviour training should be based on positive reinforcement; so praise and reward your dog when he does something good. Generally Cockapoos are very keen to please their owners, and this trait speeds up the training process. The main aim of training is to build a good understanding between you and your dog

6. **Ignore bad behaviour**, no matter how hard this may be. If, for example, your dog is chewing his way through your shoes, couch or toilet rolls, remove him from the situation and then ignore him. For some dogs even negative attention is some attention. Or if he is constantly demanding your attention, ignore him. Remove yourself from the room so he

learns that you give attention when you want to give it, not when he demands it. The more time you spend praising and rewarding good behaviour while ignoring bad behaviour, the more likely he is to respond to you. If your pup is a chewer – and most are - make sure he has plenty of durable toys to keep him occupied. Cockapoos can chew their way through flimsy toys in no time.

7. **Take the time to learn what sort of temperament your dog has.** Is she by nature a nervous or confident girl? What was she like as a puppy, did she rush forward or hang back? Does she fight to get upright when on her back or is she happy to lie there? Is she a couch potato or a ball of fire? Your puppy's temperament will affect her behaviour and how she responds to the world around her. A timid Cockapoo will certainly not respond well to a loud approach on your part, whereas an energetic, strong-willed one will require more patience and exercise

8. **Exercise and stimulation.** A lack of either is another major reason for dogs behaving badly. Regular daily exercise, indoor or outdoor games and toys are all ways of stopping your dog from becoming bored or frustrated

9. **Learn to leave your dog.** Just as leaving your dog alone for too long can lead to problems, so can being with him 100% of the time. The dog becomes over-reliant on you and then gets stressed when you leave him. This is called *separation anxiety* and something which Cockapoos are susceptible to, like many breeds which thrive on human contact. When your dog is a puppy, or when he arrives at your house as an adult, start by leaving him for a few minutes every day and gradually build it up so that after a few weeks or months you can leave him for up to four hours

10. **Love your Cockapoo – but don't spoil him,** however difficult that might be. You don't do your dog any favours by giving him too many treats, constantly responding to his demands for attention or allowing him to behave as he wants inside the house.

Separation Anxiety

It's not just Cockapoos that experience separation anxiety - people do too. About 7% of adults and 4% of children suffer from this disorder. Typical symptoms for humans are:

> ➢ Distress at being separated from a loved one
> ➢ Fear of being left alone

Our canine companions aren't much different to us. When a dog leaves the litter, his owners become his new family or pack. It's estimated that as many as 10% to 15% of dogs suffer from separation anxiety. Both male and female Cockapoos are susceptible because they are companion dogs and thrive on being with people. It is an exaggerated fear response caused by separation from their owner.

Separation anxiety is on the increase and recognised by behaviourists as the most common form of stress for dogs. Millions of dogs suffer from separation anxiety.

It can be equally distressing for the owner - I know because our dog, Max, suffers from this. He howls whenever we leave home without him. Fortunately his problem is only a mild one. If we return after only a short while, he's usually quiet. Although if we silently sneak back home and peek in through the letterbox, he's never asleep. Instead he's waiting by the door looking and listening for our return. It can be embarrassing. Whenever I go to the Post Office, I tie him up outside and even though he can see me through the glass door, he still barks his head off - so loud that the people inside can't make themselves heard. Luckily the lady behind the counter is a dog lover and, despite the large **'GUIDE DOGS ONLY'** sign outside, she lets Max in. He promptly dashes through the door and sits down beside me, quiet as a mouse!

Tell-Tale Signs

Does your Cockapoo do any of the following?

> ➤ Follow you from room to room whenever you're home?
> ➤ Get anxious or stressed when you're getting ready to leave the house?
> ➤ Howl, whine or bark when you leave?
> ➤ Tear up paper or chew cushions, couches or other things?
> ➤ Dig, chew, or scratch at doors and windows trying to join you?
> ➤ Foul or urinate inside the house, even though he is housetrained? (This **only** occurs when left alone)
> ➤ Exhibit restlessness - such as licking his coat excessively, pacing or circling?
> ➤ Greet you ecstatically every time you come home – even if you've only been out to empty the bins?
> ➤ Wait by the window or door until you return?
> ➤ Dislike spending time alone in the garden or yard?
> ➤ Howl or whine when one family member leaves - even though others are still in the room or car?

If so, he or she may suffer from separation anxiety. Fortunately, in many cases this can be cured.

Canine Separation Anxiety Through the Ages

Dogs are pack animals and being alone is not a natural state for them. Puppies should be patiently taught to get used to isolation slowly and in a structured way if they are to be comfortable with it. A puppy will emotionally latch on to his new owner, who has taken the place of his mother and siblings.

He will want to follow you everywhere initially and, although you want to shower him with love and attention, it's important to leave your new puppy alone for short periods in the beginning to avoid him becoming totally dependent on you. In our case, I was working from home when we got Max. With hindsight, we should have regularly left him alone for short periods more often in the first few months.

Adopted dogs may be particularly susceptible to separation anxiety. They may have been abandoned once already and fear it happening again. Symptoms are not commonly seen in middle-aged dogs, although dogs that develop symptoms when young may be at risk later on. Separation anxiety is, however, common in elderly dogs. Pets age and - like humans - their senses, such as hearing and sight, deteriorate. They become more dependent on their owners and may then become more anxious when they are separated from them - or even out of view.

It may be very flattering and cute that your dog wants to be with you all the time, but insecurity and separation anxiety are forms of panic, which is distressing for your Cockapoo. If he shows any signs, help him to become more self-reliant and confident; he will be a happier dog. So what can you do if your dog is showing signs of canine separation anxiety? Every dog is different, but here are tried and tested techniques which have proved effective for some dogs.

Ten Tips to Reduce Separation Anxiety

1. Practise leaving your dog for short periods, starting with a minute or two and gradually lengthening the time you are out of sight

2. Tire your Cockapoo out before you leave him alone. Take him for a walk or play a game before leaving

3. Keep arrivals and departures low key and don't make a big fuss. For example, when I come home, Max is hysterically happy and runs round whimpering with a toy in his mouth. I make him sit and stay and then let him out into the garden without patting or acknowledging him. I pat him several minutes later

4. Leave your dog a "security blanket," such as an old piece of clothing you have recently worn which still has your scent on it, or leave a radio on - not too loud - in the room with the dog. Avoid a heavy rock station! If it will be dark when you return, leave a lamp on a timer

5. Associate your departure with something good. As you leave, give your dog a rubber toy, like a Kong, filled with a tasty treat. This may take his mind off of your departure. (We've tried this with Max, but he "punishes" us by refusing to touch the treat until we return home - and then wolfs it down)

6. If your dog is used to a crate, try crating him when you go out. Many dogs feel safe there, and being in a crate can also help to reduce destructiveness. Always take the collar off first. Pretend to leave the house, but listen for a few minutes. Never leave a dog in a crate all day. **Warning:** if your dog starts to show major signs of distress, remove him from the crate immediately as he may injure himself

7. Structure and routine can help to reduce anxiety in your Cockapoo. Carry out regular activities, such as feeding and exercising, at the same time every day

8. Dogs read body language very well, many Cockapoos are intuitive. They may start to fret when they think you are going to leave them. One technique is to mimic your departure routine when you have no intention of leaving. So put your coat on, grab your car keys, go out of the door and return a few seconds later. Do this randomly and regularly and it may help to reduce your dog's stress levels when you do it for real

9. Some dogs show anxiety in new places; get him used to different environments and people

10. Getting another dog to keep the first one company can help, but first ask yourself whether you have the time and money for two or more dogs. Can you afford double the vet's and food bills?

Sit-Stay-Down

Another technique for helping to reduce separation anxiety is to practise the common "sit-stay" or "down-stay" exercises using positive reinforcement. The goal is to be able to move briefly out of your dog's sight while he is in the "stay" position. Through this your dog learns that he can remain calmly and happily in one place while you go about your normal daily life. You have to progress slowly with this. Get your dog to sit and stay and then walk away from him for five seconds, then 10, 15 and so on, gradually increase the distance you move away from your dog. Reward your dog with a treat every time he stays calm.

Then move out of sight or out of the room for a few seconds, return and give him the treat if he is calm, gradually lengthen the time you are out of sight. If you're watching TV with your Cockapoo snuggled up at your side and you get up for a snack, say 'stay' and leave the room. When you come back, give him a treat or praise him quietly. It is a good idea to practise these techniques after exercise or when your dog is a little sleepy (but not exhausted), as he is likely to be more relaxed. Canine Separation Anxiety is NOT the result of disobedience or lack of training. It's a psychological condition; your dog feels anxious and insecure.

NEVER punish your Cockapoo for showing signs of separation anxiety – even if he has chewed your best shoes. This will only make him worse.

NEVER leave your dog unattended in a crate for long periods or if he is frantic to get out, it can cause physical or mental harm. If you're thinking of leaving an animal all day in a crate while you are out of the house, get a rabbit or a hamster - not a dog.

Excessive Barking

Cockapoos, especially youngsters and adolescents, will behave in ways you might not want them to, until they learn that this type of unwanted behaviour doesn't earn any rewards. Cockapoos are not normally excessive barkers, but any dog can bark a lot, until he learns not to. Some puppies start off by being noisy from the outset, while others hardly bark at all until they reach adolescence or adulthood. On our website we get emails from dog owners worried that their young dogs are not barking enough. However, we get many more from owners whose dogs are barking too much!

Some Cockapoos will bark if someone comes to the door – and then welcome them like old friends - while others remain quiet. However, they do not make good guard dogs, as they want to be friends with everyone.

There can be a number of reasons a Cockapoobarks too much. He may be lonely, bored or demanding your attention. He may be possessive and over-protective and so barks (or howls) his head off when others are near you.

Excessive, habitual barking is a problem which should be corrected early on before it gets out of hand and drives you and your neighbours nuts. The problem often develops during

adolescence or early adulthood as your dog becomes more confident. If your barking dog is an adolescent, he is probably still teething, so get him a good selection of hardy chews, and stuff a Kong Toy with a treat or peanut butter to keep him occupied and gnawing. But give him these when he is quiet, not when he is barking.

Your behaviour can also encourage excessive barking. If your dog barks non-stop for several minutes and then you give him a treat to quieten him, he associates his barking with getting a nice treat. A better way to deal with it is to say in a firm voice: **"Quiet"** after he has made a few barks. When he stops, praise him and he will get the idea that what you want him to do is stop. The trick is to nip the bad behaviour in the bud before it becomes ingrained.

If he's barking to get your attention, ignore him. If that doesn't work, leave the room and don't allow him to follow you, so you deprive him of your attention. Do this as well if his barking and attention-seeking turns to nipping. Tell him to **"Stop"** in a firm voice - not shouting - remove your hand or leg and, if necessary, leave the room.

As humans, we can use our voice in many different ways: to express happiness or anger, to scold, to shout a warning, and so on. Dogs are the same; different barks and noises give out different messages. **Listen** to your dog and try and get an understanding of his Cockapoo language. Learn to recognise the difference between an alert bark, an excited bark, a demanding bark, a nervous, high pitched bark, an aggressive bark or a plain "I'm barking 'coz I can bark" bark!

If your Cockapoo is barking at other dogs, arm yourselves with lots of treats and spend time calming your dog down. When he or she starts to bark wildly at another dog - usually this happens when your Cockapoo is on a lead – distract your dog by letting them sniff a treat in your hand. Make your dog sit down and give him or her a treat. Talk in a gentle manner and keep showing and giving your dog a treat for remaining calm and not barking. There are several videos on YouTube which show how to deal with this problem in the manner described here.

Speak and Shush!

Cockapoos are not good guard dogs, they couldn't care less if somebody breaks in and walks off with the family silver – they are more likely to approach the burglar for a pat or a treat. But if you do have a problem with excessive barking when somebody visits your home, the Speak and Shush technique is one way of getting a dog to quieten down. If your Cockapoo doesn't bark and you want him to, a slight variation of this method can also be used to get him to bark as a way of alerting you that someone is at the door.

When your dog barks at an arrival at your house, gently praise him after the first few barks. If he persists, gently tell him that that is enough. Like humans, some dogs can get carried away with the sound of their own voice, so try and discourage too much barking from the outset. The Speak and Shush technique teaches your dog or puppy to bark and be quiet on command. Get a friend to stand outside your front door and say "Speak" - or "Woof" or "Alert." This is the cue for your accomplice to knock or ring the bell – don't worry if you both feel like idiots, it will be worth the embarrassment!

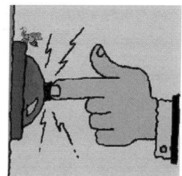

When your Cockapoo barks, praise him profusely. You can even bark yourself in encouragement. After a few good barks, say "Shush" and then dangle a tasty treat in front of his nose. He will stop barking as soon as he sniffs the treat, because it is physically impossible for a dog to sniff and woof at the same time.

Praise your dog again as he sniffs quietly and then give him the treat. Repeat this routine a few times a day and your Cockapoo will quickly learn to bark whenever the doorbell rings and you ask him to speak. Eventually your dog will bark after your request but BEFORE the doorbell rings, meaning he has learned to bark on command. Even better, he will learn to anticipate the likelihood of getting a treat following your "Shush" request and will also be quiet on command.

With Speak and Shush training, progressively increase the length of required shush time before offering a treat - at first just a couple of seconds, then three, five, 10, 20, and so on. By alternating instructions to speak and shush, the dog is praised and rewarded for barking on request and also for stopping barking on request.

To get your Cockapoo to bark on command, you need to have some treats at the ready, waiting for that rare bark. Wait until he barks - for whatever reason - then say "Speak" or whatever word you want to use, praise him and give him a treat. At this stage, he won't know why he is receiving the treat. Keep praising him every time he barks and give him a treat. After you've done this for several days, hold a treat in your hand in front of his face and say "Speak." Your Cockapoo will probably still not know what to do, but will eventually get so frustrated at not getting the treat that he will bark. At which point, praise him and give him the treat. We trained our dog to do this and now he barks his head off when anybody comes to the door or whenever we give him the command: "Speak."

Always use your 'encouraging teacher voice' when training; speak softly when instructing your dog to Shush, and reinforce the Shush with whisper-praise. The more softly you speak, the more your dog will be likely to pay attention. Cockapoos respond very well to training when it is kept fun and short.

Aggression

Some breeds are more prone to aggression than others. Fortunately, this is a problem not often seen in Cockapoos. However, given a certain set of circumstances, any dog can growl, bark or even bite. As well as snarling, lunging, barking or biting, you should also look out for other physical signs of aggression, such as: raised hackles, top lip curled back to bare teeth, ears up and tail raised.

All puppies bite; they explore the world with their noses and mouths. But it is important to train your cute little pup not to bite, as he may cause a serious injury if he continues as an adult.

Any dog can bite when under stress, and, however unlikely it may seem, there are images on the internet of people - often children - who have been bitten by Cockapoos.

Here are some different types of aggressive behaviour:

- Growling at you or other people
- Snarling or lunging at other dogs while on the lead
- Growling or biting if you or another animal goes near his food
- Growling if you pet or show attention to another animal
- Being possessive with toys
- Marking territory by urinating inside the house
- Growling and chasing other small animals
- Growling and chasing cars, joggers or strangers
- Standing in your way, blocking your path
- Pulling and growling on the lead

Cockapoos love to be the centre of attention, but they can also become possessive of you, their food or toys, which in itself can lead to bullying behaviour. Aggression may be caused by a lack of socialisation, an adolescent dog trying to see how far he can push the boundaries, nervousness, being spoiled by the owner, jealousy or even fear. This fear often comes from a bad experience the dog has suffered or from lack of proper socialisation. Another form of fear-aggression is when a dog becomes over-protective/possessive of his owner, which can lead to barking and lunging at other dogs or humans.

An owner's treatment of a dog can be a further reason. If the owner has been too harsh with the dog, such as shouting, using physical violence or reprimanding the dog too often, this in turn causes poor behaviour. Aggression breeds aggression. Dogs can also become aggressive if they are consistently left alone, cooped up, under-fed or under-exercised. A bad experience with another dog or dogs can be a further cause.

Many dogs are more combative on the lead (leash). This is because once on a lead, they cannot run away and escape - fight or flight and they know they can't run away, so they make themselves as frightening as possible. They therefore bark or growl to warn off the other dog or person. Socialising your Cockapoo when young is vital. The first four months or so of a puppy's life is the critical time for socialisation.

If your Cockapoo suddenly shows a change of behaviour and becomes aggressive, have him checked out by a vet to rule out any underlying medical reason for the crankiness, such as toothache or earache. Raging hormones can be another reason for aggressive actions. Consider having your Cockapoo spayed or neutered if he or she has not already been done. A levelling-off of hormones can lead to a more laid-back dog.

Another reason for dogs to display aggression is because they have been spoiled by their owners and have come to believe that the world revolves around them. Not spoiling your Cockapoo and teaching him or her what is acceptable behaviour in the first place is the best preventative measure. Early training, especially during puppyhood and before he or she develops unwanted habits, can save a lot of trouble in the future. Professional dog trainers employ a variety of techniques with a dog which has become aggressive. Firstly they will look at the causes and then they almost always use reward-based methods to try and cure aggressive or fearful dogs.

Counter conditioning is a positive training technique used by many professional trainers to help change a dog's aggressive behaviour towards other dogs. A typical example would be a dog which snarls, barks and lunges at other dogs while on the lead. It is the presence of other dogs which is triggering the dog to act in a fearful or anxious manner. Every time the dog sees another dog, he or she is given a tasty treat to counter the aggression. With enough steady repetition, the dog starts to associate the presence of other dogs with a tasty treat. Properly and patiently done, the final result is a dog which calmly looks to the owner for the treat whenever he or she sees another dog while on the lead.

Whenever you encounter a potentially aggressive situation, divert your Cockapoo's attention by turning his head away from the other dog and towards you, so that he cannot make eye contact with the other dog.

Aggression Towards People

Desensitisation is the most common method of treating aggression. It starts by breaking down the triggers for the behaviour one small step at a time. The aim is to get the dog to associate pleasant things with the trigger, i.e. people or a specific person whom he previously feared or regarded as a threat. This is done through using positive reinforcement, such as praise or treats. Successful desensitisation takes time, patience and knowledge. If your dog is starting to growl at people, there are a couple of techniques you can try to break him of this bad habit before it develops into full-blown biting.

One method is to arrange for some friends to come round, one at a time. When they arrive at your house, get them to scatter kibble on the floor in front of them so that your dog associates the arrival of people with tasty treats. As they move into the house, and your dog eats the kibble, praise your dog for being a good boy or girl. Manage your dog's environment. Don't over-face him.

Most Cockapoos love children, but if yours is at all anxious around them, separate them or carefully supervise their time together in the beginning. Children typically react enthusiastically to dogs and some dogs may regard this as frightening or an invasion of their space.

Some dogs, particularly spoiled companion dogs, may show aggression towards the partner of the owner. Several people have written to our website on this topic and it usually involves a partner or husband. Often the dog is jealous of the attention the owner is giving to the other person, or it could be that the dog feels threatened by him. This is not uncommon with Toy breeds.

If this does arise, the key is for the partner to gradually gain the trust of the dog. He or she should show that they are not a threat by speaking gently to the dog and giving treats for good behaviour. Avoid eye contact, as the dog may see this as a challenge. If the subject of the aggression lives in the house, then try letting this person give the dog his daily feeds. The way to a Cockapoo's heart is often through his stomach.

A crate is also a useful tool for removing an aggressive dog from the situation for short periods of time, allowing him out gradually and praising good behaviour. As with any form of aggression, the key is to take steps to deal with it immediately.

Coprophagia (Eating Faeces)

It is hard for us to understand why a dog would want to eat his or any other animal's faeces (stools, poop or poo, call it what you will), but it does happen. There is plenty of anecdotal evidence that some dogs love the stuff. Nobody fully understands why dogs do this, it may simply be an unpleasant behaviour trait or there could be an underlying reason.

It is also thought that the inhumane and useless housetraining technique of "sticking the dog's nose" in it when he has eliminated inside the house can also encourage coprophagia.

If your dog eats faeces from the cat litter tray - a problem several owners have contacted us about - the first thing to do is to place the litter tray somewhere where your dog can't get to it – but the cat can. Perhaps on a shelf or put a guard around it, small enough for the cat to get through but not your Cockapoo.

Our dog sometimes eats cow or horse manure when out in the countryside. He usually stops when we tell him to and he hasn't suffered any after effects – so far. But again, this is a very unpleasant habit as the offending material sticks to the fur around his mouth and has to be cleaned off.

Sometimes he rolls in the stuff and then has to be washed down. You may find that your Cockapoo will roll in fox poo to cover the fox's scent. It's a good idea to avoid areas you know are frequented by foxes if you can, as their faeces can transmit several diseases, including Canine Parvovirus or lungworm – neither of these should pose a serious health risk if your dog is up to date with vaccinations and worming medication.

Vets have found that canine diets with low levels of fibre and high levels of starch increase the likelihood of coprophagia. If your dog is exhibiting this behaviour, first check that the diet you are feeding is nutritionally complete. Look at the first ingredient on the dog food packet or tin – is it corn or meat? Does he look underweight? Check that you are feeding the right amount. If there is no underlying medical reason, you will have to try and modify your dog's behaviour. Remove cat litter trays, clean up after your dog and do not allow him to eat his own faeces. If it's not there, he can't eat it. Don't reprimand the dog for this behaviour. A better technique is to distract him while he is in the act and then remove the offending material.

Coprophagia is sometimes seen in pups aged between six months to a year and often disappears after this age.

In extreme cases, when a dog exhibits persistent bad behaviour that the owner is unable to correct, a canine professional may be the answer. However, this is not an inexpensive option. Far better to spend time training and socialising your dog as soon as you get him or her.

Important: This chapter provides just a general overview of canine behaviour. If your Cockapoo exhibits persistent behavioural problems, particularly if he or she is aggressive towards people or other dogs, you should consider seeking help from a reputable canine behaviourist, such as those listed the Association of Professional Dog Trainers at https://apdt.com.

9. Cockapoo Health

The Cockapoo is generally regarded as a healthy dog. Responsible breeders are playing their part in producing healthy pups from healthy breeding stock.

However, there is not a single breed or crossbreed (hybrid) without the potential for some genetic weaknesses. All dogs - whether pedigrees, crossbreeds or Heinz 57s - can develop genetic health problems, just as people can inherit diseases from their parents and grandparents. It's all to do with genes passed down through the generations.

Specific genetic diseases within purebreds are not uncommon. For example, German Shepherds are more prone to hip problems than some other breeds, and 30% of Dalmatians have problems with their hearing. If you get a German Shepherd or a Dalmatian, your dog will not automatically suffer from these issues, but he or she will statistically be more likely to have them than a breed with no history of the complaint.

The way that these problems are being reduced within the breeds is by health testing dams and sires and selective breeding by responsible breeders, i.e. NOT breeding from dogs which carry the gene or genes for specific health issues. DNA testing is key to identifying which dogs may pass on the disease.

However, mating two dogs from two different breeds does not necessarily mean that a healthier pup will emerge. For more details, read the section on **Hybrid Vigour** in **Chapter 1**.

The Cockapoo, for example, is a crossbreed, yet can be susceptible to eye problems or hip dysplasia; and Cavapoos are at medium risk of suffering from cataracts and other eye issues. Cockapoos often live to a ripe old age in the mid to high teens – but this does not mean that by choosing one you are guaranteed a healthy dog. It is, however, true to say that your chance of getting a puppy with no hereditary problems is greatly increased if you buy from a good breeder who DNA health tests her dogs.

Many people believe that a crossbreed – particularly a first generation (F1) cross - will naturally be healthier than a pedigree or purebred dog. This can be true, but is not automatically the case. A Cockapoo may be susceptible to health problems associated with the original breeds, which are Poodles, along with English or American Cocker Spaniels. However, there's also a belief that a bigger gene pool caused by mixing these two breeds may lower the chances of a dog developing certain inherited diseases.

But if a breeder interbreeds her dogs (i.e. breeds from closely related dogs, as has often happened with purebred lines in the past), then the gene pool becomes reduced again, which is one of the reasons why health testing of breeding dogs is so important. You can't see inside your Cockapoo, but you can reduce the risk of inherited diseases by buying from an approved breeder, by physically seeing the parents (or at least the mother) and asking to see all of their and the puppy's health certificates.

The Cockapoo Club of GB states: "Within the gene pool that affects Cockapoo breeding, there are some known genetic diseases that can cause serious illness later in life that will not be apparent as puppies. The Cockapoo Club of GB is promoting health testing awareness and following procedures to minimise the occurrence of the diseases now and in future Cockapoos in this country."

The American Cockapoo Club's Code of Ethics for registered breeders, Point 7, states: "Use for breeding only those dogs which they believe to be healthy and free from serious congenital and hereditary defects."

Cockapoo Insurance

Another point to consider is insurance for your new puppy or adult dog. The best time to get pet insurance is BEFORE you bring your dog home and before any health issues develop. Don't wait until you need to seek veterinary help – bite the bullet and take out annual insurance. If you can afford it, take out life cover. This may be more expensive, but will cover your dog throughout his or her lifetime - including for recurring or chronic ailments, such as ear or joint problems.

Insuring a healthy puppy or adult dog is the only sure fire way to ensure vets' bills are covered before anything unforeseen happens - and you'd be a rare owner if you didn't use your policy at least once during your dog's lifetime. Fortunately, Cockapoos are not one of the most expensive dogs to insure - even so, it's not cheap. Typical Cockapoo insurance may cost anything from £20 to £50 a month in the UK, depending on the level of cover ($30 to $75 in the US) - and if you make a claim, the monthly premium will increase. On the plus side, you'll have peace of mind and you'll know how much you have to shell out every month.

The other side of the coin is that with advances in veterinary science, there is so much more vets can do to help an ailing dog - but at a cost. Surgical procedures often rack up bills of thousands of pounds or dollars.

In the UK, Bought By Many has teamed up with insurers to launch a pet insurance policy specifically for Cockapoos which offers a 20% discount on their normal rates. Visit https://boughtbymany.com/offers/Cockapoo-insurance for details. Owners first have to join the Cockapoo Group, which currently has more than 800 members.

Bought By Many says: "Although Cockapoos sometimes develop problems with their knees, eyes, and ears, as a crossbreed they typically experience fewer health issues than pure breed dogs. That means they also spend relatively little time at the vet – and that makes them attractive to pet insurance companies."

Another point to consider is that desirable purebreds and crossbreeds like the Cockapoo are at increasing risk of theft by criminals, including organised gangs. With the purchase price of puppies rising, dognapping more than quadrupled in the UK between 2010 and 2015. Some 49% of dogs are snatched from owners' gardens and 13% from people's homes. If you take out a policy, check that theft is included. Although nothing can ever replace your beloved Cockapoo, a good insurance policy will ensure that you are not out of pocket.

In the US, Consumers' Advocate have named the top 10 pet insurance companies, taking into account reimbursement policies, coverage and customers' reviews. Here is their league table: 1.

Healthy Paws, 2. PetPlan, 3. Trupanion, 4. Embrace, 5. Pets Best, 6. PetFirst, 7. VPI Pet Insurance, 8. Pet Partners, 9. ASPCA Pet Health Insurance, 10. Pet Premium.

The information in this chapter is not written to frighten new owners, but to help you to recognise symptoms of the main conditions affecting Cockapoos and enable you to take prompt action should the need arise. There are also a number of measures you can take to prevent or reduce the chances of certain physical and behavioural problems developing, including keeping your dog's weight in check and giving him regular daily exercise.

Three Golden Tips

There are three golden tips for anybody thinking about owning a Cockapoo which will in all likelihood save you a lot of money and heartache.

Tip Number 1: **Buy a well-bred puppy**

Scientists have come to realise the important role that genetics play in determining a person's long-term health – and the same is true of dogs. This means ensuring your puppy comes from a reputable breeder who selects the parents based on a number of factors, mainly health and temperament. A good Cockapoo breeder selects their stock based on:

- ➢ **General health and DNA testing of the parents**
- ➢ **temperament**
- ➢ **conformation (physical structure)**
- ➢ **coat**

Although well-bred Cockapoo puppies are expensive, many responsible breeders do not make a lot of money from their sale, often incurring high bills for health checks, veterinary fees, specialised food, etc. The main concern of a good breeder is to produce healthy puppies with good temperaments.

It's better to spend time beforehand choosing a puppy which has been properly bred than to spend a great deal of time and money later as your wonderful pet bought from an online advert or pet shop develops health problems due to poor breeding, not to mention the heartache that causes.

So spend some time to find a reputable breeder and read **Chapter 2. Choosing a Puppy** for information on finding a good breeder and knowing the right questions to ask.

- ➢ Don't buy a puppy from a pet shop. No reputable breeder allows their pups to end up in pet shops

- ➢ Don't buy a puppy from a small ad on a general website

- ➢ Don't buy a pup or adult Cockapoo unseen with a credit card – you are storing up trouble and expense for yourself

Tip Number 2: Get pet insurance as soon as you get your dog

Don't wait until he or she has a health issue and needs to see a vet. Most insurers will exclude all pre-existing conditions on their policies. When choosing insurance check the small print to make sure that any condition which might occur is covered, and that if the problem is a chronic (long term) or recurring one, then it will continue to be covered year after year. When you are working out costs for getting a Cockapoo, factor in the annual or monthly cost of good pet insurance and trips to a vet for check-ups, annual vaccinations, etc.

Tip Number 3: Find a good vet

Ask around your pet-owning friends, rather than just going to the first one you find. A vet that knows your dog from his or her vaccinations as a puppy and then right through their life is more likely to understand your dog and diagnose quickly and correctly when something is wrong. If you visit a big veterinary practice, ask for the vet by name when you make an appointment.

We all want our dogs to be healthy - so how can you tell if yours is? Well, here are some positive things to look for in a healthy Cockapoo.

Top 11 Signs of a Healthy Cockapoo

1. **Ears** – If you are choosing a puppy, gently clap your hands behind the pup (not so loud as to frighten him) to see if he reacts. If not, this may be a sign of deafness. As with Spaniels, ears can be a problem with some Cockapoos. The folded ear flaps can hide dirt and dust and should be inspected regularly for infection or ear mites as part of your normal grooming process. An unpleasant smell, redness or inflammation are all signs of infection. Some wax inside the ear – usually brown or yellowy - is normal; lots of wax or crusty wax is not. Tell-tale signs of an ear infection are scratching the ears or shaking the head a lot, usually accompanied by an unpleasant odour around the ears.

2. **Coat and skin** – These are easy-to-monitor indicators of a healthy dog. A Cockapoo's coat, regardless of length, should be glossy and soft to the touch. Dandruff, bald spots, a dull lifeless coat, a discoloured or oily coat, or one which loses excessive hair, can all be signs that something is amiss. Skin should be smooth without redness. (Normal Cockapoo skin pigment can vary from pale pink to brown, black or mottled, depending on coat colour). If your dog is scratching, licking or biting himself a lot, he may have a condition which needs addressing before he makes it worse. Open sores, scales, scabs, red patches or growths can be a sign of a problem. Signs of fleas, ticks and other external parasites should be treated immediately. Check there are no small black specks, which may be fleas, on the coat or bedding.

3. **Mouth** – Gums should be a healthy pink or with black pigmentation. A change in colour can be an indicator of a health issue. Paleness or whiteness can be a sign of anaemia or lack of oxygen due to heart or breathing problems. Blue gums or tongue area sign that your Cockapoo is not breathing properly. Red, inflamed gums can be a sign of gingivitis or other tooth disease. Again, your dog's breath should smell OK. Young dogs will have sparkling white teeth, whereas older dogs will have darker teeth, but they should not have any hard white, yellow, green or brown bits.

4. **Weight** – Dogs may have weight problems due to factors such as diet, overfeeding, lack of exercise, allergies, diabetes, thyroid or other problems. A general rule of thumb is that your dog's stomach should be above his rib cage when standing, and you should be able to feel his

ribs beneath his coat without too much effort. If his stomach hangs below, he is overweight or may have a pot belly, which can also be a symptom of other conditions.

5. **Nose** – A dog's nose is an indicator of health symptoms. It should normally be moist and cold to the touch as well as free from clear, watery secretions. Any yellow, green or foul smelling discharge is not normal - in younger dogs this can be a sign of canine distemper. A Cockapoo's nose can be black, pink or a similar colour to the coat.

6. **Eyes** – A healthy Cockapoo's eyes are dark and shiny with no yellowish tint. The area around the eyeball (the conjunctiva) should be a healthy pink; paleness could be a sign of underlying problems. A red swelling in the corner of one or both eyes could by a sign of cherry eye. Sometimes the dog's third eyelid (the nictating membrane) is visible at the eye's inside corner - this is normal. There should be no thick, green or yellow discharge from the eyes. A cloudy eye could be a sign of cataracts.

7. **Temperature** – The normal temperature of a dog is 101°F to 102.5°F. (A human's is 98.6°F). Excited or exercising dogs may run a slightly higher temperature. Anything above 103°F or below 100°F should be checked out. The exceptions are female dogs about to give birth that will often have a temperature of 99°F. If you take your dog's temperature, make sure he or she is relaxed and **always** use a purpose-made canine thermometer.

8. **Attitude** – A generally positive attitude and personality is the sign of good health. Cockapoos are engaged, enthusiastic dogs, so symptoms of illness may include one or all of the following: not eating food, a general lack of interest in his or her surroundings, lethargy and sleeping a lot (more than normal). The important thing is to look out for any behaviour which is out of the ordinary for your individual dog.

9. **Energy** – The Cockapoo is generally regarded as a dog with medium to high energy levels. Your dog should have good energy levels with fluid and pain-free movements. Lethargy or lack of energy – if it is not the dog's normal character – could be a sign of an underlying problem.

10. **Stools** – Poo, poop, business, faeces – call it what you will - it's the stuff that comes out of the less appealing end of your Cockapoo on a daily basis! It should be firm and brown, not runny, with no signs of worms or parasites. Watery stools or a dog not eliminating regularly are both signs of an upset stomach or other ailments. If it continues for a day or two, consult your vet. If puppies have diarrhoea they need checking out much quicker as they can soon dehydrate.

11. Smell – Cockapoos are known for not having an unpleasant 'doggie odour' your dog should smell good! If there is a musty, 'off' or generally unpleasant smell coming from his body, it could be a sign of yeast infection. There can be a number of reasons for this, often his ears not being cleaned and groomed properly, or occasionally an allergy to a certain type of food. You need to get to the root of the problem.

So now you know some of the signs of a healthy dog – what are the signs of an unhealthy one? There are many different symptoms that can indicate that your beloved canine companion isn't feeling great. If you don't yet know your dog, his habits, temperament and behaviour patterns, then we recommend you spend some time to get acquainted with him.

What are his normal character and temperament? Lively or calm, playful or serious, a joker or an introvert, bold or nervous, happy to be left alone or loves to be with people, a keen appetite or a fussy eater? How often does he empty his bowels, does he ever vomit? (Dogs will often eat grass to make themselves sick, this is perfectly normal and a canine's natural way of cleansing the digestive system).

You may think your Cockapoo can't talk, **but he can!** If you really know your dog, his character and habits, then he CAN tell you when he's not well. He does this by changing his patterns. Some symptoms are physical, some emotional and others are behavioural.

It's important for you to be able to recognise these changes as soon as possible. Early treatment can be the key to keeping a simple problem from snowballing into a serious illness. If you think your Cockapoo is unwell, it is useful to keep an accurate and detailed account of his symptoms to give to the vet, perhaps even take a video of him on your mobile phone. This will help the vet to correctly diagnose and effectively treat your dog.

Four Vital Signs of Illness

1. **Temperature -** A new-born puppy will have a temperature of 94-97ºF. This will reach the normal adult body temperature of 101ºF at about four weeks old. Anything between 100ºF and 103ºF is regarded as normal. A dog's temperature is normally taken via the rectum. If you do this, be very careful. It's easier if you get someone to hold your dog while you do this.

   Digital thermometers are a good choice, but **only use one specifically made for rectal use,** as normal glass thermometers can easily break off in the rectum. Ear thermometers are now available, making the task much easier, although they can be expensive and don't suit all dogs' ears. (Walmart has started stocking them).

   Remember that exercise or excitement can cause the temperature to rise by 2ºF to 3ºF when your dog is actually in good health, so better to wait until he is relaxed and calm before taking his temperature. If it is above or below the norms, give your vet a call.

2. **Respiratory Rate -** Another symptom of canine illness is a change in breathing patterns. This varies a lot depending on the size and weight of the dog. An adult dog will have a respiratory rate of 15-25 breaths per minute when resting. You can easily check this by counting your dog's breaths for a minute with a stopwatch handy. Don't do this if he is panting; it doesn't count.

Ear Thermometer

3. **Heart Rate -** You can feel your Cockapoo's heartbeat by placing your hand on his lower ribcage – just behind the elbow. Don't be alarmed if the heartbeat seems irregular compared to a human. It IS irregular in some dogs. Your Cockapoo will probably love the attention, so it should be quite easy to check his heartbeat. Just lay him on his side and bend his left front leg at the elbow, bring the elbow in to his chest and place your fingers or a stethoscope on this area and count the beats.

> ➤ **Small dogs have a normal rate of 90 to 140 beats per minute**
> ➤ **Medium-sized dogs have a normal rate of 80 to 120 beats per minute**
> ➤ **Big dogs have a normal rate of 70 to 120 beats per minute**
> ➤ **A young puppy has a heartbeat of around 220 beats per minute**
> ➤ **An older dog has a slower heartbeat**

4. Behaviour Changes

Classic symptoms of illness are any inexplicable behaviour changes. If there has NOT been a change in the household atmosphere, such as another new pet, a new baby, moving home, the absence of a family member or the loss of another dog, then the following symptoms may well be a sign that all is not well:

> ➤ Depression
> ➤ Anxiety and/or trembling
> ➤ Falling or stumbling
> ➤ Loss of appetite
> ➤ Walking in circles
> ➤ Being more vocal - grunting, whining and whimpering
> ➤ Aggression - Cockapoos are normally extremely friendly, so this can be a sign of ill health
> ➤ Tiredness - sleeping more than normal and/or not wanting to exercise
> ➤ Abnormal posture

Your Cockapoo may normally show some of these signs, but if any of them appear for the first time or worse than usual, you need to keep him under close watch for a few hours or even days. Quite often he will return to normal of his own accord. Like humans, dogs have off-days too.

If he is showing any of the above symptoms, then don't over-exercise him, and avoid stressful situations and hot or cold places. Make sure he has access to clean water. There are many other signals of ill health, but these are four of the most important. Keep a record for your vet; if your dog does need professional medical attention, most vets will want to know:

WHEN the symptoms first appeared in your dog

WHETHER they are getting better or worse, and

HOW FREQUENT the symptoms are. Are they intermittent, continuous or increasing?

We have highlighted some of the indicators of good and poor health to help you monitor your dog's wellbeing. Getting to know his or her character, habits and temperament will go a long way towards spotting the early signs of ill health. The next section looks in detail at some of the most common ailments affecting Cockapoos, with complicated medical terminology explained in simple terms. We also cover the symptoms and treatments of various conditions.

The Cockapoo Dog Club of GB advises testing for the following conditions: prcd-PRA (Progressive Retinol Atrophy), Primary Glaucoma, Hip Dysplasia, PFK (Phosphofructokinase), Retinal Dysplasia, FN (Familial Nephropathy) and von Willebrands Disease Type1. The last two do NOT affect Cockapoos bred from American Cocker Spaniels.

What the Breeders Say

The Cockapoo Handbook asked breeders about Cockapoo health and this is what some of them said, starting in North America.

Jeanne Davis, of Wind Horse Offering, Maryland, USA, believes that in general the Cockapoo is a healthy dog, saying: "I have not had long-term experience with any on-going health issues, although I have heard of ear problems. I have not had any soundness issues."

Jessica Sampson, of Legacy Cockapoos, Ontario, Canada, said: "For American Cockapoos, PRA-prcd (Progressive Retinal Atrophy- Progressive Rod Cone Degeneration) and Luxating Patella are the big ones. But we also test their hips/eyes and DNA test for glycogen storage disease VII/ PFK Deficiency, Degenerative Myelopathy, Exercise-Induced Collapse, and von Willebrand Disease. The current biggest threat to the Cockapoo is uneducated breeders and lack of health/DNA screenings of breeding stock."

Jackie Stafford, of Dj's Cockapoos, Rusk, Texas, added: "The biggest problem I have seen in Cockapoos is luxated patellas. Usually the smaller the dog, the more prevalent it can be."

Rebecca Goins, of MoonShine Cockapoos, agrees: "The main health issues with Cockapoos would be Patella Luxation - Poodles are susceptible to this. Progressive Retinal Atrophy (PRA) is another issue as both parent breeds are susceptible, although the rate of incidence is currently lower in Cockapoos than it is for either Poodles or Cockers.

"Ear infections also occur, with both Poodles and Cockers being susceptible to ear infections. The Cocker's long ears prevent air flow, as does the hair growth in the ear canal of the Poodle. If this is not kept trimmed on the underside of the ear and the hair plucked from the inside of the ear canal, warm moist conditions can result which can promote fungal and bacterial growth."

UK breeder Pat Pollington, of Polycinders Cockapoos, Devon, outlines some of the extensive health testing that responsible breeders undertake: "The main problem with crossbreeds is that you are putting two different breeds together and both have their own health problems. The most important thing when buying any puppy is that both parents are fully health tested. The good thing with F1 crossbreeds is that because you have two different breeds, there is no interbreeding."

She continued: "The main health issue with Cockapoos is prcd–PRA. This is a disease in the eye which will make your dog go blind at a very young age. You need to buy from health tested parents. Always make sure both parents are tested and that one parent is clear.

The English Cocker Spaniel also needs to be FN (Familial Nephropathy) tested. This is a kidney disorder which will kill the dog around the age of two. Both of these diseases are well documented in Cockapoos, and they are both very cruel. Poodles should also be BVA (British Veterinary Association) eye tested. This is an annual test necessary because Poodles are susceptible to Glaucoma. Miniature Poodles should also be hip scored.

"There are some other tests that you can have done, but they are tests for any breed and are highly uncommon. As long as one parent is prcd-PRA clear, the Cocker is FN clear and the Poodles are BVA clear and hip scored, then the breeder has done everything to make sure the puppy has no health issues from the start." Pictured is Pat's healthy and beautiful F1 bitch Cherry.

Karol Watson Todd, of KaroColin Cockapoos, Sleaford, Lincolnshire, UK, said: "The biggest threat to health is PRA, as both parent breeds have this as a possibility. I think some of the health testing is irrelevant as neither parent breed greatly show the issues, e.g. hip testing. However luxating patella is an issue and should be tested for, but is not a requirement. As my vet stated: we are testing for things most of the dogs should pass, so not testing for the real issues. As you get into F2s and further, then health testing should be more stringent."

PRA (Progressive Retinal Atrophy)

PRA is the name for several progressive diseases which lead to blindness. First recognised at the beginning of the 20th century in Gordon Setters, this inherited condition has been documented in over 100 breeds and some mixed breeds.

Miniature and Toy Poodles, English Cocker Spaniels, American Cocker Spaniels, Labrador Retrievers, Cockapoos, Labradoodles and Goldendoodles are all recognised as being among the breeds and crossbreeds which can be affected by the disease. Puppies are born with normal eyesight and this generally begins to deteriorate from around the age of three to five in Cockapoos.

The specific genetic disorder which can affect Cockapoos is called prcd-PRA - progressive rod-cone degeneration PRA. (It is sometimes also called GPRA - General Progressive Retinal Atrophy). It causes cells in the retina at the back of the eye to degenerate and die, even though the cells seem to develop normally early in life. The rod cells operate in low light levels and are the first to lose normal function, and so the first sign is night blindness.

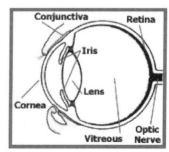

Then the cone cells gradually lose their normal function in full light situations. Most affected dogs will eventually go blind. (Conditions that might look like prcd-PRA could be another disease and might not be inherited. Not all retinal disease is PRA and not all PRA is the prcd form of PRA). Annual eye exams by a veterinary ophthalmologist will build a history of eye health that will help to diagnose disease.

Prcd-PRA is inherited as a recessive trait. This means that the faulty gene must be inherited **from both parents** in order to cause disease in an offspring. In other words, for a puppy to get the disease, both its father and mother were either a carrier or sufferer. A dog that inherits only one copy of the abnormal gene (from its mother OR father) will have no signs of the disease, but will be a carrier and may pass the gene on to any future offspring. It's been proven that all breeds tested for prcd-PRA have the same mutated gene, even though the disease may develop at different ages or severities from one breed to another. Testing for prcd-PRA is mandatory for all Cockapoos registered with The Cockapoo Club of GB (Great Britain). One parent must show Normal/Clear.

Sadly, there is no cure, but prcd-PRA can be avoided in future generations by DNA testing of breeding dogs. If your Cockapoo is affected, it may be helpful to read other owners' experiences of living with blind dogs at www.eyevet.org and www.blinddogs.com.

Eye Testing

There are various ways of testing for hereditary eye conditions. In North America there is the OptiGen prcd-*PRA* Test and the Canine Eye Registration Foundation (CERF). Breeders using the Optigen test get one of three results:

CLEAR: these dogs have two normal copies of DNA. Clear dogs will not develop PRA as a result of the mutation

CARRIER: these dogs have one copy of the mutation and one normal copy of DNA. These dogs will not develop PRA themselves as a result of the mutation, but they will pass the mutation on to half of their offspring.

GENETICALLY AFFECTED: these dogs have two copies of the mutation and will almost certainly develop PRA during their lifetime.

In the UK there is the British Veterinary Association (BVA) Eye Test, which is carried out each year due to the fact some diseases have a late onset. If you are buying a puppy, it is highly advisable to check if the parents have been tested and given the all-clear. Always ensure the breeder lets you see the original certificate (which is white in the UK) and not a photocopy. The UK tests also give one of three results: CLEAR, CARRIER and AFFECTED. In the US, the OFA (Orthopedic Foundation for Animals) statistics show that 9.4% of all Poodles tested were carriers for PRA, as were 1.9% of Cocker Spaniels.

Identifying dogs which carry the diseased genes and NOT breeding from them is the key to eradicating the problem.

Hip Dysplasia

Canine Hip Dysplasia (CHD) is the most common cause of hind leg lameness in dogs; dysplasia means 'abnormal development'. It is also the most common heritable orthopaedic problem seen in dogs, affecting virtually all breeds, but is more common in large breeds. The condition develops into degenerative osteoarthritis of the hip joints. CHD is known in Cocker Spaniels - both English and American – as well as all three sizes of Poodle. Some 11.7% of Poodles and 6.4% of Cocker Spaniels tested in the USA by the OFA had abnormal hips.

The hip is a ball and socket joint. Hip dysplasia is caused when the head of the femur (thigh bone) fits loosely into a shallow and poorly-developed socket in the pelvis. Most dogs with dysplasia are born with normal hips, but due to their genetic make-up (and possibly other factors such as diet) the soft tissues that surround the joint develop abnormally.

The joint carrying the weight of the dog becomes loose and unstable, muscle growth lags behind normal development and is often followed by degenerative joint disease or osteoarthritis, which is the body's attempt to stabilise the loose hip joint. Early diagnosis gives your vet the best chance to tackle the problem as soon as possible, minimising the chance of arthritis developing. Symptoms range from mild discomfort to extreme pain. A puppy with canine hip dysplasia usually starts to show signs between five and 13 months old.

The right hand side of our picture shows a shallow hip socket and a deformed femur head, causing hip dysplasia. The healthy joint is on the left.

Symptoms

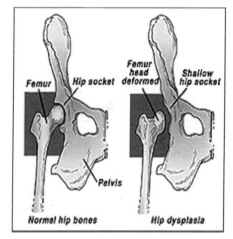

> ➢ Lameness in hind legs, particularly after exercise
> ➢ Difficulty or stiffness when getting up or climbing uphill
> ➢ A 'bunny hop' gait
> ➢ Dragging the rear end when getting up
> ➢ Waddling rear leg gait
> ➢ A painful reaction to stretching the hind legs, resulting in a short stride
> ➢ A side-to-side sway of the croup (area above the tail) with a tendency to tilt the hips down if you push down on the croup
> ➢ A reluctance to jump, exercise or climb stairs

Causes and Triggers - Canine hip dysplasia is usually inherited, but there are also factors which can trigger or worsen the condition, including:

1. Overfeeding, especially on a diet high in protein and calories
2. Excess calcium, also usually due to overfeeding
3. Extended periods without exercise – or too much vigorous exercise - especially when your dog's bones are growing
4. Obesity

Advances in nutritional research have shown that diet plays an important role in the development of hip dysplasia. Feeding a high-calorie diet to growing dogs can trigger a predisposition to hip dysplasia, as the rapid weight gain places increased stress on the hips. During their first year of life, Cockapoo puppies should be fed a diet which contains the correct amount of calories, minerals and protein, thereby reducing the risk of hip dysplasia. Ask your breeder or vet for advice on the best diet.

Exercise may be another risk factor. Dogs that have a predisposition to the disease may have an increased chance of getting it if they are over-exercised at a young age. On the other hand, dogs with large leg muscle mass are **less** likely to get dysplasia than dogs with small muscle mass. The key here is moderate, low impact exercise for fast-growing young dogs. Activities which strengthen the gluteus muscles, such as running and swimming, are probably a good idea. However, high impact activities that apply a lot of force to the joint, such and jumping and catching Frisbees, are not recommended with young Cockapoos.

Treatment - As with most conditions, early detection leads to a better outcome. Your vet will take X-rays to make a diagnosis. Treatment is geared towards preventing the hip joint getting worse and decreasing pain. Various medical and surgical treatments are now available to ease the dog's discomfort and restore some mobility. Treatment depends upon several factors, such as the dog's age, how bad the problem is and, sadly, how much money you can afford to spend on treatment.

Management of the condition usually consists of restricting exercise, keeping body weight down and then managing pain with analgesics and anti-inflammatory drugs. As with humans, cortisone injections may sometimes be used to reduce inflammation and swelling. Cortisone can be injected directly into the affected hip to provide almost immediate relief for a tender, swollen joint. In severe cases, surgery may be an option, especially with older dogs.

Hip Testing

Both the dam and sire of your puppy should have been 'hip scored' - or tested - for hip dysplasia and the results available for you to see. Thirty years ago the British Veterinary Association (BVA) and Kennel Club set up a hip screening programme for dogs in the UK, which tests them using radiology and gives them a rating or 'hip score'. In the USA the OFA (Orthopedic Foundation for Animals) administers the tests.

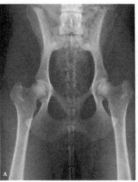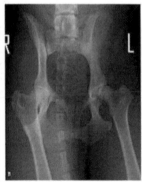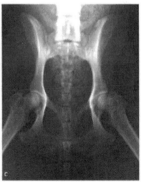

In these X rays, Figure A (left) is the healthy hip, Figure B shows lateral tilting, C shows outward rotation

The hip score is the total number of points given for nine points examined by X-ray, the lower the score the better. The best score for each hip is 0 and the worst is 53 and, as a dog has two hips, the total score will be between 0 and 106. The suggested mean score for Cockapoos is 12-13. Responsible breeders should only breed from stock which has a hip score below 13. The Kennel Club is responsible for publishing hip dysplasia results for all pedigree dogs in the Kennel Club Breed Records. However, as the Cockapoo is a crossbreed, the KC does not hold the information.

In the UK, the current cost of a hip score is only £57; the cost of a joint hip and elbow test is £105. The tests are much cheaper in the US: hip testing costs $35 for an individual pup or $90 for the whole litter, and $40 for a joint hip and elbow test. With the price of a Cockapoo puppy running to many hundreds of pounds (or dollars), all breeders can afford to have their potential breeding stock tested. Ethically, they should have all stock tested, as non-breeding from dogs carrying the hip dysplasia genes is the way to reduce this painful disease.

When buying a Cockapoo pup, ask to see the original hip score certificate, which is green in the UK. If the breeder does not own the stud dog, a photocopy of his results should also be available. The same applies with elbow tests outlined below, when results are on a gold-coloured form. Veterinary MRI and radiology specialist Ruth Dennis, of the Animal Health Trust, states: *"For dogs intended for breeding, it is essential that the hips are assessed before mating to ensure that they are free of dysplastic changes or only minimally affected."*

Luxating Patella

Luxating patella, also called 'floating kneecap' or 'slipped stifle' is a painful condition similar to a dislocated knee cap. It is often congenital (present from birth) and typically affects small and miniature breeds. Cockapoos bred from Miniature or Toy Poodles may be susceptible to luxating patella although, as yet, testing is not routinely carried out on breeding stock.

Symptoms - A typical sign would be if your dog is running across the park when he suddenly pulls up short and yelps with pain. He might limp on three legs and then after a period of about 10 minutes, drop the affected leg and start to walk normally again. If the condition is severe, he may hold up the affected leg for a few days. Dogs that have a luxating patella on both hind legs may change their gait completely, dropping their hindquarters and holding the rear legs further out from the body as they walk. In extreme cases they might not even use their rear legs, but walk like a circus act by balancing on their front legs so their hindquarters don't touch the ground.

Genetics, injury and malformation during development can all cause this problem. Because the most common cause is genetics, a dog with luxating patella should never be used for breeding. If you are buying a puppy, ask if there is any history in either parent. Typically, most sufferers are middle-aged dogs with a history of intermittent lameness in the affected rear leg or legs, although the condition may appear as early as four to six months old.

A groove in the end of the femur (thigh bone) allows the knee cap to glide up and down when the knee joint is bent, while keeping it in place at the same time. If this groove is too shallow, the knee cap may luxate – or dislocate. It can only return to its natural position when the quadricep muscle relaxes and increases in length, which is why a dog may have to hold his leg up for some time after the dislocation. Sometimes the problem can be caused by obesity, the excess weight putting too much strain on the joint – another good reason to keep your Cockapoo's weight in

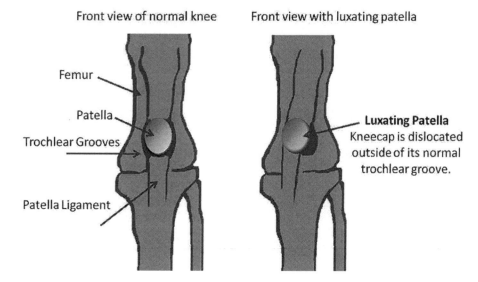

Front view of normal knee   Front view with luxating patella

Femur

Patella

Trochlear Grooves

Patella Ligament

Luxating Patella
Kneecap is dislocated outside of its normal trochlear groove.

check.

Treatment - There are four grades of patellar luxation, ranging from Grade I, which causes a temporary lameness in the joint, to Grade IV, in which the patella cannot be realigned manually. This gives the dog a bow-legged appearance. If left untreated, the groove will become even shallower and the dog will become progressively lamer, with arthritis prematurely affecting the joint. This will cause a permanently swollen knee and reduce your dog's mobility. It is therefore important to get your Cockapoo in for a veterinary check-up ASAP if you suspect he may have a luxating patella.

In severe cases, surgery is an option, although this should not be undertaken lightly. The groove at the base of the femur may be surgically deepened to better hold the knee cap in place. This operation is known as a **trochlear modification**. The good news is that dogs generally respond well, whatever the type of surgery, and are usually completely recovered within one to two months.

Primary Glaucoma

Glaucoma is a condition which puts pressure on the eye, and if the condition becomes chronic or continues without treatment, it will eventually cause permanent damage to the optic nerve, resulting in blindness.

A normal eye contains a fluid called aqueous humour to maintain its shape, and the body is constantly adding and removing fluid from inside of the eye to maintain the pressure inside the eye at the proper level. Glaucoma occurs when the pressure inside the eyeball becomes higher than normal. Just as high blood pressure can damage the heart, excessive pressure inside the eye can damage the eye's internal structures. Unless glaucoma is treated quickly, temporary loss of vision or even total blindness can result.

The cornea and lens inside the eye are living tissues, but they have no blood vessels to supply the oxygen and nutrition they need; these are delivered through the aqueous humour. In glaucoma, the increased pressure is most frequently caused by this fluid not being able to properly drain away from the eye. Fluid is constantly being produced and if an equal amount does not leave the globe, then the pressure starts to rise, similar to a water balloon. As more water is added the balloon stretches more and more. The balloon will eventually burst, but the eye is stronger so this does not happen. Instead the eye's internal structures are damaged irreparably.

Secondary glaucoma means that it is caused by another problem, such as a wound to the eye. Primary glaucoma is normally inherited and this is the type of glaucoma which Cockapoos should be tested for. All types of Cocker Spaniel are listed as being susceptible as well as Poodles.

Symptoms – Even though Even though a puppy may carry the gene for this disorder, the disease itself does not usually develop until a Cockapoo is at least two or three years old. The dog has to first reach maturity, then live a little longer before the first signs appear. With primary glaucoma, both eyes are rarely affected equally or at the same time, it usually starts in one eye several months or even years before it affects the second one. Glaucoma is a serious disease and it's important for an owner to be able to immediately recognise initial symptoms. If treatment is not started within a few days - or even hours in some cases - of the pressure increasing, the dog will probably lose sight in that eye. Here are the early signs:

- ➢ Pain
- ➢ A dilated pupil or one pupil looks bigger than the other
- ➢ Rapid blinking
- ➢ Cloudiness in the cornea at the front of the eye
- ➢ The whites of an eye look bloodshot
- ➢ One eye looks larger or sticks out further than the other one
- ➢ Loss of appetite, which may be due to headaches
- ➢ Change in attitude, less willing to play, etc.

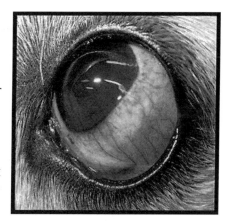

Most dogs will not display all of these signs at first, perhaps just one or two. A dog rubbing his eye with his paw, against the furniture or carpet or your leg is a common - and often unnoticed- early sign. Some dogs will also seem to flutter the eyelids or squint with one eye.

The pupil of the affected eye will usually dilate (get bigger) in the early stages of glaucoma. It may still react to all bright light, but it will do so very slowly. Remember that glaucoma, even primary glaucoma, is usually going to initially affect just one of the eyes. If the pupil in one eye is larger than in the other, something is definitely wrong and it could be glaucoma.

If you suspect your dog has glaucoma, get him to the vet as soon as possible, i.e. **immediately,** not the day after, this is a medical emergency. The vet will carry out a manual examination and test your dog's eye pressure using a tonometer on the surface of the eye. There is still a fair chance that the dog may lose sight in this eye, but a much better chance of saving the second eye with the knowledge and preventative measures learned from early intervention.

Treatment will revolve around reducing the pressure within the affected eye, draining the aqueous humour and providing pain relief, as this can be a painful condition for your dog. There are also surgical options for the long-term control of glaucoma. As yet it cannot be cured.

Familial Nephropathy (FN)

Familial nephropathy is an inherited disease which leads to early kidney failure and death. Around 11% of English Cocker Spaniels – both show and working - are carriers of the genetic mutation responsible, but American Cockers are not affected.

There is a 99% reliable FN DNA test to determine affected dogs, and these should not be used for breeding. Without testing, an unsuspecting breeder can mate a male carrier and a female carrier without knowing it and produce a litter containing affected puppies.

The test is mandatory for breeders registered with the Cockapoo Club of GB. Results show if the dog is Clear, Carrier or Affected, and if one parent has a Clear result, the puppy will not inherit the disease, as the gene is recessive. If you are buying a Cockapoo puppy where English Cockers are in the bloodline, ask to see the parents' certificates for FN.

Sadly, the disease usually affects puppies and young dogs between the age of six months and two years. Symptoms are:

- ➢ Excessive thirst
- ➢ Excessive urine
- ➢ Weight loss
- ➢ A slowdown in growth
- ➢ Reduced appetite
- ➢ Vomiting and diarrhoea

All these are signs of the kidney ceasing to function, leading to the death of the dog.

PFK Deficiency

PFK (Phosphofructokinase) Deficiency is a genetic metabolic disorder affecting American Cocker Spaniels and their offspring, but not English Cocker Spaniels. It prevents the glucose metabolising into energy. Phosphofructokinase is the name of the enzyme responsible for this metabolic action.

The technical description of PK is 'an autosomal recessive genetic disease.' This means that dogs which are carriers show no signs of PFK deficiency, but can pass the gene on to their puppies, thereby spreading the disease. Some 10% of American Cockers are thought to be affected, but **both** parents have to be Carriers or Affected for the puppy to inherit PFK deficiency.

Symptoms vary depending on how serious the condition is, but typical signs are:

- ➢ An intolerance to exercise
- ➢ Lethargy or general weakness
- ➢ Muscle wasting and cramping
- ➢ Blood in the dog's urine (haematuria)
- ➢ Fever
- ➢ Depression
- ➢ Pale gums

Affected dogs have persistent mild anaemia (low levels of red blood cells), but can usually compensate for this. They also have intermittent bouts of red blood cell breakdown (haemolysis), when they become lethargic and weak and may even bleed. This usually happens after intense exercise, excessive barking or panting. The dog's gums are pale or jaundiced and he or she usually has a high fever. You may notice your dog's urine is brown, this is due to blood breakdown products in the urine and at these times the dog needs veterinary attention.

Your vet will examine the dog and take blood tests before diagnosing PFK Deficiency. There is no specific treatment, but the condition can be managed with the help of your vet. You have to play your part by keeping on the lookout for symptoms and avoiding certain situations, such as increased stress for your dog, strenuous exercise, excitement that causes lots of barking and hot conditions.

Retinal Dysplasia

This is another disease which affects American Cocker Spaniels but not English Cockers. Retinal dysplasia is a disorder in which the cells and layer of retinal tissue at the back of the eye do not develop properly. One or both eyes may be affected. It can be detected by a vet using an ophthalmoscope when the puppy is six weeks old or even younger. The retina looks like layers of folded tissue rather than one flat layer.

There are different types of the condition; American Cockers can have Focal and Multifocal Retinal Dysplasia, which appear as streaks and dots in the central retina. Some dogs have no symptoms, while more severely affected puppies may have symptoms such as a reluctance to walk into dark areas, bumping into things and obvious sight problems. There is no treatment for the condition.

von Willebrand's Disease

Von Willebrand's Disease is a common inherited bleeding disorder similar to haemophilia in humans. In von Willebrand's Disease (vWD), the dog lacks a substance which helps to form blood clots.

Technically speaking this substance (called 'von Willebrand's factor') forms clots and stabilises something called Factor VIII in the normal clotting process. Dogs with von Willebrand's Disease bleed excessively as their blood does not clot properly. Some breeds have a higher incidence of vWD than others - including Poodles - which can be passed on to Cockapoos. However, if Cockapoos are affected by the condition, it will be Type 1 von Willebrand's, which is the least severe form of the disease.

Humans can also suffer from vWD. This disease is named after Erik Adolf von Willebrand, a Finnish doctor who documented and studied a rare bleeding disorder in an isolated group of people in 1924. He showed that the disease was inherited, rather than caught by infection.

Symptoms - The main one is excessive bleeding:

> Nosebleeds
> Blood in the faeces (black or bright red blood)
> Bloody urine
> Bleeding from the gums
> Females bleeding excessively from the vagina
> Bruising of skin
> Prolonged bleeding after surgery or trauma
> Blood loss anaemia if there is prolonged bleeding

If bleeding occurs in the stomach or intestine, you may notice something unusual in your dog's faeces; his stools may have blood in them or be black and tarry or bright red. Some dogs will have blood in their urine, while others may have bleeding in their joints. In this last case, the symptoms are similar to those of arthritis.

The diagnosis is made through a test to check the levels of von Willebrand's factor in the blood. If you are buying a puppy, you can check that the parents have been DNA tested for vWD and ask to see the certificate giving them the all-clear.

Treatment - Sadly, as yet, there is no cure for von Willebrand's Disease. The only way to stop the spread of the disease is to have dogs tested and to prevent breeding from affected animals. Without treatment, a dog can bleed to death after surgery or what otherwise might normally be considered a less than life-threatening injury. The only proven way to treat vWD is with transfusions of blood collected from healthy dogs.

Some dogs with von Willebrand's Disease also are **hypothyroid**, meaning they have lower than normal levels of thyroid hormone. These dogs benefit from thyroid hormone replacement therapy. A drug called DDAVP may help dogs with bleeding episodes. It can be administered into the nose to increase clotting, but opinion is still divided as to whether this treatment is effective.

Hypothyroidism

Hypothyroidism is a common hormonal disorder in dogs and is due to an under-active thyroid gland. The gland (located on either side of the windpipe in the dog's throat) does not produce enough of the hormone thyroid, which controls the speed of the metabolism. Dogs with very low thyroid levels have a slow metabolic rate. It occurs mainly in dogs over the age of five. Some Cockapoos have been known to have been affected by this condition.

Generally, hypothyroidism occurs most frequently in larger, middle-aged dogs of either gender. The symptoms are often non-specific and quite gradual in onset, and they may vary depending on breed and age. Most forms of hypothyroidism are diagnosed with a blood test.

Common Symptoms - These have been listed in order, with the most common ones being at the top of the list:

- High blood cholesterol
- Lethargy
- Hair loss
- Weight gain or obesity
- Dry coat or excessive shedding
- Hyper pigmentation or darkening of the skin, seen in 25% of cases
- Intolerance to cold, seen in 15% of dogs with the condition

Treatment - Although hypothyroidism is a type of auto-immune disease and cannot be prevented, symptoms can usually be easily diagnosed and treated. Most affected dogs can be well-managed on thyroid hormone replacement therapy tablets. The dog is placed on a daily dose of a synthetic thyroid hormone called thyroxine (levothyroxine).

The patient is usually given a standard dose for his weight and then blood samples are taken periodically to monitor him and the dose is adjusted accordingly. Depending upon your dog's preferences and needs, the medication can be given in different forms, such as a solid tablet, in liquid form, or a gel that can be rubbed into your Cockapoo's ears. Once treatment has started, he will be on it for the rest of his life.

In some less common situations, surgery may be required to remove part or all of the thyroid gland. Another treatment is radioiodine, where radioactive iodine is used to kill the overactive cells of the thyroid. While this is considered one of the most effective treatments, not all dogs are suitable for the procedure and lengthy hospitalisation is often required. Happily, once the diagnosis has been made and treatment has started, whichever treatment your dog undergoes, the majority of symptoms disappear.

NOTE: **Hyper**thyroidism (as opposed to **hypo**thyroidism) is caused by the thyroid gland producing **too much** thyroid hormone. It's quite rare in dogs, more often seen in cats. A common symptom is the dog being ravenously hungry, but losing weight.

Canine Bloat (Gastric Torsion)

Canine bloat is a serious medical condition which requires urgent medical attention. Without it, the affected dog can die. Bloat is known by several different names: twisted stomach, gastric torsion or, to give the ailment its medical term, Gastric Dilatation-Volvulus (GDV). It occurs when the dog's body becomes overstretched with too much gas.

The reasons for it are not fully understood, but there are some well-known risk factors. Bloat occurs mainly in larger breeds, particularly those with deep chests like Great Danes, Doberman Pinschers and Setters, but these are not the only breeds affected and it can happen to smaller dogs. It also happens more - but not exclusively- to dogs over seven years of age and it is more common in males than in females. The risks increase if the stomach is very full, either with food or with water. A dog which is fed once daily and eats very quickly, or gets access to the food store and gorges itself, could be at higher risk. Exercising after eating or after a big drink increases the risk, and stress can also act as a trigger.

Bloat occurs when gas is taken in as the dog eats or drinks. It can occur with or without the stomach twisting (volvulus). As the stomach swells with gas, it can rotate 90° to 360°. The twisting stomach traps air, food and water inside, and the bloated organ stops blood flowing properly to veins in the abdomen. This leads to low blood pressure, shock and even damage to internal organs.

Bloat can kill a dog in less than one hour. If you suspect your Cockapoo has bloat, get him into the car and off to the vet immediately. Even with treatment, mortality rates range from 10% to 60%. With surgery, this drops to 15% to 33%.

Causes

The causes are not completely clear, despite research being carried out into the condition. However, the following conditions are generally thought to be contributory factors:

> Air is gulped down as the dog eats or drinks. This is thought more likely to cause a problem when the dog's bowls are on the floor. Some owners buy or construct a frame for the bowls so they are at chest height. However, some experts believe that this may actually increase the risk of bloat. Discuss the situation with your vet. You can buy a plastic bowl with moulded lumps in the base (pictured), which is effective in slowing dog when eating Another option is to moisten your dog's food to slow him down.

> A large meal eaten once a day. For this reason, many owners of large dogs feed their dog two smaller feeds every day

- ➢ Diet may be a factor: avoid dog food with high fats or which use citric acid as a preservative; also avoid food with tiny pieces of kibble. Don't overfeed your dog; try and prevent him from eating too fast and avoid feeding scraps, as these may upset his stomach and lead to bloat

- ➢ Drinking too much water just before, during or after eating. Remove the water bowl just before mealtimes, but be sure to return it soon after

- ➢ Vigorous exercise before or after eating. Allow one hour either side of mealtimes before allowing your dog strenuous exercise

- ➢ Age, temperament and breeds: older dogs are more susceptible than younger ones and more males suffer than females. Deep-chested dogs are most at risk

- ➢ Stress can possibly be a trigger, with nervous and aggressive dogs being more prone to the illness. Try and maintain a peaceful environment for your dog

Symptoms - Bloat is extremely painful and the dog will show signs of distress, although it may be difficult to distinguish them from other types of stress. He may stand uncomfortably or seem to be anxious for no apparent reason. Another symptom is dry retching: the dog will often attempt to vomit every five to 30 minutes, but nothing is fetched up, except perhaps foam.

Other signs include swelling of the abdomen – this will usually feel firm like a drum – general weakness, difficulty breathing or rapid panting, drooling or excessive drinking. His behaviour will change and he may do some of the following: whine, pace up and down, look for a hiding place or lick the air. Bloat is an emergency condition. Get your dog to a veterinary surgery immediately.

———————————

Epilepsy

Thanks to **www.canineepilepsy.co.uk** for assistance with this article. If your Cockapoo has epilepsy, we recommend reading this excellent website to gain a greater understanding of the illness.

Poodles and Cocker Spaniels are breeds which are at a slightly higher risk than average of having epilepsy. The characteristics of genetic epilepsy tend to show up between 10 months and three years of age, but dogs as young as six months or as old as five years can show signs.

Anyone who has witnessed their dog having a seizure (convulsion) knows how frightening it can be. Seizures are not uncommon in dogs, but many dogs only ever have one. If your dog has had more than one seizure, it may be that he or she is epileptic. Just as with people, there are medications to control seizures in dogs, allowing them to live more normal lives.

Epilepsy means repeated seizures due to abnormal activity in the brain and is caused by an abnormality in the brain itself. It can affect any breed of dog and in fact affects around four or five dogs in every 100. In some breeds it can be hereditary. If seizures happen because of a problem somewhere else in the body, such as heart disease (which stops oxygen reaching the brain), this is not epilepsy. Your vet may do tests to try to find the reason for the epilepsy, but in many cases no cause can be identified.

Symptoms - Some dogs seem to know when they are about to have a seizure and may behave in a certain way. You will come to recognise these signs as meaning that a seizure is likely. Often dogs just seek out their owner's company and come to sit beside them when a seizure is about to start. Once the seizure starts, the dog is unconscious – he cannot hear or respond to you (unlike with head tremors). Most dogs become stiff, fall onto their side and make running movements with their legs. Sometimes they will cry out and may lose control of their bowels or bladder.

Most seizures last between one and three minutes - **it is worth making a note of the time the seizure starts and ends** because it often seems that a seizure goes on for a lot longer than it actually does.

After a seizure, dogs behave in different ways. Some dogs just get up and carry on with what they were doing, while others appear dazed and confused for up to 24 hours afterwards. Most commonly, dogs will be disoriented for only 10 to 15 minutes before returning to their old self.

They often have a set pattern of behaviour that they follow - for example going for a drink of water or asking to go outside to the toilet. If your dog has had more than one seizure, you may well start to notice a pattern of behaviour which is typically repeated.

Most seizures occur while the dog is relaxed and resting quietly. It is very rare for a seizure to occur while exercising. They often occur in the evening or at night. In a few dogs, seizures seem to be triggered by particular events or stress. It is common for a pattern to develop and, should your dog suffer from epilepsy, you will gradually recognise this as specific to your dog.

The most important thing is to **stay calm**. Remember that your dog is unconscious during the seizure and is not in pain or distressed. It is likely to be more distressing for you than for him. Make sure that he is not in a position to injure himself, for example by falling down the stairs, but otherwise do not try to interfere with him. Never try to put your hand inside his mouth during a seizure or you are very likely to get bitten. Seizures can cause damage to the brain and if your dog has repeated occurrences, it is likely that further seizures will occur in the future. The damage caused is cumulative and after a lot of seizures there may be enough brain damage to cause early senility (with loss of learned behaviour and housetraining or behavioural changes).

It is very rare for dogs to injure themselves during a seizure. Occasionally they may bite their tongue and there may appear to be a lot of blood, but is unlikely to be serious; your dog will not swallow his tongue. If a seizure goes on for a very long time (more than 10 minutes), his body temperature will rise and this can cause damage to other organs, such as the liver and kidneys as well as the brain. In very extreme cases, some dogs may be left in a coma after severe seizures. If you can, record your dog's seizure on a mobile phone, as it will be most useful in helping the vet.

When Should I Contact the Vet?

Generally, if your dog has a seizure lasting more than five minutes, or is having more than two or three a day, you should contact your vet. When your dog starts fitting, make a note of the time. If he comes out of it within five minutes, allow him time to recover quietly before contacting your vet. It is far better for him to recover quietly at home rather than be bundled into the car and carted off to the vet right away.

However, if your dog does not come out of the seizure within five minutes, or has repeated seizures close together, contact your vet immediately, as he or she will want to see your dog as soon as possible. If this is his first seizure, your vet may ask you to bring him in for a check and some routine blood tests. Always call your vet's practice before setting off to be sure that there is someone there who can help your dog.

There are many things other than epilepsy which cause seizures in dogs. When your vet first examines your dog, he or she will not know whether your dog has epilepsy or another illness. It's unlikely that the vet will see your dog during a seizure, so it is **vital** that you're able to describe in some detail just what happens. You might want to make notes or record it on your mobile phone.

Your vet may need to run a range of tests to ensure that there is no other cause of the seizures. These may include blood tests, possibly X-rays, and maybe even a scan (MRI) of your dog's brain. If no other cause can be found, then a diagnosis of epilepsy may be made. If your Cockapoo already has epilepsy, remember these key points:

> **Don't change or stop any medication without consulting your vet**
> **See your vet at least once a year for follow-up visits**
> **Be sceptical of 'magic cure' treatments**

Remember, live **with** epilepsy not **for** epilepsy. With the proper medical treatment, most epileptic dogs have far more good days than bad ones. Enjoy all those good days.

Treatment - It is not usually possible to remove the cause of the seizures, so your vet will use medication to control them. Treatment will not cure the disease, but it will manage the signs – even a well-controlled epileptic will have occasional seizures.

Sadly, as yet, there is no cure for epilepsy, so don't be tempted with 'instant cures' from the internet.

There are many drugs used in the control of epilepsy in people, but very few of these are suitable for long-term use in a dog. Two of the most common are Phenobarbital and Potassium Bromide (check that these drugs are suitable for Cockapoos, some dogs can have negative results with Phenobarbital). There are also a number of holistic remedies advertised, but we have no experience of them or any idea if any are effective.

Many epileptic dogs require a combination of one or more types of drug to achieve the most

effective control of their seizures. Treatment is decided on an individual basis and it may take some time to find the best combination and dose of drugs for your pet. You need patience when managing an epileptic pet. It is important that medication is given at the same time each day.

Once your dog has been on treatment for a while, he will become dependent on the levels of drug in his blood at all times to control seizures. If you miss a dose of treatment, blood levels can drop and this may be enough to trigger a seizure. Each epileptic dog is an individual and a treatment plan will be designed specifically for him. It will be based on the severity and frequency of the seizures and how they respond to different medications.

Keep a record of events in your dog's life, note down dates and times of episodes and record when you have given medication. Each time you visit your vet, take this diary along with you so he or she can see how your dog has been since his last check-up. If seizures are becoming more frequent, it may be necessary to change the medication. The success or otherwise of treatment may depend on YOU keeping a close eye on your Cockapoo to see if there are any physical or behavioural changes.

It is rare for epileptic dogs to stop having seizures altogether. However, provided your dog is checked regularly by your vet to make sure that the drugs are not causing any side effects, there is a good chance that he will live a full and happy life. Visit www.canineepilepsy.co.uk for more information.

Heart Problems

Cockapoos are not particularly prone to heart problems, but they are relatively common among the canine population in general. **Heart failure, or congestive heart failure (CHF),** occurs when the heart is not able to pump enough blood around the dog's body.

The heart is a mechanical pump. It receives blood in one half and forces it through the lungs, then the other half pumps the blood through the entire body. The two most common forms of heart failure in dogs are Degenerative Valvular Disease (DVD) and Dilated Cardiomyopathy (DCM), also known as an enlarged heart.

In people, heart disease usually involves the arteries that supply blood to the heart muscle becoming hardened over time, causing the heart muscles to receive less blood than they need. Starved of oxygen, the result is often a heart attack. In dogs, hardening of the arteries (arteriosclerosis) and heart attacks are very rare. However, heart disease is very common.

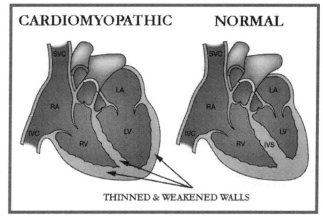

In dogs, heart disease is often seen as heart failure, which means that the muscles 'give out.' This is usually caused by one chamber or side of the heart being required to do more than it is physically able to do. It may be that excessive force is required to pump the blood through an area and over time the muscles fail.

Unlike a heart attack in humans, heart failure in the dog is a slow insidious process that occurs over months or years. In these cases, once symptoms are noted, they will usually worsen over time until the animal is placed on treatment. Heart failure in older dogs is usually due to problems with the mitral valve of the heart, and occurs most commonly in smaller breeds, including small Poodles, Yorkshire Terriers, Lhasa Apsos and Pomeranians.

Symptoms – you may notice one or more of these:

> **Tiredness**
> **Decreased activity levels**
> **Restlessness,** pacing around instead of settling down to sleep

- ➤ **Intermittent coughing** - especially during exertion or excitement. This tends to occur at night, sometimes about two hours after the dog goes to bed or when he wakes up in the morning. This coughing is an attempt to clear fluid in the lungs and is often the first clinical sign of a mitral valve disorder. As the condition worsens, other symptoms may appear:
- ➤ **Lack of appetite**
- ➤ **Rapid breathing**
- ➤ **Abdominal swelling (due to fluid)**
- ➤ **Noticeable loss of weight**
- ➤ **Fainting (syncope)**
- ➤ **Paleness**

Diagnosis - If your dog is exhibiting a range of the above symptoms, the vet may suspect congestive heart failure. He will carry out tests to make sure. These may include listening to the heart, chest X-rays, blood tests, electrocardiogram (a record of your dog's heartbeat) or an echocardiogram (ultrasound of the heart).

Treatment - If the heart problem is due to an enlarged heart (DCM) or valve disease, the condition cannot be reversed. Instead, treatment focuses on managing the symptoms with various medications, which may change over time as the condition worsens. The vet may also prescribe a special low salt diet for your dog, as sodium (found in salt) determines the amount of water in the blood, and the amount of exercise your dog has will have to be controlled. There is some evidence that vitamin and other supplements may be beneficial; discuss this with your vet.

The prognosis (outlook) for dogs with congestive heart failure depends on the cause and severity, as well as their response to treatment. Sadly, CHF is progressive, so your dog can never recover from the condition. But once diagnosed, he can live a longer, more comfortable life with the right medication and regular check-ups.

Heart Murmurs

Heart murmurs are not uncommon in dogs. Our dog was diagnosed with a Grade 2 murmur a few years ago and, of course, your heart sinks when the vet gives you the terrible news. But once the shock is over, it's important to realise that there are several different severities of the condition and, at its mildest, it is no great cause for concern.

Our dog is 11 now and, as the saying goes: "fit as a butcher's dog," with seemingly no signs of the heart murmur (except through the vet's stethoscope). However, we are always on alert for a dry, racking cough, which is a sign of fluid in the lungs. So far it hasn't happened, touch wood.

Literally, a heart murmur is a specific sound heard through a stethoscope; it results from the blood flowing faster than normal within the heart itself or in one of the two major arteries. Instead of the normal 'lubb dupp' noise, an additional sound can be heard that can vary from a mild 'pshhh' to a loud 'whoosh'. The different grades are:

- ♦ **Grade 1**—barely audible
- ♦ **Grade 2**—soft, but easily heard with a stethoscope
- ♦ **Grade 3**—intermediate loudness; most murmurs which are related to the mechanics of blood circulation are at least grade III

- ♦ **Grade 4**—loud murmur that radiates widely, often including opposite side of chest
- ♦ **Grade 5 and Grade 6**—very loud, audible with stethoscope barely touching the chest; the vibration is also strong enough to be felt through the animal's chest wall

Murmurs are caused by a number of factors; it may be a problem with the heart valves or could be due to some other condition, such as hyperthyroidism, anaemia, or heartworm.

In puppies, there are two major types of heart murmurs, and they will probably be detected by your vet at the first or second vaccinations. The most common type is called an innocent "flow murmur." This type of murmur is soft - typically Grade 2 or less - and is not caused by underlying heart disease. An innocent flow murmur typically disappears by four to five months of age.

However if a puppy has a loud murmur - Grade 3 or louder - or if the heart murmur is still easily heard with a stethoscope after four or five months of age, the likelihood of the puppy having an underlying congenital (from birth) heart problem becomes much higher. The thought of a puppy having congenital heart disease is extremely worrying, but it is important to remember that the disease will not affect all puppies' life expectancy or quality of life.

A heart murmur can also develop suddenly in an adult dog with no prior history of the problem. This is typically due to heart disease that develops with age. In toy and small breeds, a heart murmur may develop in middle-aged to older dogs due to an age-related thickening and degeneration of one of the valves in the heart, the mitral valve. (This is the type our dog has).

This thickening of the valve prevents it from closing properly and as a result it starts to leak; this is known as mitral valve disease. The more common type of heart disease affecting larger dog breeds in middle age is Dilated Cardiomyopathy (DCM). The best way to investigate the cause of the heart murmur is with an ultrasound examination of the heart (an echocardiogram).

Canine Diabetes

This is not an issue which particularly affects Cockapoos any more than any other type of dog, but can affect dogs of all breeds, sizes and both genders. It does, however, affect obese dogs more than ones of a normal weight.

There are two types: **diabetes mellitus** and **diabetes insipidus**. Diabetes mellitus (sugar diabetes) is the most common form and affects one in 500 dogs. Cockapoos are regarded as having a moderate risk of contracting this.

Thanks to modern veterinary medicine, the condition is now treatable and need not shorten your Cockapoo's lifespan or interfere with his quality of life. Diabetic dogs undergoing treatment now have the same life expectancy as non-diabetic dogs of the same age and gender.

However, if left untreated, the disease can lead to cataracts, increasing weakness in the legs (neuropathy), other ailments and even death. In dogs, diabetes is typically seen anywhere between the ages of four to 14, with a peak at seven to nine years. Both males and females can develop it; unspayed females have a slightly higher risk. The typical canine diabetes sufferer is middle-aged, female and overweight, but there are also juvenile cases.

What is Diabetes?

Diabetes insipidus is caused by a lack of vasopressin, a hormone which controls the kidneys' absorption of water. **Diabetes mellitus** occurs when the dog's body does not produce enough insulin and cannot successfully process sugars.

Dogs, like us, get their energy by converting the food they eat into sugars, mainly glucose. This glucose travels in the dog's bloodstream and individual cells then remove some of that glucose from the blood to use for energy. The substance that allows the cells to take glucose from the blood is a protein called **insulin.**

Insulin is created by beta cells that are located in the pancreas, next to the stomach. Almost all diabetic dogs have Type 1 diabetes: their pancreas does not produce any insulin. Without it, the cells have no way to use the glucose that is in the bloodstream, so the cells 'starve' while the glucose level in the blood rises. Your vet will use blood samples and urine samples to check glucose concentrations in order to diagnose diabetes. Early treatment helps to prevent further complications developing.

Common Symptoms

> ➢ Extreme thirst
> ➢ Excessive urination
> ➢ Weight loss
> ➢ Increased appetite
> ➢ Coat in poor condition
> ➢ Lethargy
> ➢ Vision problems due to cataracts

Cataracts and Diabetes - Some diabetic dogs do go blind. Cataracts may develop due to high blood glucose levels causing water to build up in the eyes' lenses. This leads to swelling, rupture of the lens fibres and the development of cataracts. In many cases, the cataracts can be surgically removed to bring sight back to the dog. Vision is restored in 75% to 80% of diabetic dogs that undergo cataract removal.

However, some dogs may stay blind even after the cataracts are gone, and some cataracts simply cannot be removed. Blind dogs are often able to get around surprisingly well, particularly in a familiar home.

Treatment – this starts with the right diet. Your vet will prescribe meals low in fat and sugars. He will also recommend medication. Many cases of canine diabetes can be successfully treated with diet and medication. More severe cases may require insulin injections. In the newly-diagnosed dog, insulin therapy begins at home.

Normally, after a week of treatment, you return to the vet who will do a series of blood sugar tests over a 12-14 hour period to see when the blood glucose peaks and when it hits its lows. Adjustments are then made to the dosage and timing of the injections. Your vet will explain how to prepare and inject the insulin. You may be asked to collect urine samples using a test strip (a small piece of paper that indicates the glucose levels in urine).

If your dog is already having insulin injections, beware of a 'miracle cure' offered on some internet sites. It does not exist. There is no diet or vitamin supplement which can reduce your dog's dependence on insulin injections because vitamins and minerals cannot do what insulin does in the dog's body. If you think that your dog needs a supplement, discuss it with your vet first to make sure that it does not interfere with any other medication.

Exercise - Managing your dog's diabetes also means managing his activity level. Exercise burns up blood glucose the same way that insulin does. If your dog is on insulin, any active exercise on top of the insulin might cause him to have a severe low blood glucose episode, called **'hypoglycaemia'.**

Keep your dog on a reasonably consistent exercise routine. Your usual insulin dose will take that amount of exercise into account. If you plan to take your dog out for some extra demanding exercise, such as running round with other dogs, give him only half of his usual insulin dose.

Tips

> ➤ You can usually buy specially formulated diabetes dog food from your vet

> ➤ You should feed the same type and amount of food at the same time every day

> ➤ Most vets recommend twice-a-day feeding for diabetic pets. It is OK if your dog prefers to eat more often

> ➤ If you have other pets in the home, they should also be placed on a twice-a-day feeding schedule, so that the diabetic dog cannot eat from their bowls. Help your dog to achieve the best possible blood glucose control by not feeding him table scraps or treats between meals

> ➤ Watch for signs that your dog is starting to drink more water than usual. Call the vet if you see this happening, as it may mean that the insulin dose needs adjusting. Remember these simple points:

Food raises blood glucose

Insulin and exercise lower blood glucose

Keep them in balance

For more information on canine diabetes visit **www.caninediabetes.org**

Canine Cancer

This is the biggest single killer of dogs of whatever breed and will claim the lives of one in four dogs. It is the cause of nearly half the deaths of all dogs aged 10 years and older, according to the American Veterinary Medical Association.

Symptoms - Early detection is critical, some things to look out for are:

- ➢ **Swellings anywhere on the body**
- ➢ **Lumps in a dog's armpit or under his jaw**
- ➢ **Sores that don't heal**
- ➢ **Bad breath**
- ➢ **Weight loss**
- ➢ **Poor appetite, difficulty swallowing or excessive drooling**
- ➢ **Changes in exercise or stamina level**
- ➢ **Laboured breathing**
- ➢ **Change in bowel or bladder habits**

If your dog has been spayed or neutered, the risk of certain cancers decreases. These cancers include uterine and breast/mammary cancer in females, and testicular cancer in males (if the dog was neutered before he was six months old). Along with controlling the pet population, spaying is especially important because mammary cancer in female dogs is fatal in about 50% of all cases.

Diagnosis - Just because your dog has a skin growth doesn't mean that it's cancerous. As with humans, tumours may be benign (harmless) or malignant (harmful). Your vet will probably confirm the tumour using X-rays, blood tests and possibly ultrasounds. He or she will then decide whether it is benign or malignant via a biopsy in which a tissue sample is taken from your dog and examined under a microscope. If your dog is diagnosed with cancer, there is hope. Advances in veterinary medicine and technology offer various treatment options, including chemotherapy, radiation and surgery. Unlike with humans, a dog's hair will not fall out with chemotherapy.

Treatment - Canine cancer is growing at an ever-increasing rate. One of the difficulties is that your pet cannot tell you when a cancer is developing, but if cancers can be detected early enough through a physical or behavioural change, they often respond well to treatment.

Over recent years, we have all become more aware of the risk factors for human cancer. Responding to these by changing our habits is having a significant impact on human health. For example, stopping smoking, protecting ourselves from over-exposure to strong sunlight and eating a healthy, balanced diet all help to reduce cancer rates. We know to keep a close eye on ourselves, go for regular health checks and report any lumps and bumps to our doctors as soon as they appear. Increased cancer awareness is definitely improving human health. The same is true

with your dog.

While it is impossible to completely prevent cancer from occurring, a healthy lifestyle with a balanced diet and regular exercise can help to reduce the risk. Also, be aware of any new lumps and bumps on your dog's body and any changes in his behaviour.

The success of treatment will depend on the type of cancer, the treatment used and on how early the tumour is found. The sooner treatment begins, the greater the chances of success. One of the best things you can do for your dog is to keep a close eye on him for any tell-tale signs.

This shouldn't be too difficult and can be done as part of your regular handling and grooming. If you notice any new bumps, for example, monitor them over a period of days to see if there is a change in their appearance or size. If there is, then make an appointment to see your vet as soon as possible. It might only be a cyst, but better to be safe than sorry.

Research into earlier diagnosis and improved treatments is being conducted at veterinary schools and companies all over the world. Advances in biology are producing a steady flow of new tests and treatments which are now becoming available to improve survival rates and canine cancer care. If your dog is diagnosed with cancer, do not despair, there are many options and new, improved treatments are constantly being introduced.

Our Happy Ending

We know from personal experience that canine cancer can be successfully treated if it is diagnosed early enough. Our dog was diagnosed with T-cell lymphoma when he was four years old.

We had noticed a black lump on his anus which grew to the size of a small grape. We took him to the vet within the first few days of seeing the lump and, after a test, he was diagnosed with the dreaded T-cell lymphoma. This is a particularly nasty and aggressive form of cancer which can spread to the lymph system and is often fatal for dogs.

As soon as the diagnosis was confirmed, our vet Graham operated and removed the lump. He also had to remove one of his anal glands, but as dogs have two this was not a serious worry. Afterwards, we were on tenterhooks, not knowing if another lump would grow or if the cancer had already spread to his lymph system.

After a few months, Max had another blood test and was finally given the all-clear. Max is now happy, healthy and 11 years old. We were very lucky. I would strongly advise anyone who suspects that their dog has cancer to get him or her to your local vet as soon as possible.

———————————

Disclaimer: The author of this book is not a qualified veterinarian. This chapter is intended to give owners an indication of some of the illnesses which may affect their dogs and the symptoms to look out for. If you have any concerns regarding the health of your dog, our advice is always the same: consult a veterinarian.

10. Skin and Allergies

Allergies are a growing concern for owners of many breeds and crossbreeds. Visit any busy vet's surgery these days – especially in spring and summer – and it's likely that one or more of the dogs will be there because of some type of sensitivity. When bred from healthy parents, Cockapoos are known for being robust and lively dogs with few problems reported as far as allergies and skin problems are concerned. However, visit any Cockapoo forum and you'll see there are plenty of itchy dogs out there.

While some breeds and crossbreeds are more prone to develop issues – and the Cockapoo is not generally regarded as one of them - any individual dog can have issues. Skin conditions, allergies and intolerances are on the increase in the canine world as well as the human world. How many children did you hear of having asthma or a peanut allergy when you were at school? Not many, I'll bet, yet allergies and adverse reactions are now relatively common – and it's the same with dogs. As yet the reasons are not clear; it could be to do with breeding, but there is no clear scientific evidence to back this up.

This is a complicated topic and a whole book could be written on this subject alone. While many dogs have no problems at all, some suffer from sensitive skin, allergies, yeast infections and/or skin disorders, causing them to scratch, bite or lick themselves excessively on the paws and other areas. Symptoms may vary from mild itchiness to a chronic reaction.

The Cockapoo breeders and owners we asked about this topic were mainly of the opinion that their dog(s) have had no problems, but they had often heard of other Cockapoos with issues. If you haven't already bought your puppy, it would be one question to ask the breeder. One quite common condition with Cockapoos is ear infections due to their long, floppy Spaniel-type ears – more about these later.

As with humans, the skin is the dog's largest organ. It acts as the protective barrier between your dog's internal organs and the outside world; it also regulates temperature and provides the sense of touch. Surprisingly, a dog's skin is actually thinner than ours, and it is made up of three layers:

1. **Epidermis** or outer layer, the one that bears the brunt of your dog's contact with the outside world

2. **Dermis** is the extremely tough layer mostly made up of collagen, a strong and fibrous protein. This where blood vessels deliver nutrients and oxygen to the skin, and it also acts as your dog's thermostat by allowing his body to release or keep in heat, depending on the outside temperature and your dog's activity level

3. **Subcutis** is a dense layer of fatty tissue that allows your dog's skin to move independently from the muscle layers below it, as well as providing insulation and support for the skin

Human allergies often trigger a reaction within the respiratory system, causing us to wheeze or sneeze, whereas allergies or hypersensitivities in a dog often cause a reaction in his or her **skin.**

Skin can be affected from the **inside** by things that your dog eats or drinks.

Skin can be affected from the **outside** by fleas, parasites, inhaled or contact allergies triggered by grass, pollen, man-made chemicals, dust, mould etc. These environmental allergies are especially common in some Terriers as well as the Miniature Schnauzer, Bulldog and certain other breeds.

Like all dogs, a Cockapoo can suffer from food allergies or intolerances as well as environmental allergies. Canine skin disorders are a complex subject. Some dogs can run through fields, digging holes and rolling around in the grass with no after-effects at all. Others may spend a lot of time indoors and have an excellent diet, but still experience severe itching.

Skin problems may be the result of one or more of a wide range of causes - and the list of potential remedies and treatments is even longer. It's by no means possible to cover all of them in this chapter. The aim here is to give a broad outline of some of the ailments most likely to affect Cockapoos and how to deal with them. We have also included remedies tried with some success by ourselves (our dog has skin issues) and other owners of dogs with skin problems, as well as advice from a holistic specialist.

This information is not intended to take the place of professional help. We are not animal health experts and you should always contact your vet as soon as your dog appears physically unwell or uncomfortable. This is particularly true with skin conditions:

If a vet can find the source of the problem early on, there is more chance of successfully treating it before it has chance to develop into a more serious condition with secondary issues.

There is anecdotal evidence from some owners that switching to a raw diet or raw meaty bones diet can significantly help some canines with skin issues. See **Chapter 6. Feeding a Cockapoo** for more information.

One of the difficulties with this type of ailment is that the exact cause is often difficult to diagnose, as the symptoms may also be common to other issues. If environmental allergies are involved, some specific tests are available costing hundreds of pounds or dollars. You will have to take your vet's advice on this, as the tests are not always conclusive and if the answer is dust or pollen, it can be difficult to keep your lively dog away from the triggers while still having a normal life - unless you and your Cockapoo spend all your time in a spotlessly clean city apartment (which is, frankly, unlikely!). It is often a question of managing a skin condition, rather than curing it.

Skin issues and allergies often develop in adolescence or early adulthood, which in a Cockapoo may be anything from a few months to two or three years old. Our dog Max was perfectly normal until he reached two when he began scratching, triggered by environmental allergies - most likely pollen. He's now 11 and over the years he's been on various different remedies which have all worked for a time. As his allergies are seasonal, he normally does not have any medication between October and March. But come spring and as sure as daffodils are daffodils, he starts scratching again. Luckily, they are manageable and Max lives a happy, normal life.

Another issue reported by some dog owners is food allergy or intolerance (there is a difference) – often to grain.

Allergies and their treatment can cause a lot of stress for dogs and owners alike. The number one piece of advice is that if you suspect your Cockapoo has an allergy or skin problem, try to deal with it right away - either via your vet or natural remedies – before the all-too-familiar scenario kicks in and it develops into a chronic (long term) condition.

Whatever the cause, before a vet can diagnose the problem you have to be prepared to tell him or her all about your dog's diet, exercise regime, habits, medical history and local environment. The vet will then carry out a thorough physical examination, possibly followed by further (expensive) tests, before a course of treatment can be prescribed. You'll have to decide whether these tests are worth it and whether they are likely to discover the exact root of the problem.

Types of Allergies

'*Canine dermatitis*' means inflammation of a dog's skin and it can be triggered by numerous things, but the most common by far is allergies. Vets estimate that one in four dogs at their clinics is there because of some kind of allergy.

Symptoms

> ➢ Chewing on paws
> ➢ Rubbing the face on the carpet
> ➢ Scratching the body
> ➢ Scratching or biting the anus
> ➢ Itchy ears, head shaking
> ➢ Hair loss
> ➢ Mutilated skin with sore or discoloured patches or hot spots

A Cockapoo who is allergic to something will show it through skin problems and itching; your vet may call this '*pruritus*'.

It may seem logical that if a dog is allergic to something he inhales, like certain pollen grains, his nose will run; if he's allergic to something he eats, he may vomit, or if allergic to an insect bite, he may develop a swelling. But in practice this is seldom the case. The skin is an organ and with dogs it is this organ which is often affected by allergies. So instead, he will have a mild to severe itching sensation over his body and maybe a chronic ear infection.

Dogs with allergies often chew their feet until they are sore and red. You may see your Cockapoo rubbing his face on the carpet or couch or scratching his belly and flanks. Because the ear glands produce too much wax in response to the allergy, ear infections can occur, with bacteria and yeast - which is a fungus - often thriving in the excessive wax and debris. But your Cockapoo doesn't have to suffer from allergies to get ear infections, the lack of air flow under the floppy hairy ears make them prone to the condition. By the way, if your Cockapoo does develop a yeast infection and you decide to switch to a grain-free diet, try and avoid those which are potato-based, as these contain high levels of starch.

Holistic vet Dr Jodie Gruenstern says: "Grains and other starches have a negative impact on gut health, creating insulin resistance and inflammation. It's estimated that up to 80% of the immune system resides within the gastrointestinal system; building a healthy gut supports a more appropriate immune response. The importance of choosing fresh proteins and healthy fats over processed, starchy diets (such as kibble) can't be overemphasized."

An allergic dog may cause skin lesions or 'hot spots' by constant chewing and scratching. Sometimes he will lose hair, which can be patchy, leaving a mottled appearance. The skin itself may be dry and crusty, reddened, swollen or oily, depending on the dog. It is very common to get secondary bacterial skin infections due to these self-inflicted wounds. An allergic dog's body is reacting to certain molecules called 'allergens.' These may come from:

> Trees
> Grass
> Pollens
> Foods and food additives, such as specific meats, grains or colourings
> Milk products
> Fabrics, such as wool or nylon
> Rubber and plastics
> House dust and dust mites
> Mould
> Flea bites
> Chemical products used around the house

These allergens may be **inhaled** as the dog breathes, **ingested** as the dog eats or caused by **contact** with the dog's body when he walks or rolls. However they arrive, they all cause the immune system to produce a protein (IgE), which causes various irritating chemicals, such as histamine, to be released. In dogs these chemical reactions and cell types occur in sizeable amounts only within the skin, hence the scratching.

Inhalant Allergies (Atopy)

The most common allergies in dogs are inhalant and seasonal (at least at first, some allergies may develop and worsen). Substances which can cause an allergic reaction in dogs are similar to those causing problems for humans.

While any dog can suffer from them, some breeds may have a higher incidence of them and there is some evidence that this includes American Cocker Spaniels and Cockapoos bred from American Cockers. There is anecdotal evidence from owners that some English Cockapoos also suffer from atopy.

A clue to diagnosing these allergies is to look at the timing of the reaction. Does it happen all year round? If so, this may be mould, dust or some other trigger which is permanently in the environment. If the reaction is seasonal, then pollens may well be the culprit.

A diagnosis can be made by allergy testing - either a blood or skin test where a small amount of antigen is injected into the dog's skin to test for a reaction. The blood test can give false positives, so the skin test is many veterinarians' preferred method.

Whether or not you take this route will be your

decision; allergy testing is not cheap, it takes time and may require your dog to be sedated. And there's also no point doing it if you are not going to go along with the recommended method of treatment afterwards, which is immunotherapy, or **'hyposensitisation',** and this can also be an expensive and lengthy process.

It consists of a series of injections made specifically for your dog and administered over weeks or months to make him more tolerant of specific allergens. It may have to be done by a veterinary dermatologist if your vet is not familiar with the treatment. Vets in the US claim that success rates can be as high as 75% of cases. These tests work best when carried out during the season when the allergies are at their worst.

But before you get to this stage, your vet will have had to rule out other potential causes, such as fleas or mites, fungal, yeast or bacterial infections and hypothyroidism. Due to the time and cost involved in skin testing, most mild cases of allergies are treated with a combination of avoidance, fatty acids and antihistamines.

Environmental or Contact Irritations

These are a direct reaction to something the dog physically comes into contact with. It could be as simple as grass, specific plants, dust or other animals. If the trigger is grass or other outdoor materials, the allergies are often seasonal. The dog may require treatment (often tablets, shampoo or localised cortisone spray) for spring and summer, but be perfectly fine with no medication for the other half of the year. This is the case with our dog.

If you suspect your Cockapoo may have outdoor contact allergies, here is one very good tip guaranteed to reduce his scratching: get him to stand in a tray or large bowl of water on your return from a walk. Washing his feet and under his belly will get rid of some of the pollen and other allergens, which in turn will reduce his scratching and biting. This can help to reduce the allergens to a tolerable level. Other possible triggers include dry carpet shampoos, caustic irritants, new carpets, cement dust, washing powders or fabric conditioners. If you wash your dog's bedding or if he sleeps on your bed, use a fragrance-free - if possible, hypoallergenic - laundry detergent and avoid fabric conditioner.

The irritation may be restricted to the part of the dog - such as the underneath of the paws or belly - which has touched the offending object. Symptoms are skin irritation - either a general problem or specific hotspots - itching (pruritis) and sometimes hair loss. Readers sometimes report to us that their dog will incessantly lick one part of the body, often the paws, anus, belly or back.

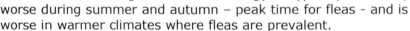

Flea Bite Allergies

These are a very common canine allergy and affect dogs of all breeds. To compound the problem, many dogs with flea allergies also have inhalant allergies. Flea bite allergy is typically seasonal,

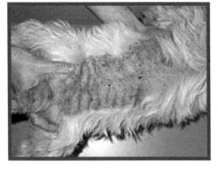

worse during summer and autumn – peak time for fleas - and is worse in warmer climates where fleas are prevalent.

This type of allergy is not the flea itself, but to proteins in flea saliva, which are deposited under the dog's skin when the insect feeds. Just one bite to an allergic Cockapoo will cause intense and long-lasting itching. If affected, the dog will try to bite at the base of his tail and scratch a lot. Most of the damage is done by the dog's scratching, rather than the flea bite, and can result in his fur falling out or skin abrasions.

Some Cockapoos will develop hot spots. These can occur anywhere, but are often along the back and base of the tail. Flea bite allergies can only be totally prevented by keeping all fleas away from the dog. Various flea prevention treatments are available – see the section on **Parasites**. If you suspect your dog may be allergic to fleas, consult your vet for the proper diagnosis and medication.

Diet and Food Allergies

Food is the third most common cause of allergies in dogs. Cheap dog foods bulked up with grains and other ingredients can cause problems. Some Cockapoo owners have reported their dogs having problems with wheat and other grains. If you feed your dog a dry commercial dog food, make sure that it's a high quality, preferably hypoallergenic, one and that the first ingredient listed on the sack is meat or poultry, not grain.

Without the correct food, a dog's whole body - not just his skin and coat - will continuously be under stress and this manifests itself in a number of ways. The symptoms of food allergies are similar to those of most allergies:

➢ Itchy skin affecting primarily the face, feet, ears, forelegs, armpits and anus
➢ Excessive scratching
➢ Chronic or recurring ear infections
➢ Hair loss
➢ Hot spots
➢ Skin infections that clear up with antibiotics, but return after the antibiotics have finished
➢ Possible increased bowel movements, maybe twice as many as normal

The bodily process which occurs when an animal has a reaction to a particular food agent is not very well understood, but the veterinary profession does know how to diagnose and treat food allergies. As many other problems can cause similar symptoms to food allergies (and also the fact that many sufferers also have other allergies), it is important that any other problems are identified and treated before food allergies are diagnosed.

Atopy, flea bite allergies, intestinal parasite hypersensitivities, sarcoptic mange and yeast or bacterial infections can all cause similar symptoms. This can be an anxious time for owners as vets try one thing after another to get to the bottom of the allergy.

The normal method for diagnosing a food allergy is elimination. Once all other causes have been ruled out or treated, then a food trial is the next step – and that's no picnic for owners either. See **Chapter 6. Feeding a Cockapoo** for more information. As with other allergies, dogs may have short-term relief by taking fatty acids, antihistamines, and steroids, but removing the offending items from the diet is the only permanent solution.

Acute Moist Dermatitis (Hot Spots)

Acute moist dermatitis or 'hot spots' are not uncommon. A hot spot can appear suddenly and is a raw, inflamed and often bleeding area of skin. The area becomes moist and painful and begins spreading due to continual licking and chewing. They can become large, red, irritated lesions in a short pace of time. The cause is often a local reaction to an insect bite; fleas, ticks, biting flies and even mosquitoes have been known to cause acute moist dermatitis. Other causes of hot spots include:

- ➢ Allergies - inhalant allergies and food allergies
- ➢ Mites
- ➢ Ear infections
- ➢ Poor grooming
- ➢ Burs or plant awns
- ➢ Anal gland disease
- ➢ Hip dysplasia or other types of arthritis and degenerative joint disease

Diagnosis and Treatment - The good news is that, once diagnosed and with the right treatment, hot spots disappear as soon as they appeared. The underlying cause should be identified and treated, if possible. Check with your vet before treating your Cockapoo for fleas and ticks at the same time as other medical treatment (such as anti-inflammatory medications and/or antibiotics), as he or she will probably advise you to wait.

Treatments may come in the form of injections, tablets or creams – or your dog might need a combination of them. Your vet will probably clip and clean the affected area to help the effectiveness of any spray or ointment and your poor Cockapoo might also have to wear an E-collar until the condition subsides, but usually this does not take long.

Interdigital Cysts

If you've ever noticed a fleshy red lump between your dog's toes that looks like an ulcerated sore or a hairless bump, then it was probably an interdigital cyst - or 'interdigital furuncle' to give the condition its correct medical term.

These can be very difficult to get rid of, since they are not the primary issue, but often a sign of some other condition. Actually they are not cysts, but the result of **furunculosis**, a condition of the skin which clogs hair follicles and creates chronic infection. They can be caused by a number of factors, including allergies, obesity, poor foot conformation, mites, yeast infections, ingrown hairs or other foreign bodies, and obesity.

These nasty-looking bumps are painful for your dog and will probably cause him to limp. Vets might recommend a whole range of treatments to get to the root cause of the problem. It can be extremely expensive if your dog is having a barrage of tests or biopsies and even then you are not guaranteed to find the underlying cause.

The first thing he or she will probably do is put your dog in an E-collar to stop him licking the affected area, which will never recover properly as long as he's constantly licking it. This again is stressful for your dog. Here are some remedies your vet may suggest:

- ➢ Antibiotics and/or steroids and/or mite killers
- ➢ Soaking his feet in Epsom salts twice daily to unclog the hair follicles
- ➢ Testing him for allergies or thyroid problems
- ➢ Starting a food trial if food allergies are suspected
- ➢ Shampooing his feet
- ➢ Cleaning between his toes with medicated (benzoyl peroxide) wipes
- ➢ A referral to a veterinary dermatologist
- ➢ Surgery

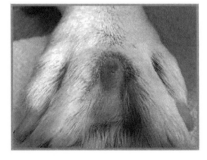

If you suspect your Cockapoo has an interdigital cyst, take him to the vet for a correct diagnosis and then discuss the various options.

A course of antibiotics may be suggested initially, along with switching to a hypoallergenic diet if a food allergy is suspected. If the condition persists, many owners get discouraged, especially when treatment may go on for many weeks.

Before you resort to any drastic action, first try soaking your Cockapoo's affected paw in Epsom

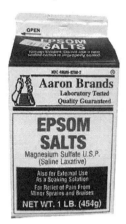

salts for five or 10 minutes twice a day. After the soaking, clean the area with medicated wipes, which are antiseptic and control inflammation. In the US these are sold under the brand name Stridex pads in the skin care section of any grocery, or from the pharmacy. If you think the cause may be an environmental allergy, wash your dog's paws and under his belly when you return from a walk, this will help to remove pollen and other allergens from his body.

Surgery can be effective, but it is a drastic option and although it might solve the immediate problem, it will not deal with whatever is triggering the interdigital cysts in the first place. Not only is healing after this surgery a lengthy and difficult process, it also means your dog will never have the same foot as before - future orthopaedic issues and a predisposition to more interdigital cysts are a couple of problems which can occur afterwards.

All that said, your vet will understand that interdigital cysts aren't so simple to deal with, but they are always treatable. Get the right diagnosis as soon as possible, limit all offending factors and give medical treatment a good solid try before embarking on more drastic cures.

Parasites

Demodectic Mange

Demodectic mange is also known as red mange, follicular mange or puppy mange. It is caused by the tiny mite Demodex canis – pictured - which can only be seen through a microscope. The mites actually live inside the hair follicles on the bodies of virtually every adult dog, and most humans, without causing any harm or irritation. In humans, the mites are found in the skin, eyelids and the creases of the nose … try not to think about that!

The demodectic mite spends its entire life on the host dog. Eggs hatch and mature from larvae to nymphs to adults in 20 to 35 days and the mites are transferred directly from the mother to the puppies within the first week of life by direct physical contact. Demodectic mange is not a disease of poorly kept or dirty kennels. It is generally a disease of young dogs with inadequate or poorly developed immune systems (or older dogs suffering from a suppressed immune system).

Vets currently believe that virtually every mother carries and transfers mites to her puppies, and most are immune to the mite's effects, but a few puppies are not and they develop full-blown mange. They may have a few (less than five) isolated lesions and this is known as localised mange – often around the head. This happens in around 90% of cases, but in the other 10% of cases, it develops into generalised mange which covers the entire body or region of the body. This is most likely to develop in puppies with parents that have suffered from mange. Most lesions in either form develop after four months of age. It can also develop around the time when females have their first season, typically around nine months old, and may be due to a slight dip in the bitch's immune system.

Symptoms – Bald patches are usually the first sign, usually accompanied by crusty, red skin which sometimes appears greasy or wet. Usually hair loss begins around the muzzle, eyes and other areas on the head. The lesions may or may not itch. In localised mange, a few circular crusty areas appear, most frequently on the head and front legs of three to six-month-old puppies. Most will self-heal as the puppies become older and develop their own immunity, but a persistent problem needs treatment.

With generalised mange there are bald patches over the entire coat, including the head, neck, body, legs, and feet. The skin on the head, side and back is crusty, often inflamed and oozes a clear fluid. The skin itself will often be oily to touch and there is usually a secondary bacterial infection. Some puppies can become quite ill and can develop a fever, lose their appetites and become lethargic. If you suspect your puppy has generalised demodectic mange, get him to a vet straight away.

There is also a condition called pododermatitis, when the mange affects a puppy's paws. It can cause bacterial infections and be very uncomfortable, even painful. The symptoms of this mange include hair loss on the paws, swelling of the paws (especially around the nail beds) and red/hot/inflamed areas which are often infected. Treatment is always recommended, and it can take several rounds to clear it up.

Diagnosis and Treatment – The vet will normally diagnose demodectic mange after he or she has taken a skin scraping. As these mites are present on every dog, they do not necessarily mean the dog has mange. Only when the mite is coupled with lesions will the vet diagnose mange. Treatment usually involves topical (on the skin) medication and sometimes tablets. Localised demodectic mange often resolves itself as the puppy grows.

If the dog has just one or two lesions, these can usually be successfully treated using specific creams and spot treatments. With generalised demodectic mange, treatment can be lengthy and expensive. The vet might prescribe Amitraz anti-parasitic dips every two weeks. It is an organophosphate available only on prescription under the name Mitaban. Owners should always wear rubber gloves when treating their dog, and it should be applied in an area with adequate ventilation. It should also be noted that **some dogs – especially Toy breeds - can react to this**, so check very carefully with your vet as to whether it will be suitable. Most dogs with the severe form of the condition need from six to 14 dips every two weeks. After the first three or four dips, your vet will probably take another skin scraping to check that the mites have gone. Dips continue for one month after the mites have disappeared, but dogs shouldn't be considered cured until a year after their last treatment.

Other options include the heartworm treatment Ivermectin. This isn't approved by the FDA for treating mange, but is often used to do so. It is usually given orally every one to two days, or by injection, and can be very effective. Again, some dogs react badly to it. Another drug is Interceptor (Milbemycin oxime), which can be expensive as it has to be given daily. However, it is effective on up to 80% of the dogs who did not respond to Mitaban dips – but should be given with caution to pups under 21 weeks of age. Dogs that have the generalised condition may have underlying skin infections, so antibiotics are often given for the first several weeks of treatment. Because the mite flourishes on dogs with suppressed immune systems, you should try to get to the root cause of immune system disease, especially if your Cockapoo is older when he or she develops demodectic mange.

Sarcoptic Mange

Also known as canine scabies, this is caused by the parasite *Sarcoptes scabiei*. This microscopic mite can cause a range of skin problems, the most common of which is hair loss and severe itching. The mites can infect other animals such as foxes, cats and even humans, but prefer to live their short lives on dogs. Fortunately, there are several good treatments for this mange and the disease can be easily controlled.

In cool, moist environments, they live for up to 22 days. At normal room temperature they live from two to six days, preferring to live on parts of the dog with less hair. These are the areas you may see him scratching, although it can spread throughout the body in severe cases.

Diagnosing canine scabies can be somewhat difficult, and it is often mistaken for inhalant allergies. Once diagnosed, there are a number of effective treatments, including selamectin (Revolution), a topical solution applied once a month which also provides heartworm prevention, flea control and some tick protection. Various Frontline products are also effective – check with your vet for the correct ones.

Because your dog does not have to come into direct contact with an infected dog to catch scabies, it is difficult to completely protect him. Foxes and their environment can also transmit the mite, so keep your dog away from areas where you know foxes are present.

Fleas

When you see your dog scratching and biting, your first thought is probably: "He's got fleas!" and you may well be right. Fleas don't fly, but they do have very strong back legs and they will take any opportunity to jump from the ground or another animal into your Cockapoo's lovely warm coat. You can sometimes see the fleas if you part your dog's fur.

And for every flea that you see on your dog, there is the awful prospect of hundreds of eggs and larvae in your house or apartment. So if your Cockapoo is unlucky enough to catch fleas, you'll have to treat your environment as well as your dog in order to completely get rid of them.

The best form of cure is prevention. Vets recommend giving dogs a preventative flea treatment every four to eight weeks. This may vary depending on your climate, the season - fleas do not breed as quickly in the cold - and how much time your dog spends outdoors.

Once-a-month topical (applied to the skin) insecticides - like Frontline and Advantix - are the most commonly used flea prevention products on the market. You part the skin and apply drops of the liquid on to a small area on your dog's back, usually near the neck. Some kill fleas and ticks, and others just kill fleas - check the details.

It is worth spending the money on a quality treatment, as cheaper brands may not rid your Cockapoo completely of fleas, ticks and other parasites. Sprays, dips, shampoos and collars are other options, as are tablets and injections in certain cases, such as before your dog goes into boarding kennels or has surgery. Incidentally, a flea bite is different from a flea bite allergy.

NOTE: There is considerable anecdotal evidence from dog owners of various breeds that the US flea and worm tablet *Trifexis* may cause severe side effects in some dogs. You may wish to read some owners' comments at: www.max-the-schnauzer.com/trifexis-side-effects-in-schnauzers.html

Ticks

A tick is not an insect, but a member of the arachnid family, like the spider. There are over 850 types of them, divided into two types: hard shelled and soft shelled. Ticks don't have wings - they can't fly, they crawl. They have a sensor called Haller's organ which detects smell, heat and humidity to help them locate food, which in some cases is a Cockapoo. A tick's diet consists of one thing and one thing only – blood! They climb up onto tall grass and when they sense an animal is close, crawl on him.

Ticks can pass on a number of diseases to animals and humans, the most well-known of which is Lyme Disease, a serious condition which causes lameness and other problems. Dogs which spend a lot of time outdoors in high risk areas, such as woods, can have a vaccination against Lime Disease.

If you do find a tick on your Cockapoo's coat and are not sure how to get it out, have it removed by a vet or other expert. Inexpertly pulling it out yourself and leaving a bit of the tick behind can be detrimental to your dog's health. Prevention treatment is similar to that for fleas. If your Cockapoo has particularly sensitive skin, he might do better with a natural flea or tick remedy.

Heartworm

Heartworm is a serious and potentially fatal disease affecting pets in North America and many other parts of the world. It is caused by foot-long worms (heartworms) that live in the heart, lungs and associated blood vessels of affected pets, causing severe lung disease, heart failure and damage to other organs in the body.

The dog is a natural host for heartworms, which means that heartworms living inside the dog mature into adults, mate and produce offspring. If untreated, their numbers can increase; dogs have been known to harbour several hundred worms in their bodies. Heartworm disease causes lasting damage to the heart, lungs and arteries, and can affect the dog's health and quality of life long after the parasites are gone. For this reason, prevention is by far the best option and treatment - when needed - should be administered as early as possible.

The mosquito (pictured) plays an essential role in the heartworm life cycle. When a mosquito bites and takes a blood meal from an infected animal, it picks up baby worms which develop and mature into 'infective stage' larvae over a period of 10 to 14 days. Then, when the infected mosquito bites another dog, cat or susceptible wild animal, the infective larvae are deposited onto the surface of the animal's skin and enter the new host through the mosquito's bite wound. Once inside a new host, it takes approximately six months for the larvae to develop into adult heartworms. Once mature, heartworms can live for five to seven years in a dog.

In the early stages of the disease, many dogs show few or no symptoms. The longer the infection persists, the more likely symptoms will develop. These include:

> ➢ A mild persistent cough
> ➢ Reluctance to exercise
> ➢ Tiredness after moderate activity
> ➢ Decreased appetite
> ➢ Weight loss

As the disease progresses, dogs may develop heart failure and a swollen belly due to excess fluid in the abdomen. Dogs with large numbers of heartworms can develop sudden blockages of blood flow within the heart leading to the life-threatening caval syndrome. This is marked by a sudden onset of laboured breathing, pale gums and dark, bloody or coffee-coloured urine. Without prompt surgical removal of the heartworm blockage, few dogs survive.

Although more common in the south eastern US, heartworm disease has been diagnosed in all 50 states. And because infected mosquitoes can fly indoors, even Cockapoos which spend much time inside the home are at risk. For that reason, the American Heartworm Society recommends that you get your dog tested every year and give your dog heartworm preventive treatment for 12 months of the year.

Thanks to the American Heartworm Society for assistance with the section

---

Ringworm

This is not actually a worm, but a fungus and is most commonly seen in puppies and young dogs. It is highly infectious and often found on the face, ears, paws or tail. The ringworm fungus is most prevalent in hot, humid climates but, surprisingly, most cases occur in autumn and winter. Ringworm infections in dogs are not that common; in one study of dogs with active skin problems, less than 3% had ringworm.

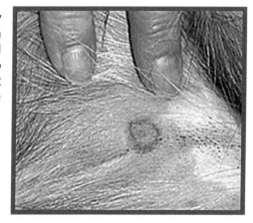

Ringworm is transmitted by spores in the soil and by contact with the infected hair of dogs and cats, which can be typically found on carpets, brushes, combs, toys and furniture. Spores from infected animals can be shed into the environment and live for over 18 months, but fortunately most healthy adult dogs have some resistance and never develop symptoms.

The fungi live in dead skin, hairs and nails - and the head and legs are the most common areas affected. Tell-tale signs are bald patches with a roughly circular shape (see photo). Ringworm is relatively easy to treat with fungicidal shampoos or antibiotics from a vet.

Humans can catch ringworm from pets, and vice versa. Children are especially susceptible, as are adults with suppressed immune systems and those undergoing chemotherapy. Hygiene is extremely important. If your dog has ringworm, wear gloves when handling him and wash your hands well afterwards. And if a member of your family catches ringworm, make sure they use separate towels from everyone else or the fungus may spread. (As an adolescent I caught ringworm from horses at stables where I worked at weekends - much to my mother's horror - and was treated like a leper by the rest of the family until it had cleared up!).

Bacterial infection (Pyoderma)

Pyoderma literally means 'pus in the skin' (yuk!) and fortunately this condition is not contagious. Early signs of this bacterial infection are itchy red spots filled with yellow pus, similar to pimples or spots in humans. They can sometimes develop into red, ulcerated skin with dry and crusty patches.

Pyoderma is caused by several things: a broken skin surface, a skin wound due to chronic exposure to moisture, altered skin bacteria, or impaired blood flow to the skin. Dogs have a higher risk of developing an infection when they have a fungal infection or an endocrine (hormone gland) disease such as hyperthyroidism, or have allergies to fleas, food or parasites.

Pyoderma is often secondary to allergic dermatitis and develops in the sores on the skin which happen as a result of scratching. Puppies often develop 'puppy pyoderma' in thinly-haired areas such as the groin and underarms. Fleas, ticks, yeast or fungal skin infections, thyroid disease, hormonal imbalances, heredity and some medications can increase the risk. If you notice symptoms, get your dog to the vet quickly before the condition develops from **superficial pyoderma** into **severe pyoderma**, which is very unpleasant and takes a lot longer to treat.

Bacterial infection, no matter how bad it may look, usually responds well to medical treatment, which is generally done on an outpatient basis. Superficial pyoderma will usually be treated with a two to six-week course of antibiotic tablets or ointment. Severe or recurring pyoderma looks awful, causes your dog some distress and can take months of treatment to completely cure. Medicated shampoos and regular bathing, as instructed by your vet, are also part of the treatment. It's also important to ensure your dog has clean, dry, padded bedding.

Ear Infections

The Cockapoo has a reputation for being a healthy hybrid, but ear infections are the crossbreed's Achilles' heel. Infection of the external ear canal (outer ear infection) is called otitis externa and is one of the most common types seen. The fact that your dog has recurring ear infections does not necessarily mean that his ears are the source of the problem – although they might be.

One common reason for them in Cockapoos is moisture in the ear canal, which in turn allows bacteria to flourish there. However, some Cockapoos with chronic or recurring ear infections have inhalant or food allergies or low thyroid function (hypothyroidism).

Sometimes the ears are the first sign of allergy. The underlying problem must be treated or the dog will continue to have chronic ear problems. Tell-tale signs include your dog shaking his head, scratching or rubbing his ears a lot, or an unpleasant odour coming from the ears.

If you look inside the ears, you may notice a reddy brown or yellow discharge, it may also be red and inflamed with a lot of wax. Sometimes a dog may appear depressed or irritable; ear infections are painful. In chronic cases, the inside of his ears may become crusty or thickened. Dogs can have ear problems for many different reasons, including:

> ➤ Allergies, such as environmental or food allergies
> ➤ Ear mites or other parasites
> ➤ Bacteria or yeast infections
> ➤ Injury, often due to excessive scratching

> Hormonal abnormalities, e.g. hypothyroidism
> The ear anatomy and environment, e.g. excess moisture
> Hereditary or immune conditions and tumours

In reality, many Cockapoos have ear infections due to the structure of the ear. The long, hairy ears often prevent sufficient air flow inside the ear. This can lead to bacterial or yeast infections - particularly if there is moisture inside. These warm, damp and dark areas under the ear flaps provide an ideal breeding ground for bacteria.

Treatment depends on the cause and what – if any - other conditions your dog may have. Antibiotics are used for bacterial infections and antifungals for yeast infections. Glucocorticoids, such as dexamethasone, are often included in these medications to reduce the inflammation in the ear. Your vet may also flush out and clean the ear with special drops, something you may have to do daily at home until the infection clears.

A dog's ear canal is L-shaped, which means it can be difficult to get medication into the lower (horizontal) part of the ear. The best method is to hold the dog's ear flap with one hand and put the ointment or drops in with the other, if possible tilting the dog's head away from you so the liquid flows downwards **with gravity**. Make sure you then hold the ear flap down and massage the medication into the horizontal canal before letting go of your dog, as the first thing he will do is shake his head – and if the ointment or drops aren't massaged in, they will fly out.

Nearly all ear infections can be successfully managed if properly diagnosed and treated. But if an underlying problem remains undiscovered, the outcome will be less favourable. Deep ear infections can damage or rupture the eardrum, causing an internal ear infection and even permanent hearing loss. Closing of the ear canal (*hyperplasia* or *stenosis)* is another sign of severe infection. Most extreme cases of hyperplasia will eventually require surgery as a last resort; the most common procedure is called a 'lateral ear resection'.

Our dog had a lateral ear resection two or three years ago following years of recurring ear infections and the growth of scar tissue. It was surgery or deafness, the vet said. We opted for surgery and our dog has been free of ear infections ever since. However, it is an **extremely** painful procedure for the dog and should only be considered as a very last resort.

To avoid or alleviate recurring ear infections, check your dog's ears and clean them regularly. Hair should be regularly plucked from inside your Cockapoo's ears – either by you or a groomer, or both. If your Cockapoo is one of the very many who enjoys swimming, great care should be taken to ensure the inside of the ear is thoroughly dry afterwards - and after bathing at home. There is more information in **Chapter 11. Grooming.**

When cleaning or plucking your dog's ears, be very careful not to put anything too far down inside. Visit YouTube to see videos of how to correctly clean without damaging them. In a nutshell, DO NOT use cotton buds, these are too small and can damage the ear. Some owners recommend regularly cleaning the inside of ears with cotton wool and a mixture of water and white vinegar once a week or so.

If your dog appears to be in pain, has smelly ears, or if his ear canals look inflamed, contact your vet straight away. If you can nip the first infection in the bud, there is a chance it will not return. If your dog has a ruptured or weakened eardrum, ear cleansers and medications could do more harm than good. Early treatment is the best way of preventing a recurrence.

Canine Acne

This is not uncommon and - just as with humans - generally affects teenagers, often between five and eight months of age with canines. Acne occurs when oil glands become blocked causing bacterial infection and these glands are most active in teenagers. Acne is not a major health problem as most of it will clear up once the dog becomes an adult, but it can recur. Typical signs are pimples, blackheads or whiteheads around the muzzle, chest or groin. If the area is irritated, then there may some bleeding or pus that can be expressed from these blemishes.

Hormonal Imbalances

These occur in dogs of all breeds. They are often difficult to diagnose and occur when a dog is producing either too much (hyper) or too little (hypo) of a particular hormone. One visual sign is often hair loss on both sides of the dog's body. The condition is not usually itchy. Hormone imbalances can be serious as they are often indicators that glands which affect the dog internally are not working properly. However, some types can be diagnosed by special blood tests and treated effectively.

Some Allergy Treatments

Treatments and success rates vary tremendously from dog to dog and from one allergy to another, which is why it is so important to consult a vet at the outset. Earlier diagnosis is more likely to lead to a successful treatment. Some owners whose Cockapoos have recurring skin issues find that a course of antibiotics or steroids works wonders for their dog's sore skin and itching. However, the scratching starts all over again shortly after the treatment stops.

Food allergies require patience, a change of diet and maybe even a food trial, and the specific trigger is notoriously difficult to isolate – unless you are lucky and hit on the culprit straight away. With inhalant and contact allergies, blood and skin tests are available, followed by hypersensitisation treatment. However, these are expensive and often the specific trigger for many dogs remains unknown. So the reality for many owners of Cockapoos with allergies is that they manage the ailment with various medications and practices, rather than curing it completely.

Our Personal Experience

After corresponding with numerous other dog owners and consulting our vet, Graham, it seems that our experiences with allergies are not uncommon. This is borne out by the dozens of dog owners who have contacted our website about their pet's allergy or sensitivities. Our dog was perfectly fine until he was about two years old when he began to scratch a lot. He scratched more in spring and summer, which meant that his allergies were almost certainly inhalant or contact-based and related to pollens, grasses or other outdoor triggers.

One option was for Max to have a barrage of tests to discover exactly what he was allergic to. We decided not to do this, not because of the cost, but because our vet said it was highly likely that he was allergic to pollens. If we had confirmed an allergy to pollens, we were not going to stop taking him outside for walks, so the vet treated him on the basis of seasonal inhalant or contact allergies, probably related to pollen.

As mentioned, one method is to have a shallow bath or hose outside and to rinse the dog's paws and underbelly after a walk in the countryside. This is something our vet does with his own dogs and has found that the scratching reduces as a result. Regarding medications, Max was at first put on to a tiny dose of Piriton, an antihistamine for hay fever sufferers (human and canine) and for the first few springs and summers, this worked well.

Allergies can often change and the dog can also build up a tolerance to a treatment, which is why they can be so difficult to treat. This has been the case with our dog over the years. The symptoms change from season to season, although the main ones remain and they are: general scratching, paw biting and ear infections. One year he bit the skin under his tail a lot (near the anus) and this was treated effectively with a single steroid injection followed by spraying the area with cortisone once a day at home for a period. This type of spray can be very effective if the itchy area is small, but no good for spraying all over a dog's body.

A couple of years ago Max started nibbling his paws for the first time - a habit he persists with - although not to the extent that they become red and raw. Over the years we have tried a number of treatments, all of which have worked for a while, before he comes off the medication in autumn for six months when plants and grasses stop growing outdoors. He manages perfectly fine the rest of the year without any treatment.

If we were starting again from scratch, knowing what we know now, I would investigate a raw diet, if necessary in combination with holistic remedies. Our dog is now 11; we feed him a high quality hypoallergenic dry food. His allergies are manageable, he loves his food, is full of energy and otherwise healthy, and so we are reluctant to make such a big change at this point in his life.

According to Graham, more and more dogs are appearing in his waiting room every spring with various types of allergies. Whether this is connected to how we breed our dogs remains to be seen. One season he put Max on a short course of steroids. These worked very well for five months, but steroids are not a long-term solution, as prolonged use can cause organ damage.

Another spring Max was prescribed a non-steroid daily tablet called Atopica, sold in the UK only through vets. (The active ingredient is **cyclosporine**, which suppresses the immune system. Some dogs can get side effects, although Max didn't, and holistic practitioners believe that it is harmful to the dog). This treatment was expensive, but initially extremely effective – so much so that we thought we had cured the problem completely. However, after a couple of seasons on cyclosporine he developed a tolerance to the drug and started scratching again.

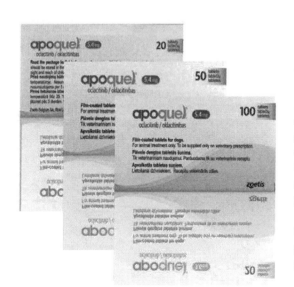

A few years ago he went back on the antihistamine Piriton, a higher dose than when he was two years old, and this worked very well again. One advantage of this drug is that is it manufactured by the million for dogs and is therefore very inexpensive.

In 2013 the FDA approved **Apoquel** (oclacitinib) to control itching and inflammation in allergic dogs. In some quarters it has been hailed a **'wonder drug'** for canine allergies. In fact it has proved so popular in the UK and North America that there has been a shortage of supply, with the manufacturers not being able to produce it fast enough.

We have tried it with excellent results. There was some tweaking at the beginning to get the daily dose right, but it really has proved effective for us. Max still scratches, but not so much – all dogs scratch a bit - and he is still on Apoquel today for six months of the year. Normally dogs start with a double dose for 10 days to suppress the allergic reaction and then go on to a single tablet a day mixed into one of their feeds. The tablets cost around £1 or $1.50 each, so it's not cheap.

Many vets recommend adding fish oils (which contain Omega-3 fatty acids) to a daily feed to keep your dog's skin and coat healthy all year round – whether or not he has problems. We add a liquid supplement called Yumega Plus, which contains Omegas 3 and 6, to one of his two daily feeds all year round and this definitely seems to help his skin. In the past when the scratching has got particularly bad, we have bathed Max in an antiseborrhoeic shampoo (called Malaseb) twice a week for a limited time. This also helped, although this has not been necessary since he started on the Apoquel.

The main point is that most allergies are manageable. They may change throughout the life of the dog and you may have to alter the treatment. Our Max still scratches, but not as much as when he was younger. He may have allergies, but he wouldn't miss his walks for anything and, all in all, he is one contented canine. We've compiled some anecdotal evidence from our website from owners of dogs with various allergies. Here are some of their suggestions for alleviating the problems:

Bathing - Bathing your dog using shampoos that break down the oils which plug the hair follicles. These shampoos contain antiseborrhoeic ingredients such as benzoyl peroxide, salicylic acid, sulphur or tar. One example is Sulfoxydex shampoo, which can be followed by a cream rinse such as Episoothe Rinse afterwards to prevent the skin from drying out.

Dabbing – Using an astringent such as witch hazel or alcohol on affected areas. We have heard of zinc oxide cream being used to some effect. In the human world, this is rubbed on to mild skin abrasions and acts as a protective coating. It can help the healing of chapped skin and nappy rash in babies. Zinc oxide works as a mild astringent and has some antiseptic properties and is safe to use on dogs, *as long as you do not allow the dog to lick it off*.

Daily supplements - Vitamin E, vitamin A, zinc and omega oils all help to make a dog's skin healthy. Feed a daily supplement which contains some of these, such as fish oil, which provides omega.

Here are some specific remedies from owners. We are not endorsing them; we're just passing on the information. **Check with your vet before trying any new remedies.**

A medicated shampoo with natural tea tree oil has been suggested by one owner. Some have reported that switching to a fish-based diet has helped lessen scratching. Ann G. said: "Try Natural Balance Sweet Potato and Fish formula. My dog Charlie has skin issues and this food has helped him tremendously! Plus he LOVES it!" Others have suggested home-cooked food is best, if you have the time to prepare the food.

This is what another reader had to say: "My eight-month-old dog also had a contact dermatitis around his neck and chest. I was surprised how extensive it was. The vet recommended twice-a-week baths with an oatmeal shampoo. I also applied organic coconut oil daily for a few weeks. This completely cured the dermatitis. I also put a capsule of fish oil with his food once a day and continue to give him twice-weekly baths. His skin is great now."

Several owners have tried coconut oil with some success. Here is a link to an article on the benefits of coconut oils and fish oils, check with your vet first: www.cocotherapy.com/fishoilsvsvirginoil_coconutoil.htm

And from another reader: "I have been putting a teaspoon of canola (rapeseed) oil in my dog's food every other day and it has helped with the itching. I have shampooed the new carpet in hopes of removing any of the chemicals that could be irritating her. And I have changed laundry detergent. After several loads of laundry everything has been washed."

The Holistic Approach

As canine allergies become increasingly common, more and more owners of dogs with allergies and sensitivities are looking towards natural foods and remedies to help deal with the issues. Some others are finding that their dog does well for a time with injections or medication, but then the symptoms slowly start to reappear. A holistic practitioner looks at finding the root cause of the problem and treating that, rather than just treating the symptoms.

Dr Sara Skiwski is a holistic vet working in California. She writes here about canine environmental allergies: "Here in California, with our mild weather and no hard freeze in Winter, environmental allergens can build up and cause nearly year-round issues for our beloved pets. Also seasonal allergies, when left unaddressed, can lead to year-round allergies. Unlike humans, whose allergy symptoms seem to affect mostly the respiratory tract, seasonal allergies in dogs often take the form of skin irritation/inflammation.

"Allergic reactions are produced by the immune system. The way the immune system functions is a result of both genetics and the environment: Nature versus Nurture. Let's look at a typical case. A puppy starts showing mild seasonal allergy symptoms, for instance a red tummy and mild itching in Spring. Off to the vet!

"The treatment prescribed is symptomatic to provide relief, such as a topical spray. The next year when the weather warms up, the patient is back again - same symptoms but more severe this time. This time the dog has very itchy skin. Again, the treatment is symptomatic - antibiotics, topical spray (hopefully no steroids), until the symptoms resolve with the season change. Fast forward to another Spring ... on the third year, the patient is back again but this time the symptoms last longer, (not just Spring but also through most of Summer and into Fall). By year five, all the symptoms are significantly worse and are occurring year round.

"This is what happens with seasonal environmental allergies. The more your pet is exposed to the allergens they are sensitive to, the more the immune system over-reacts and the more intense and long-lasting the allergic response becomes. What to do?

"In my practice, I like to address the potential root cause at the very first sign of an allergic response, which is normally seen between the ages of six to nine months old. I do this to circumvent the escalating response year after year. Since the allergen load your environmentally-sensitive dog is most susceptible to is much heavier outdoors, I recommend two essential steps in managing the condition. They are vigilance in foot care as well as fur care.

"What does this mean? A wipe down of feet and fur, especially the tummy, to remove any pollens or allergens is key. This can be done with a damp cloth, but my favorite method is to get a spray bottle filled with Witch Hazel and spray these areas. First, spray the feet then wipe them off with a cloth, and then spray and wipe down the tummy and sides. This is best done right after the pup has been outside playing or walking. This will help keep your pet from tracking the environmental allergens into the home and into their beds. If the feet end up still being itchy, I suggest adding foot soaks in Epsom salts."

Dr Sara also stresses the importance of keeping the immune system healthy by avoiding unnecessary vaccinations or drugs: "The vaccine stimulates the immune system, which is the last thing your pet with seasonal environmental allergies needs. I also will move the pet to an anti-inflammatory diet. Foods that create or worsen inflammation are high in carbohydrates. An allergic pet's diet should be very low in carbohydrates, especially grains. Research has shown that 'leaky gut,' or dysbiosis, is a root cause of immune system overreactions in both dog and cats (and some humans).

"Feed a diet that is not processed, or minimally processed; one that doesn't have grain and takes a little longer to get absorbed and assimilated through the gut. Slowing the assimilation assures that there are not large spikes of nutrients and proteins that come into the body all at once and overtax the pancreas and liver, creating inflammation.

"A lot of commercial diets are too high in grains and carbohydrates. These foods create inflammation which overtaxes the body and leads not just to skin inflammation, but also to other inflammatory conditions, such as colitis, pancreatitis, arthritis, inflammatory bowel disease and ear infections. Also, these diets are too low in protein, which is needed to make blood. This causes a decreased blood reserve in the body and in some of these animals this can leads to the skin not being properly nourished, starting a cycle of chronic skin infections which produce more itching."

After looking at diet, check that your dog is free from fleas and then these are some of her suggested supplements:

> **Raw (Unpasteurised) Local Honey** - an alkaline-forming food containing natural vitamins, enzymes, powerful antioxidants and other important natural nutrients, which are destroyed during the heating and pasteurisation processes.

Raw honey has anti-viral, anti-bacterial and anti-fungal properties. It promotes body and digestive health, is a powerful antioxidant, strengthens the immune system, eliminates allergies, and is an excellent remedy for skin wounds and all types of infections. Bees collect pollen from local plants and their honey often acts as an immune booster for dogs living in the locality.

Dr Sara says: "It may seem odd that straight exposure to pollen often triggers allergies, but that exposure to pollen in the honey usually has the opposite effect. But this is typically what we see. In honey, the allergens are delivered in small, manageable doses and the effect over time is very much like that from undergoing a whole series of allergy immunology injections."

> **Mushrooms -** make sure you choose the non-poisonous ones! Dogs don't like the taste, so you may have to mask it with another food. Medicinal mushrooms are used to treat and prevent a wide array of illnesses through their use as immune stimulants and modulators, and antioxidants. The most well-known and researched are reishi, maitake, cordyceps, blazei, split-gill, turkey tail and shiitake.

The mushrooms stabilise mast cells in the body, which have the histamines attached to them. Histamine is what causes much of the inflammation, redness and irritation in allergies. By helping to control histamine production, the mushrooms can moderate the effects of inflammation and even help prevent allergies in the first place.

WARNING! Mushrooms can interact with some over-the-counter and prescription drugs, so do your research as well as checking with your vet first.

> ➢ **Stinging Nettles** - contain biologically active compounds that reduce inflammation. Nettles have the ability to reduce the amount of histamine the body produces in response to an allergen. Nettle tea or extract can help with itching. Nettles not only help directly to decrease the itch, but also work overtime to desensitise the body to allergens, helping to reprogramme the immune system.

> ➢ **Quercetin** – is an over-the-counter supplement with anti-inflammatory properties. It is a strong antioxidant and reduces the body's production of histamines.

> ➢ **Omega-3 Fatty Acids** - these help decrease inflammation throughout the body. Adding them into the diet of all pets - particularly those struggling with seasonal environmental allergies – is very beneficial. If your dog has more itching along the top of their back and on their sides, add in a fish oil supplement. Fish oil helps to decrease the itch and heal skin lesions. The best sources of Omega 3s are krill oil, salmon oil, tuna oil, anchovy oil and other fish body oils, as well as raw organic egg yolks. If using an oil alone, it is important to give a vitamin B complex supplement.

> ➢ **Coconut Oil** - contains lauric acid, which helps decrease the production of yeast, a common opportunistic infection. Using a fish body oil combined with coconut oil before inflammation flares up can help moderate or even suppress your dog's inflammatory response.

Dr Sara adds: "Above are but a few of the over-the-counter remedies I like. In non-responsive cases, Chinese herbs can be used to work with the body to help to decrease the allergy threshold even more than with diet and supplements alone. Most of the animals I work with are on a program of Chinese herbs, diet change and acupuncture.

"So, the next time Fido is showing symptoms of seasonal allergies, consider rethinking your strategy to treat the root cause instead of the symptom."

With thanks to Dr Sara Skiwski, of the Western Dragon Integrated Veterinary Services, San Jose, California, for her kind permission to use her writings as the basis for this section.

This chapter has only just touched on the complex subject of skin disorders. As you can see, the causes and treatments are many and varied. One thing is true: whatever the condition, if your Cockapoo has a skin issue, seek a professional diagnosis as soon as possible before attempting to treat it yourself and before the condition becomes entrenched. Early diagnosis and treatment can sometimes nip the problem in the bud. Some skin conditions cannot be completely cured, but they can be successfully managed, allowing your Cockapoo to live a happy, pain-free life.

If you haven't got your puppy yet, ask the breeder if there is a history of skin issues in her bloodlines. Once you have your Cockapoo, remember that good quality diet and attention to cleanliness and grooming go a long way in preventing and managing canine skin problems and ear infections.

11. Grooming a Cockapoo

Cockapoos have many advantages over other breeds and crossbreeds: they get along with everybody, they are usually non-aggressive towards other dogs, they generally shed very little, they are often suitable for allergy sufferers, they love children and the elderly, they can work as therapy dogs, and they are easy to obedience train and housetrain. These are just a few of their outstanding qualities.

However, one of the very reasons why you have chosen a Cockapoo – namely, the very fact that most of them are minimal shedders - also has a downside. And that is that these dogs are relatively high maintenance when it comes to grooming. Regular home grooming and trips to the grooming parlour (unless you learn to trim the dog yourself) are an essential part of looking after your Cockapoo.

Your dog can't shed and replace his hair like most other breeds and, without regular attention, his hair will become dirty and matted, he will overheat in summer and he will in all likelihood pick up ear infections - leading to a lot of pain for your dog and several expensive and frustrating trips to the vet when the infections recur.

Routine grooming sessions help your Cockapoo to look and feel his best. They also allow you to examine his coat, ears, teeth, eyes and nails for signs of problems. How much attention your dog needs will depend to some extent on exactly what type of coat he has.

Cockapoos normally have a soft, silky and wavy coat – although there are variations, even within litters. There are three types of coat, although all are known for their low shedding/low dander properties – unlike many other types of dog which often have coarser or wirier hair.

Some Cockapoos may take more after the Poodle and have a tight curly coat – similar to the wool coat of the Poodle. If your dog has inherited more of the Cocker Spaniel genes, his coat will be straighter. The third type of coat is the loose wavy coat. A general rule of thumb is that the curly/wavier coats tend to shed less.

You cannot simply leave the coat unkempt, and you will also have to decide how short to keep your Cockapoo's coat. If you are experienced, you can clipper or hand strip the dog yourself, otherwise it's regular trips to a professional groomer approximately every two months. This is an additional expense every owner has to factor in. But whichever way you look at it, a well-groomed Cockapoo is a joy to behold.

Here are some general tips for keeping all Cockapoos in tip top condition.

Brushing and Clipping

We are very grateful to Jessica Sampson, of Legacy Cockapoos, Beaverton, Ontario, Canada, for writing this section for The Cockapoo Handbook. Jessica got her first Cockapoo in 1996 and started breeding five years later. She is a registered American Cockapoo Club breeder and breeds only F2 and F3 Cockapoos, with coat colours ranging from black, phantom, sable, apricot, red and chocolate to merle and parti. For 15 years she was a professional dog groomer.

Jessica starts off by explaining a little about the different generations of Cockapoos:

"As far as grooming is concerned, the generation of the Cockapoo generally makes no difference. The only time it does make a difference for grooming and clipping is if your Cockapoo has a smooth/flat coat like a Cocker Spaniel. In this case they look beautiful in a Cocker-style clip, with full fluffy ear featherings. The smooth coat's brushing requirements are also much lighter in the maintenance department as they have far less coat to contend with.

When breeding Cockapoos, we strive for a soft, silky, full, wavy, fleecy coat type. Smooth/flat and curly coated Cockapoos are considered to have the less desirable coat type. But you can get all three coat types in any given litter. After the third generation, things start to stabilize out and you start seeing less and less of the other coat types.

The majority of F1s have a full, wavy, fleecy coat type, although you will get a few smooth and curly coated dogs as well. The second generation has the most diversity in coat type. All three coat types can be born to a litter of F2s. By the time you reach F3s, things start to stabilize out. This is, of course, if you have been selectively breeding only the dogs with the desired coat type. If you continue to breed down your lines with all three coat types, you will continue to have all three coat types. There is little difference in temperament within the generations.

Brushing

Cockapoos require regular grooming to keep their coat healthy and free of matting. One of the most important parts of grooming your Cockapoo is brushing. One thorough brushing a week is usually adequate, but the right tools and technique are very important.

Tools - the most important tools you will ever own are a soft slicker brush, and a fine tooth steel comb. A dematting comb can also be useful but, if you are brushing your dog regularly and thoroughly, there should be no need for it. With these tools and the proper technique, you will be able to achieve a professional quality brush out. I can attest to this as I am a professional grooming veteran of over 15yrs. I rarely found use for any other type of brushes and found many of them to be a waste of money and time.

Technique – this is your secret weapon! This is very important to get a thorough brush that penetrates right down to the skin and not just brushes the surface fur. The technique is called 'Line Brushing' and here's how to do it:

1. First separate the hair. Make a line going horizontally along the dog from nose to tail so you can see the skin

2. Using your soft slicker brush, brush the hair up across the entire line against the natural lie of the coat

3. Separate a new line 1/4 inch below the first line and repeat over the entire dog

4. Repeat the line brushing technique with your fine tooth steel comb as well. Make sure you pay special attention to the armpit, groin and behind the ears, as these are typical spots where matting forms. If the fine tooth comb does not easily pass through the coat with no hang ups, your dog is not thoroughly brushed and you need to repeat the process where needed

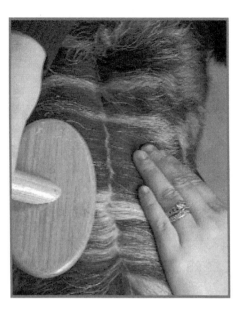

Clipping

Clipping should always be done on a clean dog to preserve the life of your grooming equipment.

When clipping a Cockapoo the look we are trying to achieve is that of a 'teddy bear'. Generally we strive for a clip of about 2"-3" in length. The top of the head is the same length as the body. If the tail is docked (in the USA and Canada), it is clipped the same length as the body. If the dog's tail has been left natural, the tail featherings should be left long and natural.

The face should have hair and a beard, all flowing into one another and trimmed no longer than 4". The ears should be left long and trimmed even with the bottom of the beard. The face and body should never be shaved. If the dog is not being shown, then a shorter or longer coat is allowed. Remember to keep the eyes clear of fur and well brushed. If you choose to leave your Cockapoo Au Naturel, they tend to resemble a shaggy sheepdog and his or her coat will require much more maintenance to stay matt free.

Bathing

The Cockapoo is considered a low odor dog. With regular brushing the natural oils in the dog's coat tend to repel dirt, leaving him or her needing very little bathing. You should only bath your Cockapoo when it is needed - and no more than once a month if you bath regularly. Over-bathing your Cockapoo will lead to your dog having a dry skin and coat.

To maintain a matt-free coat, make sure you thoroughly brush your Cockapoo before you bath him or her. Matts stretch when wet and tighten when they dry, resulting in stubborn matts. Trying to remove them can be very difficult and painful for your dog, and the result is quite often having these matts shaved/clipped out of the coat. Here is the technique I use:

1. Put cotton balls into you Cockapoo's ear canals to help prevent water from entering

2. Thoroughly wet your Cockapoo. Be very careful not to get any water down the ear canals, which can cause ear infections

3. Apply a good quality dog shampoo, NEVER use a human shampoo as this is too harsh for a dog's skin and can lead to skin irritation and/or possible hair loss

4. Work up a good lather working the suds deep into the coat

5. Rinse and repeat with a second shampoo. The first shampoo quite often does not penetrate all the way to the skin. A second shampoo will leave your Cockapoo smelling fresh and sparkling. (This is a groomer's secret! If you've ever wondered why your dog comes home smelling and feeling so much better than when you have bathed him, this is why)

6. Rinse and then rinse again. This is the most important step in bathing, which many overlook. If your dog is not rinsed thoroughly, his or her coat will look dull and the skin will become flaky and itchy, making your Cockapoo very uncomfortable. The soap left behind in the hair will also attract dirt, resulting in your dog needing to be bathed once again

7. Remove the cotton balls and fill the ear canal with doggy ear cleaner, rub the base of the ears and allow your dog to shake his or her head. This will remove any water that may have snuck by your cotton balls. Use this opportunity to gently wipe out any waxy build-up in the ear. CAUTION! Only clean as far as you can see to avoid damaging your dog's eardrum

8. After your Cockapoo is dry, thoroughly brush him again

Ear Cleaning

Cockapoos have inherited very furry ears from their Cocker Spaniel parents and grandparents. And, like Cockers, they are prone to ear infections. Ear canals surrounded by lots of hair are generally warm and moist, making them a haven for bacteria. This can lead to recurring infections and, in severe cases, the dog going deaf or needing an operation to change the shape of his ear canal.

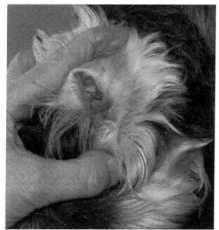

If your dog is a low or minimal shedder, the hair inside the ear flap should be regularly plucked. You can do this at home or ask your groomer to do it during routine visits. If you do pluck the hair yourself, don't overdo it. Keep an eye out for redness or inflammation of the ear flap or inner ear. Ask your groomer for tips. Some owners also regularly bathe the inner ear with cotton wool and warm water or a veterinary ear cleaner.

If your Cockapoo's ears have an unpleasant smell, if he scratches them a lot, rubs them on the carpet or they look red, consult your vet ASAP, as simple routine cleaning won't clear up an infection - and they are notoriously difficult to rid the dog of once he's had one.

The trick is to keep your dog's ears clean and free from too much hair right from puppyhood and hope that he never gets an ear infection.

Jessica says: "There are two ways to go about cleaning your Cockapoo's ears. Method One is to use a good quality ear cleaning solution, which you can pick up at your vet's or local pet/grooming supply shop. Fill your Cockapoo's ear canal with ear cleaner and then rub their ears at the base next to the skull. Allow your dog to shake his or her head and use a cotton ball to gently wipe out any dirt and waxy build up in the ear canal.

"Method Two is to use a baby wipe and gently wipe away any dirt and waxy build up. In both cases it is important to only clean as far down the ear canal as you can see to avoid damaging the eardrum. Method One is the preferred method if you are also bathing your dog, as it will remove any unwanted water that may have got down into the ears during the bath. Clean the ears after bathing."

Teeth Cleaning

Veterinary studies show that by the age of three, 80% of dogs exhibit signs of gum disease. Symptoms include yellow and brown build-up of tartar along the gum line, red inflamed gums and persistent bad breath. You can give your dog a daily dental treat, such as Dentastix, to help keep his mouth and teeth clean, but you should also brush your Cockapoo's teeth as well.

It shouldn't be a chore, but a pleasant experience for both of you. Take things slowly in the beginning, give him lots of praise and many dogs will start looking forward to teeth brushing sessions. Use a pet toothpaste (the human variety can upset a canine's stomach); many have flavours which your dog will find tasty. The real benefit comes from the actual action of the brush on the teeth. Various brushes, sponges and pads are available; the choice depends on factors such as the health of your dog's gums, the size of his mouth and how good you are at teeth cleaning!

Get your dog used to the toothpaste by letting him lick some off your finger. If he doesn't like the flavour, try a different one. Continue this until he looks forward to licking the paste – it might be instant or take days. Put a small amount on your finger and gently rub it on one of the big canine teeth at the front of his mouth. Then get him used to the toothbrush or dental sponge you will be using, praise him when he licks it – do this for several days. The next step is to actually start brushing. Talk to your Cockapoo in an encouraging way and praise him when you're finished.

Lift his upper lip gently and place the brush at a 45º angle to the gum line. Gently move the brush backwards and forwards. Start just with his front teeth and then gradually do a few more. You don't need to brush the inside of his teeth as his tongue keeps them relatively free of plaque. Cockapoos love games and, with a bit of encouragement and patience, it can become a fun task for both of you. There are various videos on YouTube which demonstrate how to clean a dog's teeth.

Jessica adds: "Bad oral hygiene is the leading cause of many diseases in dogs and cats - heart, liver, kidneys, etc. You should brush your Cockapoo's teeth at least once a week to maintain good oral hygiene. There are many fun and enjoyable flavors of doggy toothpaste available on the market today.

"If introduced properly, many dogs look forward to having their teeth brushed. I brush my dogs' teeth once a week after they have received their grooming. They look at teeth brushing as a treat for a job well done and get excited when their grooming is done and it is time to brush!"

Nail Trimming

Nails must be kept short for the paws to remain healthy. Long nails interfere with the dog's gait, and can make walking awkward or painful. They can also break easily. This usually happens at the base of the nail, where blood vessels and nerves are located and results in a trip to the vet's. If you can hear the nails clicking on the floor, they're too long. Dogs which are exercised on hard

surfaces such as pavements (sidewalks) naturally wear down their nails more quickly than dogs which are exercised on soft surfaces such as grass.

You can ask your groomer to trim your dog's nails. If you do it yourself, you will need a specially designed clipper. Most have safety guards to prevent you from cutting the nails too short. You want to trim only the ends, before the 'quick,' which is a blood vessel inside the nail. (It is also where we get the expression 'cut to the quick' from). You can see where the quick ends on a white nail, but not on a dark nail. Clip only the hook-like part of the nail that turns down. It's fair to say that many dogs dislike having their nails trimmed.

You can make it a painless procedure by getting him used to having his paws handled in puppyhood. Start trimming gently, a nail or two at a time, and your dog will learn that you're not going to hurt him. If you accidentally cut the quick, stop the bleeding with some styptic powder. Another option is to file your dog's nails with a nail grinder tool. Some dogs may have tough nails which are hard to trim and this may be less stressful for your dog, with less chance of pain or bleeding. It may take a little while for your dog to get used to the sound of the grinder, so start with very short sessions. If you find it impossible to clip your dog's nails, or you are at all worried about doing it, take him to a vet or a groomer.

Eyes - If your dog's eye(s) has a discharge, if they get a little sticky, or if he has dried deposits in the corner of his eyes, clean them gently with damp cotton wool. Do not use anything else unless instructed to do so by your vet.

Anal Glands – The two anal glands are located on each side of your dog's anus (butt). They give off a scent when your dog has a bowel movement. Squeezing them is normally done if you take your dog to a groomer's, as the glands can get full. You can also ask your vet to do this. If you notice your dog dragging himself along on his rear end or licking or scratching his anus, he may have impacted anal glands - or he may have worms or allergies. Either way, he needs some attention!

12. The Birds and the Bees

Judging by the number of questions our website receives from owners who ask about the canine reproductive cycle and breeding their dogs, there is a lot of confusion out there about the doggie facts of life. Some owners want to know whether they should mate their dog, while others ask at what age they should have their dog spayed (females) or neutered (males).

Owners of females often ask when she will come on heat, how long this will last and how often it will occur. Sometimes they want to know how you can tell if a female is pregnant or how long a pregnancy lasts. So here, in a nutshell, is a short chapter on the facts of life as far as Cockapoos are concerned.

Should I Breed From My Cockapoo?

The short and simple answer is: Unless you know exactly what you are doing or have a mentor, **NO, leave it to the experts.** You need specialist knowledge to successfully breed healthy Cockapoos to type. The rising popularity and cost of puppies is tempting more people to consider breeding their dogs. Prices may be as high as £1,000 or more in the UK and $1,500 – even several thousand dollars - in the US for a puppy from a good breeder with a proven track record. But anyone who thinks it is easy money should bear in mind that responsible Cockapoo breeding is an expensive and time-consuming business when all the fees, DNA and health tests, care, nutrition and medical expenses have been taken into account.

You can't just put any two dogs together and expect perfect, healthy Cockapoos every time; ethical and successful breeding is much more scientific than that. A good breeder is one whose main aim is to improve the Cockapoo hybrid by producing healthy puppies with good temperaments and physical structures with consistently low shedding coats. This doesn't happen by accident or happy coincidence.

Pictured is a beautiful litter of one-week-old F1 English Cockapoo puppies from fully health-tested parents, bred by Pat Pollington, of Polycinders Cockapoos, Devon, UK. Pat has been breeding dogs since 1980 and Cockapoos since 2004. Note the consistent appearance of the puppies.

If you are determined to breed from your Cockapoo, you must first learn a lot. If you are in the UK, visit the annual Cockapoo Games and talk to breeders and people showing their dogs, or search the Cockapoo Club of GB's list of approved breeders and select one near you, all are at www.cockapooclubgb.co.uk. In the USA visit www.americancockapooclub.com for their list of approved breeders near you. Ask one to become a mentor. Regardless of where you live, you can visit online Cockapoo forums where other owners are willing to share their experiences. If you have provisionally selected a breeder, ask other owners if anyone has one of their puppies.

If you want to breed first generation (F1) puppies, make sure you are very familiar with the parent breeds of Cocker Spaniel and Poodle (of whichever size) and the potential health issues.

Approved Canadian breeder Jessica Samson, of Legacy Cockapoos, Ontario, tells a cautionary tale to explain how she first got involved with breeding Cockapoos: "My love affair with Cockapoos started in the 1990s when I received my first Cockapoo, a beautiful sable girl which I named Samantha. I quickly fell in love with her many wonderful qualities. Sadly I was told, like many people, that 'hybrid dog' means 'hybrid vigor' and that my dog would be healthier than any purebred dog because of this.

"WRONG! This is a half-truth. While combining two different breeds does limit the amount of genetic disorders passed on, any genetic disorder carried by both parent breeds can be passed onto their offspring. Unfortunately, Samantha developed Progressive Rod Cone Atrophy (prcd-PRA) and this meant she went completely blind at a young age when her retinas detached. This is a well-known disorder in both Cockers and Poodles. I also had a friend with a Cockapoo from the same breeder (but different litter) that also developed prcd-PRA.

"Imagine my frustration and anger to learn that this is a hereditary disorder that had been passed on from their parents due to bad breeding practices. This experience spurred me into researching Cockapoos and their breeders. I was shocked that I could find no breeders doing any health/DNA testing/screenings of any kind on their Cockapoo parents in Canada at that time. As far as I could tell, 90% of 'breeders' were backyard breeders with a Cocker and a Poodle looking to make a quick buck! And the other 10% wanted you to be impressed with their breeding dog's fancy purebred registration papers - which mean nothing for a hybrid puppy.

"No one really seemed to care about the genetic soundness of their dogs. Shouldn't hybrid dogs be held to the same health standards as purebred dogs? I thought so and so started this wonderful life-fulfilling adventure of breeding Cockapoos." Pictured is Jessica's F2 female, Nessa, who was born white as snow before her wavy fleece coat changed to a rich dark apricot.

"All our breeding dogs are pets first and foremost and remain in our home or in their guardian home their entire lives; they are never re-homed when they are no longer suitable for breeding. We only breed a few litters a year to ensure we have time to care for each puppy born to us properly - the health and happiness of our dogs comes first and foremost.

"Sound health and temperaments come first for us. We believe that strong genetics, not 'hybrid vigor,' makes healthy dogs."

Before you think of breeding from your dog, ask yourself these questions:

1. **Did you get your Cockapoo from a good, ethical breeder?** Dogs sold in pet stores and on general sales websites are seldom good specimens and can be unhealthy

2. **Is your dog, and his or her close relatives, free from a history of eye trouble?** Have you got the relevant eye certificates for your dog and seen those for his or her parents? Progressive Retinal Atrophy Progressive Rod Cone Degeneration (prcd-PRA) can be passed on to Cockapoo puppies if the parents aren't clear, as can Glaucoma and other eye problems

3. **Is your dog, and his or her close relatives, free from other health issues?** Hip Dysplasia, Patella Luxation, von Willebrand's Disease, PFK (American Cockapoos) and Familial Nephropathy (English Cockapoos) are just some of the illnesses which Cockapoo puppies can inherit. Are you 100% sure your breeding dog is free from them all? Also, an unhealthy female is more likely to have trouble with pregnancy and whelping

4. **Does your Cockapoo have a good temperament? Does he or she socialise well with people and other animals?** If you can't tell, take your dog to training classes where the instructor can help you evaluate the dog's temperament. Dogs with poor temperaments should not be bred from, regardless of how good they look and what sort of coat they have

5. **Has your dog got a healthy, low shedding coat and were the parents' coats similar?** If you are breeding for consistency, the coat is an important factor as many potential owners choose Cockapoos for their hypoallergenic characteristics

6. **Does your dog conform to the standard/type?** Although there is no Kennel Club or AKC breed standard (as the Cockapoo is a hybrid not a purebred), the Cockapoo Club of GB has a strict Code of Ethics and promotes a breeding standard, as does the American Cockapoo Club. Do not breed from a Cockapoo which is not a good specimen, hoping that somehow the puppies will turn out better. They won't. Talk with experienced breeders and ask them for an honest assessment of your dog

7. **Is your female two years old or older and at least in her second heat cycle?** Females should not be bred until they are fully physically mature, when they are able to carry a litter to term, and are robust enough to whelp and care for a litter. Even then, not all females are suitable. Some are simply poor mothers who don't care for their puppies - which means you have to do it – others may not be able to produce enough milk

8. **Do you know exactly what type of Cockapoo you are going to produce** – F1s, F2s, F1bs? What size?

9. **Do you understand COI and its implications?** COI stands for Coefficient of Inbreeding. It measures the common ancestors of a dam and sire and indicates the probability of how genetically similar they are. In the UK, the COI should remain below 6.25%, according to the Cockapoo Club of GB

10. **Are you financially able to provide good veterinary care for the mother and puppies, particularly if complications occur?** Have you considered these costs: DNA and health testing, medical care and vets' fees, supplements, whelping equipment, vaccinations and worming, extra food and stud fees? Health can be expensive, and that's in addition to routine veterinary care and the added costs of pre-natal care and immunisations for puppies. What if your female needs a Caesarean section (C-section), or the puppies need emergency treatment? Can you afford the bills? If you are not prepared to make a financial commitment to a litter that could end up costing you a significant amount of money, then do not breed from your Cockapoo

11. **Have you got the indoor space?** The mother and puppies will need their own space in your home, which will become messy as new-born pups do not come into this world housetrained. It should also be warm and draught-free

12. **Do you have the time to provide full-time care for the mother and puppies if necessary?** Caring for the mother and new-borns is a 24/7 job in the beginning, particularly the first seven or eight weeks

13. **Will you be able to find good homes for however many puppies there should be and will you be prepared to take them back if necessary?** This is an important consideration for good breeders, who will not let their precious puppies go to any old home. They want to be sure that the new owners will take good care of their Cockapoos for their lifetime

Responsible breeding is backed up by genetic information and screening as well as a thorough knowledge of the desired traits of the Cockapoo. It is definitely not an occupation for the uninformed. Breeding is not just about the look of the dogs; health and temperament are important factors too. Many dog lovers do not realise that the single most important factor governing health and certain temperament traits is genetics.

Having said that, experts are not born, they learn their trade over several years. Anyone who is seriously considering getting into Cockapoo breeding should first spend time researching the crossbreed and its genetics. Make sure you are going into breeding for the right reasons.

Don't do it to make money or to get puppies just like your perfect Cockapoo, and certainly not to show the kids "the miracle of birth." If you are determined to go into breeding, then do so for the right reason. Learn all you can beforehand, read books, visit dog shows and make contact with established breeders. Find yourself a mentor - ideally a successful breeder with a proven track record who is registered with the Cockapoo club in your country - and make sure you have a good vet on hand who is familiar with Cockapoos.

Committed breeders use their skills and knowledge to produce healthy pups with good temperaments which conform to guidelines and ultimately improve the crossbreed.

Females and Heat

Just like all other animal and human females, a female Cockapoo has a menstrual cycle - or to be more accurate, an oestrus cycle. This is the period when she is ready (and willing!) for mating and is more commonly called **heat** or being **on heat**, **in heat** or **in season**.

A female Cockapoo has her first cycle from about six to nine or 12 months old. She will generally come on heat every six to eight months, though it may be even longer between cycles, and the timescale becomes more erratic with old age. It can also be irregular with young dogs when cycles first begin.

Heat will last on average from 12 to 21 days, although it can be anything from just a few days up to four weeks. Within this period there will be several days which will be the optimum time for her to get pregnant. This middle phase of the cycle is called the *oestrus.* The third phase, called *diestrus*, then begins. During this time, her body will produce hormones whether or not she is pregnant. Her body thinks and acts like she is pregnant. All the hormones are present; only the puppies are missing. This can sometimes lead to what is known as a 'false pregnancy'.

Breeders normally wait until a female has been in heat at least twice before breeding from her. Many believe that around two years old is the right age for a first litter, as a pregnancy draws on her calcium reserves which she needs for her own growing bones. Also, Cocker Spaniels are relatively slow to reach maturity. Responsible breeders limit the number of litters from each female, as overbreeding can take too heavy a toll on her body.

While a female is on heat, she produces hormones which attract male dogs. Because dogs have a sense of smell hundreds of times stronger than ours, your girl on heat is a magnet for all the males in the neighbourhood. They may congregate around your house or follow you around the park, waiting for their chance to prove their manhood – or mutthood in their case.

Don't expect your precious Cockapoo princess to be fussy. Her hormones are raging when she is on heat and during her most fertile days, she is ready, able and … very willing! Keep her on a lead at all times when she is on heat. As she approaches the optimum time for mating, you may notice her tail bending slightly to one side. She will also start to urinate more frequently. This is her signal to all those virile male dogs out there that she is ready for mating.

The first visual sign you may notice is when she tries to lick her swollen rear end – or vulva, to be more precise. She will then bleed; this is sometimes called spotting. It will be a light red or brown at the beginning of the heat cycle; some bitches bleed a lot after the first week. Some female Cockapoos can bleed quite heavily; this is normal. But if you have any concerns about her bleeding, contact your vet to be on the safe side. She may also start to "mate" with your leg or other dogs. These are all normal signs of heat.

Breeding requires specialised knowledge on the part of the owner, but this does not stop a female Cockapoo on heat from being extremely interested in attention from any old mutt. To avoid an unwanted pregnancy, you must keep a close eye on your female and not allow her to freely wander where she may come into contact with other dogs when she is on heat.

Unlike women, female dogs do not go through the menopause and can have puppies even when they are quite old. However, a litter for an elderly Cockapoo can also result in complications.

If you don't want your female to get pregnant, you should have her spayed. In the UK, Europe and North America, humane societies, animal shelters and rescue groups urge dog owners to have their pets spayed or neutered to prevent unwanted litters which contribute to too many animals in the rescue system or, even worse, euthanasia. Normally all dogs from rescue centres and shelters are spayed or neutered. Many responsible breeders also encourage early spaying and neutering – and some may even specify it in the puppy's sale contract.

Spaying

Spaying is the term used to describe the removal of the ovaries and uterus (womb) of a female dog so that she cannot become pregnant. Although this is a routine operation, it is major abdominal surgery and she has to be anaesthetised. A popular myth is that a female dog should have her first heat cycle before she is spayed, but this is not the case. Even puppies can be spayed. You should consult your vet for the optimum time, should you decide to have your dog done. Note that if she is on heat or nearing her heat cycle, your dog cannot be spayed.

If spayed before her first heat cycle, one of the advantages is that your dog will have an almost zero risk of mammary cancer (the equivalent of breast cancer in women). Even after the first heat, spaying reduces the risk of this cancer by 92%.

Some vets claim that the risk of mammary cancer in unspayed female dogs can be as high as one in four. Some females may put weight on easier after spaying and will require slightly less food afterwards. As with any major procedure, there are pros and cons.

Spaying is a much more serious operation for a female than neutering is for a male. This is because it involves an **internal** abdominal operation, whereas the neutering procedure is carried out on the male's testicles, which are outside his abdomen.

For:

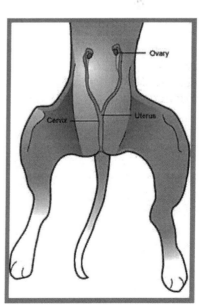

> Spaying prevents infections, mammary cancer and other diseases of the uterus and ovaries

> It reduces hormonal changes which can interfere with the treatment of diseases like diabetes or epilepsy

> Spaying can reduce behaviour problems, such as roaming, aggression to other dogs, anxiety or fear

> It eliminates the risk of the potentially fatal disease pyometra (a secondary infection that occurs as a result of hormonal changes in the female's reproductive tract), which affects unspayed middle-aged females

> A spayed dog does not contribute to the pet overpopulation problem

Against:

> ➤ Complications can occur, including an abnormal reaction to the anaesthetic, bleeding, stitches breaking and infections. This is not common

> ➤ Occasionally there can be long-term effects connected to hormonal changes. These may include weight gain, urinary incontinence or less stamina and these problems can occur years after a female has been spayed

> ➤ Older females may suffer some urinary incontinence, but it only affects a very few spayed females. Discuss it with your vet

> ➤ Cost (this is a rough estimate, vets' practices vary greatly). This can range from $160 - $480 in the USA and £100 to £300 in the UK.

If you talk to your vet or a volunteer at a rescue shelter, they will say that the advantages of spaying far outweigh any disadvantages. When you take your female Cockapoo to the vet's for her vaccinations, you can discuss with him or her at what age spaying should be considered.

Neutering

Neutering male dogs involves castration - the removal of the testicles. This can be a difficult decision for some owners, as it causes a drop in the pet's testosterone levels, which some humans – males in particular! - feel affects the quality of their dog's life.

Fortunately, dogs do not think like people and male dogs do not miss their testicles or the loss of sex. Our own experience is that male dogs are much happier once neutered. We decided to have our Max neutered after he went missing three times on walks – he ran off on the scent of a female on heat. Fortunately, he is micro-chipped and has our phone number on a tag on his collar and we were lucky that he was returned to us on all three occasions.

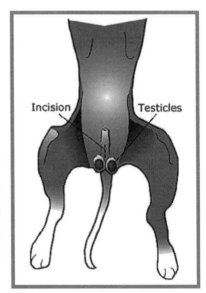

Unless you specifically want to breed from your dog, or he has a special job, neutering is recommended by animal rescue organisations and vets. Even then, Guide Dogs for the Blind, Hearing Dogs for Deaf People and Dogs for the Disabled are routinely neutered and this does not impair their ability. There are countless unwanted puppies, especially in the US, many of which are destroyed. There is also the problem of a lack of knowledge from the owners of some breeding dogs, resulting in the production of puppies with congenital health or temperament problems.

Neutering is usually performed around puberty, i.e. about six months old. It can, however, be done at any age over eight weeks, provided both testicles have descended. The operation is a relatively straightforward procedure. Dogs neutered before puberty tend to grow a little larger than dogs done later. This is because testosterone is involved in the process which stops growth, so the bones grow for longer without testosterone.

The neutering operation for a male is much less of a major operation than spaying for a female. Complications are less common and less severe than with spaying a female. Although he will feel tender afterwards, your dog should return to his normal self within a couple of days.

When he comes out of surgery, his scrotum (the sacs which held the testicles) will be swollen and it may look like nothing has been done. But it is normal for these to slowly shrink in the days following surgery. Here are the main pros and cons:

For:

➤ Behaviour problems such as aggression and wandering off are reduced

➤ Unwanted sexual behaviour, such as mounting people or objects, is reduced or eliminated

➤ Testicular problems such as infections, torsion (painful rotation of the testicle) are eradicated. Neutering also significantly reduces the number of cases of testicular cancer

➤ Prostate disease, common in older male dogs, is less likely to occur

➤ A submissive entire (uncastrated) male dog may be targeted by other dogs. After he has been neutered, he will no longer produce testosterone and so will not be regarded as much of a threat by the other males, so he is less likely to be bullied

➤ A neutered dog is not fathering unwanted puppies

Against:

➤ As with any surgery, there can be bleeding afterwards, you should keep an eye on him for any blood loss after the operation. Infections can also occur, generally caused by the dog licking the wound, so try and prevent him doing this. If he persists, use an E collar. In the **vast majority** of cases, these problems do not occur

➤ Some dogs' coats may be affected, but supplementing their diet with fish oil can compensate for this

➤ Cost. This starts at around $130 in the US, £80 in the UK

Myths - Here are some common myths about neutering and spaying:

Neutering or spaying will spoil the dog's character - There is no evidence that any of the positive characteristics of your dog will be altered. He or she will be just as loving, playful and loyal. Neutering may reduce aggression or roaming, especially in male dogs, because they are no longer competing to mate with a female.

A female needs to have at least one litter - There is no proven physical or mental benefit to a female having a litter. Pregnancy and whelping (giving birth to puppies) can be stressful and can have complications. In a false pregnancy, a female is simply responding to the hormones in her body.

Mating is natural and necessary - Dogs are not humans, they do not think emotionally about sex or having and raising a family. Because Cockapoos like the company of humans so much, we tend to ascribe human emotions to them. Unlike humans, their desire to mate or breed is entirely physical, triggered by the chemicals called hormones within their body. Without these hormones – i.e. after neutering or spaying – the desire disappears or is greatly reduced.

Male dogs will behave better if they can mate - This is simply not true; sex does not make a dog behave better. In fact it can have the opposite effect. Having mated once, a male may show an increased interest in females. He may also consider his status elevated, which may make him harder to control or call back.

Pregnancy

A canine pregnancy will normally last for 61 to 65 days - typically 63 days – regardless of the size or breed of the dog. Sometimes pregnancy is referred to as the "*gestation period.*"

It's a good idea to take a female for a pre-natal check-up after mating. The vet should answer any questions, such as the type of food, supplements and extra care needed by your female. He or she will also be able to explain any physical and psychological changes she will experience.

There is a blood test available which measures levels of **relaxin**. This is a hormone produced by the ovary and the developing placenta, and pregnancy can be detected by monitoring relaxin levels as early as three weeks after mating. The levels are high throughout pregnancy and then decline rapidly after the female has given birth.

A vet can usually see the puppies using Ultrasound from around the same time. X-rays also give the breeder an idea of the number of puppies; these can help to give the vet more information, which is particularly useful if the bitch has had previous whelping problems. Here are some of the signs of pregnancy:

➢ After mating, many females become more affectionate. (However, some will become uncharacteristically irritable and maybe even a little aggressive)

➢ The female may produce a slight clear discharge from her vagina about one month after mating

➢ Three or four weeks after mating, a few females experience morning sickness – if this is the case, feed little and often. She may seem more tired than usual

➢ She may seem slightly depressed and/or show a drop in appetite. These signs can also mean there are other problems, so you should consult your vet

➢ Her teats (nipples) will become more prominent, pink and erect 25 to 30 days into the pregnancy. Later on, you may notice a fluid coming from them

➢ After about 35 days, or seven weeks, her body weight will noticeably increase

➢ Her abdomen will become noticeably larger from around day 40, although first-time mums and females carrying few puppies may not show as much

➢ Many pregnant females' appetite will increase in the second half of pregnancy

- Her nesting instincts will kick in as the delivery date approaches. She may seem restless or scratch her bed or the floor

- During the last week of pregnancy, females often start to look for a safe place for whelping. Some seem to become confused, wanting to be with their owners and at the same time wanting to prepare their nest. Even if the female is having a C-section, she should still be allowed to nest in a whelping box with layers of newspaper, which she will scratch and dig as the time approaches

If your female becomes pregnant – either by design or accident - your first step should be to consult a vet.

False Pregnancies

As many as 50% or more of intact (unspayed) females may display signs of a false pregnancy. In the wild it was common for female dogs to have false pregnancies and to lactate (produce milk). This female would then nourish puppies if their own mother died.

False pregnancies occur 60 to 80 days after the female was in heat - about the time she would have given birth – and are generally nothing to worry about for an owner. The exact cause is unknown. However, hormonal imbalances are thought to play an important role. Some dogs have shown symptoms within three to four days of spaying. Typical symptoms include:

- Mothering or adopting toys and other objects

- Making a nest

- Producing milk (lactating)

- Appetite fluctuations

- Barking or whining a lot

- Restlessness, depression or anxiety

- Swollen abdomen

- She might even appear to go into labour

Try not to touch your dog's nipples, as touch will stimulate further milk production. If she is licking herself repeatedly, she may need an Elizabethan collar (or E-collar, a large plastic collar from the vet) to minimise stimulation.

Under no circumstances should you restrict your Cockapoo's water supply to try and prevent her from producing milk. This is dangerous as she can become dehydrated.

Some unspayed bitches may have a false pregnancy with each heat cycle. Spaying during a false pregnancy may actually prolong the condition, so better to wait until the false pregnancy is over and then have her spayed to prevent it happening again. False pregnancy is not a disease, but an exaggerated response to normal hormonal changes. Owners should be reassured that even if left untreated, the condition almost always resolves itself.

However, if your Cockapoo appears physically ill or the behavioural changes are severe enough to worry you, visit your vet. He or she may prescribe tranquilisers to relieve anxiety, or diuretics to reduce milk production and relieve fluid retention. In rare cases, hormone treatment may be necessary. Generally, dogs experiencing false pregnancies do not have serious long-term problems, as the behaviour disappears when the hormones return to their normal levels in two to three weeks.

One exception is pyometra, a disease mainly affecting unspayed middle-aged females, caused by a hormonal abnormality. Pyometra follows a heat cycle in which fertilisation did not occur and the dog typically starts showing symptoms within two to four months.

The signs are excessive drinking and urination, with the female trying to lick a white discharge from her vagina. She may also have a slight temperature. If the condition becomes severe, her back legs will become weak, possibly to the point where she can no longer get up without help.

Pyometra is serious if bacteria take a hold, and in extreme cases it can be fatal. It is also relatively common and needs to be dealt with promptly by a vet, who will give the dog intravenous fluids and antibiotics for several days. In most cases this is followed by spaying.

To recap: You may have the most wonderful Cockapoo in the world, but only enter the world of canine breeding if you have the right knowledge and motivation. Don't do it just for the money or the cute factor. Breeding poor examples only brings heartache to families in the long run when health or other issues develop.

---

13. Cockapoo Rescue

Are you thinking of adopting a Cockapoo from a rescue organisation? What could be kinder and more rewarding than giving a poor, abandoned Cockapoo a happy and loving home for the rest of his life?

Not much really; adoption saves lives. The problem of homeless dogs is truly depressing, particularly in the USA. The sheer numbers in kill shelters there is hard to comprehend. Randy Grim states in "Don't Dump The Dog" that 1,000 dogs are being put to sleep every hour in the States.

According to Jo-Anne Cousins, former Executive Director at International Doodle Owners Group (IDOG), the situations leading to a dog ending up in rescue can be summed up in one phrase: unrealistic expectations. She said: "In many situations, dog ownership was something that the family went into without fully understanding the time, money and commitment to exercise and training that it takes to raise a dog. While they may have spent hours on the internet pouring over cute puppy photos, they probably didn't read any puppy training books or look into actual costs of regular vet care, training and boarding."

Another reason some Cockapoos end up in rescue is that people get one believing they are all 'hypoallergenic', only to discover later that the dog triggers allergies in one member of the family. 'Hypoallergenic' means '**less likely** to cause an allergic reaction'; there are no sure-fire guarantees. While researching this article, I came across this advert on Preloved in the UK: "F1 Cockapoo puppy nine weeks old, selling due to my allergic reaction to her. Mum is a Cocker Spaniel KC registered, dad is a miniature Poodle, KC registered and PRA eye clear. F1 puppy, £750." Incredible to think that the puppy had only lasted a week in her new 'forever' home.

I also came across a story from my home town. A woman had gone shopping in a retail centre on Christmas Eve. She returned home with a puppy she had paid £700 ($1,050) for. The pup was in a rescue shelter by Boxing Day (December 26th).

Some of the most common reasons for rehoming include:

> A change in the owner's personal circumstances – such as a divorce or change of home or job
> The dog has too much energy, needs too much exercise, knocks the kids over and jumps on people
> The dog is growling and/or nipping at the children
> It chews or eats things it shouldn't
> It makes a mess in the house
> It needs way more time and effort than the owner is able or prepared to give

There is, however, a ray of sunshine for some of these dogs. Every year many thousands of people in North America, the UK and countries all around the world adopt a rescue dog and the story often has a happy ending.

The Dog's Point of View...

But if you are serious about adopting a Cockapoo, then you should do so with the right motives and with your eyes wide open. If you're expecting a perfect dog, you could be in for a shock. Rescue dogs can and do become wonderful companions, but much of it depends on you. Cockapoos are people-loving dogs. Some of them in rescue centres are traumatised. They don't understand why they have been abandoned by their beloved owners and may arrive at your home with problems of their own until they adjust to being part of a loving family again. Ask yourself a few questions before you take the plunge:

> ➢ Are you prepared to accept and deal with any problems - such as bad behaviour, shyness, aggression or making a mess in the house - which the dog may display when he initially arrives in your home?
> ➢ How much time are you willing to spend with your new pet to help him integrate back into normal family life?
> ➢ Can you take time off work to be at home and help the dog settle in at the beginning?
> ➢ Are you prepared to take on a new addition to your family that may live for another 10 years or more?

Think about the implications before taking on a rescue dog - try and look at it from the dog's point of view. What could be worse for the unlucky dog than to be abandoned again if things don't work out between you?

Other Considerations

Adopting a rescue dog is a big commitment for all involved. It is not a cheap way of getting a Cockapoo and shouldn't be viewed as such. It could cost you several hundred dollars - or pounds. You'll have adoption fees to pay and often vaccination and veterinary bills as well as worm and flea medication and spaying or neutering. Make sure you're aware of the full cost before committing.

Many rescue Cockapoos have had difficult lives. You need plenty of time to help them rehabilitate. Some may have initial problems with housebreaking. Others may need socialisation with people as well as other dogs.

If you are serious about adopting, you may have to wait a while until a suitable dog comes up. One way of finding out if you, your family and home are suitable is to volunteer to become a foster home for one of the rescue centres. Fosters offer temporary homes until a forever home becomes available. It's a shorter term arrangement, but still requires commitment and patience.

And it's is not just the dogs that are screened - you'll probably have to undergo a screening by the rescue organisation to ensure you are suitable. You might even have to provide references. In the UK, the Doodle Trust rescues and rehome Doodles – i.e. Labradoodles, Goldendoodles, Cockapoos and other Poodle crosses. They have a long list of "Things to Consider BEFORE Getting a Doodle," including:

- If you are just not a Poodle person, DON'T GET A DOODLE. All doodles have Poodle in them and if the word Poodle makes you cringe, then do not get a Doodle

- If you are allergic to dogs, DON'T GET A DOODLE. Doodles go through coat changes and even if you are not allergic to your Doodle's puppy coat, you may be allergic to his adult coat. Doodles are often deemed hypoallergenic by the media, but for most, this is not the case

- If you want a clean dog, DON'T GET A DOODLE. Many doodles love water, mud and rolling in smelly things. Their coats can be like Velcro and will collect twigs, dirt, burrs, leaves etc.

- If you want a low-energy dog, DON'T GET A DOODLE. Most Doodles require at least 30-60 minutes of real exercise a day. Simply letting your Doodle out in the backyard is not exercise. There are plenty of low-energy dog breeds that would be a better fit if you aren't overly active

- If you can't devote time and money into training, DON'T GET A DOODLE. Doodles are intelligent and want to please you, but they are not born with manners

- If you want an independent dog, DON'T GET A DOODLE. Doodles thrive on human companionship and most are Velcro dogs. They need your attention and will demand it

- If you want the perfect dog, DON'T GET A DOODLE. There is no such thing as a perfect dog, and just like other breeds, Doodles can have a wide variety of temperaments and health issues

- If you want a low-maintenance dog, DON'T GET A DOODLE. The look that attracts so many would-be Doodle owners requires a lot of time and money; there is major grooming involved

- If you want a dog 'for the kids', DON'T GET A DOODLE. Doodles need lots of time on a daily basis, keeping their minds stimulated and reinforcing their behaviours. Kids won't keep that commitment

To combat some unrealistic expectations about Doodles, including Cockapoos, The Trust adds a more realistic version of events: "Doodles are lively, enthusiastic and sometimes boisterous dogs that require a lot of time and attention. If you are out at work for much of the time or lead a busy life, a Doodle is NOT the right breed for you. These are people dogs and they demand human companionship, they thrive as a much loved family member. If left to their own devices for long periods, they will find their own amusement and could become destructive.

"Most Doodles love water and can be mud magnets, bringing in an enormous amount of dirt into your home. They are certainly not a breed for the house-proud. Some coat types require grooming on a daily basis in order to keep them matt free, whilst Doodles with a shorter coat will require less brushing.

"Many Doodles also need professional grooming on a regular basis in order to keep the coat manageable and this can be expensive. You should therefore consider grooming costs on top of food, insurance, toys, vaccinations, worming, etc. It all mounts up!

"Doodles are not necessarily compatible with small children and, in any case, it is unwise to leave any dog with small children. When considering a rescue Doodle, please also give some thought as to how this may affect any other pets you might own. Some cats for example may not take kindly to a big bouncy dog, and if you already own another dog, how will the new addition impact on them?

"Most Doodles coming into rescue are large boys so there may be a considerable waiting period before we can match you with the right dog. Waiting times are further increased if you specify a certain colour and coat type and our dogs will always be matched to families by their suitability, rather than looks." Another point to remember is that a rescue dog does not come free, there will be a charge of a couple of hundred pounds or dollars – or even more - to cover expenses and medical costs, worming, etc.

Rescue groups and shelters have to make sure that the people adopting their dogs are suitable and that everything has been thought through very carefully before making such a big decision. It would be a tragedy for the dog if things did not work out. To try and combat this, most charitable rescue groups will ask a raft of personal questions – some of which may seem intrusive. If you are serious about rescuing a Cockapoo, you will have to answer them. Here are some of the questions asked and information required by The Doodle Trust:

- o What is your profession and who is your employer?
- o What type of property do you live in?
- o If this is a rental property, does your lease allow pets?
- o What is the size of your garden?
- o What is the height and type of the fencing?
- o Is the garden completely secure?
- o Is there a pond or pool?
- o Does anybody in the house have asthma or other allergies?
- o If yes, what type of allergies or asthma?
- o Do you have regular visitors - canine or human? If yes, please list all regular visitors
- o Have you owned a dog before?
- o If so, what breeds or types of dogs have you owned before?
- o Please list the types/breeds (dog, cat, rabbit, etc). and ages of all pets in the home at the moment
- o Are your current dogs spayed/neutered?
- o Have you ever had to give up one of your pets?
- o Please give the name, address and telephone number of the veterinary surgery for current/past pets
- o Please provide a brief medical history of any current or previous pets
- o Do you authorise a representative of Doodle Trust to contact your veterinary surgery to confirm the medical records/history of your pets?
- o Where will your dog be when you are at home?
- o Where will your dog sleep at night?
- o Where will your dog be when you are out of the house?
- o Where will your dog go when you are on holiday?
- o Would you be prepared to use a crate for your new dog, if necessary?
- o How will you handle chewing, destruction or any other behavioural issues?
- o How far are you prepared to travel to view and/or collect a dog?

You then have to provide two personal references and agree to a home inspection visit. If you are not prepared to go through all of this, you may have to reconsider whether rescuing a Cockapoo is the right path for you.

Rescue Organisations

In the UK, The Doodle Trust can be found at: www.doodletrust.com. There are also a number of ways in which individuals living all over the UK can help this worthy cause. You could get involved by donating money, volunteering to become a foster home, a home checker or a fundraiser. Or you could help with transport; check out the website for details. The Doodle Trust has an online shop with all profits going back into rescuing Poodle crosses.

There are dog shelters and rescue groups throughout the UK which rehome dogs of all breeds; the most famous of which is Battersea Dogs' Home. There are Cockapoo forums where owners may hear of a dog which needs rehoming at www.Cockapooclubgb.co.uk/Cockapoo-club-chat.html and www.ilovemyCockapoo.com run by the Cockapoo club of GB. There are also general dog rescue websites, but you may find that these have more of certain types of dogs, such as Staffordshire Bull Terriers or German Shepherds. These include:

- o www.homes4dogs.co.uk
- o www.greenleafanimalrescue.org.uk
- o www.petfinder.com
- o www.adoptapet.com

In the USA, there are no specific Cockapoo rescue organisations, but there is the Doodle Rescue Collective at http://doodlerescuecollective.com as well as numerous websites rescuing dogs of all breeds and mixes, such as www.petsmartcharities.org and www.adoptapet.com. There is a website which lists all of the Poodle crosses, including Cockapoos, from other websites around the USA at: http://poomixrescue.com.

This is by no means an exhaustive list, but it does cover some of the main organisations involved. If you do visit these websites, you cannot presume that the descriptions are 100% accurate. They are given in good faith, but ideas of what constitutes a medium dog and what is a small or large one may vary. Some dogs advertised may be mistakenly described as "Poodle mix and Cocker Spaniel" when they may have other breeds in their genetic make-up. It does not mean they are necessarily worse dogs, but if you are attracted to the Cockapoo for its temperament and other assets, make sure you are looking at a Cockapoo.

NEVER buy a dog from eBay, Craig's List, Gumtree or any of the other advertising websites which sell old cars, washing machines, golf clubs etc. You might think you are getting a cheap dog, but in the long run you will pay the price. If the dog had been well bred and properly cared for, he or she would not be advertised on a website such as this. If you buy or get a free one, you may be storing up a whole load of trouble for yourselves in terms of health and behavioural issues, due to poor breeding and environment.

If you haven't been put you off with all of the above..... Congratulations, you may be just the family or person that poor homeless Cockapoo is looking for!

If you can't spare the time to adopt - and adoption means forever - you might want to consider fostering. Or you could help by becoming a fundraiser to generate cash to keep these very worthy rescue groups providing such a wonderful service. However you decide to get involved, Good Luck!

Saving one dog will not change the world
But it will change the world for one dog

With thanks to The Doodle Trust for their assistance with this chapter

14. Caring for Older Dogs

Cockapoos live remarkably long lives compared with many other breeds and crossbreeds. Several of the breeders we contacted thought that 15 to 17 years of age was a normal lifespan. One even knew of a dog living to the ripe old age of 20. Cockapoos can remain fit and active well into their teens. But eventually all dogs – even Cockapoos – slow down.

At some point your old dog will start to feel the effects of aging. Physically, joints may become stiffer, and organs, such as heart or liver, may not function as effectively. On the mental side - just as with humans - your dog's memory, ability to learn and awareness will all start to dim.

Your faithful companion might become a bit grumpier, stubborn or a little less tolerant of lively dogs and children. You may also notice that he doesn't see or hear as well as he used to. On the other hand, your old friend might not be hard of hearing at all. He might have developed that affliction common to many older dogs – ours included - of selective hearing. Our 11-year-old Max has bionic hearing when it comes to the word 'Dinnertime' whispered from 20 yards, yet seems strangely unable to hear the commands 'Come' or 'Down' when we are right in front of him!

Pictured is Toby, who is 16 years young. He is an F2 and was in the first litter ever bred by Jessica Sampson, of Legacy Cockapoos. He is owned by Jessica's mother, Caroline Leitch. Toby's silver sable colouring and long beard mean that he is sometimes mistaken for a Schnauzer!

You can help ease your mature dog into old age gracefully by keeping an eye on him or her, noticing the changes and taking action to help him as much as possible. This might involve a visit to the vet for supplements and/or medications, modifying your dog's environment, changing his or her diet and slowly reducing the amount of daily exercise.

Much depends on the individual dog. Just as with humans, a dog of ideal weight that has been active and stimulated all of his or her life is likely to age slower than an overweight couch potato.

Keeping Cockapoos at that optimum weight is challenging - and important – as they age. Their metabolisms slow down, making it easier to put on the pounds unless their daily calories are reduced. At the same time, extra weight places additional, unwanted stress on joints and organs, making them have to work harder than they should.

We normally talk about dogs being old when they reach the last third of their lives. This varies greatly from dog to dog and bloodline to bloodline. Some dogs may start to show signs of aging as young as eight years old while others will remain fit in mind and body long after this age.

Physical and Mental Signs of Aging

If your Cockapoo is in or approaching the last third of his life, here are some signs that his body is feeling its age:

➤ He gets up from lying down more slowly and he goes up and down stairs more slowly. He can no longer jump on to the couch or bed. These are all signs that his joints are stiffening, often due to arthritis

➤ He has generally slowed down and no longer seems as keen to go out on his walks. He tires more easily on a walk

➤ He doesn't want to go outside in bad weather

➤ He has the occasional 'accident' (incontinence) inside the house

➤ He is getting grey hairs, particularly around the muzzle

➤ He has put on a bit of weight

➤ He urinates more frequently

➤ He drinks more water

➤ He gets constipated

➤ The foot pads thicken and nails may become more brittle

➤ He has one or more lumps or fatty deposits on his body. Our 11-year-old dog developed two on his head recently and we took him straight to the vet, who performed an operation to remove them. They were benign (harmless), but you should always get them checked out ASAP in case they are an early form of cancer.

➤ He can't regulate his body temperature as he used to and so feels the cold and heat more

➤ He doesn't hear as well as he used to

➤ His eyesight may deteriorate – if his eyes appear cloudy he may be developing cataracts and you should see your vet as soon as you notice the signs

➤ He has bad breath (halitosis), which could be a sign of dental or gum disease. Brush his teeth regularly and give him a daily dental stick, such as Dentastix or similar. If the bad breath persists, get him checked out by a vet

➤ If he's inactive he may develop callouses on the elbows, especially if he lies down on hard surfaces – although this is more common with larger breeds

It's not just your dog's body which deteriorates, his mind does too. It's all part of the normal aging process. Here are some symptoms. Your dog may display some, all or none of these signs of mental deterioration:

➤ His sleep patterns change, an older dog may be more restless at night and sleepy during the day

➤ He barks more

➤ He stares at objects or wanders aimlessly around the house

➤ He forgets or ignores commands or habits he once knew well, such as housetraining and coming when called

➤ He displays increased anxiety or aggressiveness

➤ Some dogs may become more clingy and dependent, often resulting in separation anxiety. Others may become less interested in human contact

Understanding the changes happening to your dog and acting on them compassionately and effectively will help ease your dog's passage through his or her senior years. Your dog has given you so much pleasure over the years, now he or she needs you to give that bit of extra care for a happy, healthy old age. You can also help your Cockapoo to stay mentally active by playing games (not too rough) and getting new toys to stimulate interest.

Helping Seniors

The first thing you can do is monitor your dog and be on the lookout for any changes in actions or behaviour. Then there are lots of things you can do for him.

Food and Supplements - As dogs age they need fewer calories and less protein, so many owners switch to a food specially formulated for older dogs. These are labelled 'Senior,' ' Aging' or 'Mature.' Check the labelling; some are specifically for dogs aged over eight, others may be for 10 or 12-year-olds. If you are not sure if a senior diet is necessary for your Cockapoo, talk to your vet the next time you are there for annual vaccinations or a check-up. Remember, if you do change the brand, switch the food gradually over a week to 10 days. Unlike with humans, a dog's digestive system cannot cope with sudden changes of diet.

Consider feeding your Cockapoo a supplement, such as Omega-3 fatty acids for the brain and coat, or one to help joints. There are also medications and homeopathic remedies to help relieve anxiety. Again, check with your vet before introducing anything new.

Exercise – Take the lead from your dog, if he doesn't want to walk as far, then don't. But if your dog doesn't want to go out at all, you will have to coax him out. ALL senior dogs need exercise, not only to keep their joints moving, but also to keep their heart, lungs and joints exercised.

Weight – no matter how old your Cockapoo is, he still needs a waist! Maintaining a healthy weight with a balanced diet and regular, gentler exercise are the two of the most important things you can do for your dog.

Environment – Make sure your Cockapoo has a nice soft place to rest his old bones, which may mean adding an extra blanket to his bed. This should be in a place which is not too hot or cold, as he may not be able to regulate his body temperature as well as when he was younger. If his eyesight is failing, move obstacles out of his way, reducing the chance of injuries. Jumping on and off furniture or in and out of the car is high impact for his old joints and bones. He will need a helping hand on to and off the couch or your bed, if he's allowed up there, or even a little ramp to get in and out of the car. Make sure he has plenty of time to sleep and is not pestered and/or bullied by younger dogs, other animals or young children.

Consult a Professional - If your dog is showing any of the following signs, get him checked out by your vet:

> Increased urination or drinking - this can be a sign of something amiss, such as reduced liver or kidney function, Cushing's disease or diabetes

> Constipation or not urinating regularly could be a sign of something not functioning properly with the digestive system or organs

> Incontinence, which could be a sign of a mental or physical problem

> Cloudy eyes, which could be cataracts

> Lumps or bumps on the body - which are most often benign, but can occasionally be malignant (dangerous)

> Decreased appetite – most Cockapoos love their food and loss of appetite is often a sign of an underlying problem

> Excessive sleeping or a lack of interest in you and his/her surroundings

> Diarrhoea or vomiting

> A darkening and dryness of skin that never seems to get any better - this can be a sign of hypothyroidism

> Any other out-of-the-ordinary behaviour for your dog. A change in patterns or behaviour is often your dog's way of telling you that all is not well

―――――――――――――

The Last Lap

Huge advances in veterinary science have meant that there are countless procedures and medications which can prolong the life of your dog, and this is a good thing.

But there comes a time when you have to let go. If your dog is showing all the signs of aging, has an on-going medical condition from which he or she cannot recover, or is showing signs of pain, mental anxiety or distress and there is no hope of improvement, then the dreaded time has come to say goodbye.

You owe it to him or her.

There is no point keeping an old dog alive if all they have to look forward to is pain and death.

I'm even getting upset as I write this, as I think of parting from my 11-year-old dog not too many years into the future, as well as the wonderful dogs we have had in the past. But we have their lives in our hands and we can give them the gift of passing away peacefully and humanely at the end when the time is right.

Losing our beloved companion, our best friend, a member of the family, is truly heart-breaking for many owners. But one of the things we realise at the back of our minds when we get that lively little puppy is the pain that comes with it; knowing that we will live longer than him or her and that we will probably have to make this most painful of decisions at some point. It's the worst thing about being a dog owner.

If your Cockapoo has had a long and happy life, then you could not have done any more. You were a great owner and your dog was lucky to have you. Remember all the good times you had together. And try not to rush out and buy another dog; wait a while to grieve for your Cockapoo. Assess your current life and lifestyle and, if your situation is right, only then consider getting another dog and all that that entails in terms of time, commitment and expense. Cockapoos are sensitive, often intuitive, creatures. One coming into a happy, stable household will get off to a much better start in life than a dog entering a home full of grief.

Whatever you decide to do, put the dog first.

What the Cockapoo Experts Say

Let's not dwell on the end stages of our dog's life, but focus on what we can do to keep him or her fit and healthy as the years roll by.

Rebecca Mae Goins, of MoonShine Babies Cockapoos, Indiana, USA, has worked as a Pet Care Technician as well as a Companion Animal Hygienist since 1993, so she knows a thing or two about elderly dogs. She has been breeding Cockapoos since 2006 (pictured is Rebecca's service dog, Scarlett). Here's our interview:

At what age would you say a Cockapoo becomes a senior- i.e. time to look at changing to a senior diet? "I personally would say seven to nine years old is when you start looking for your Cockapoo to require a lower calorie diet, because they will start to slow down and both Cockers and Poodles can get a little chubby when they get older."

What do you feed your older Cockapoos? "I feed Royal Canin Mini from Puppy Formula to Adult. When it comes to my older Cockapoos, I switch them to Royal Canin Weight Care or Royal Canin Mature, whichever is best for the Cockapoo in need of the diet change."

Do you feed any supplements to your older dogs - or anything else which helps them as they age? "I feed all my Cockapoos NuVet Plus supplements from puppyhood to adult. When they get older I switch the seniors to NuJoint Plus, which contains all that is needed to help with the aging joints."

Are there any health issues particular to older Cockapoos? "Well since Cockapoos are a mixture of Cocker Spaniel and Poodle, you have to look at both breeds. In general Cockapoos are a hearty breed. If the parent dogs are health tested and have no health issues, then the puppies should follow suit. But even the pups of healthy parent dogs should be health tested to make sure nothing has been missed.

"There are a lot of issues that can happen to both breeds when they age, such as Luxating Patellas and several eye disorders, but the most common is Progressive Retinal Atrophy (PRA). Ear infections can occur due to the long droopy ears, and some Cockapoos have the hair that grows in the ear canal like the Poodle. If not removed by your groomer or vet, it can cause yeast and bacterial infections. Older Cockapoos can also develop lumps which will need to be looked at immediately."

How about behavioural changes? "With aging Cockapoos, behavioural changes can happen as with any aging dog. They can forget the training they have learned, so you will need to keep a steady schedule during your Cockapoo's lifetime so that there are fewer chances for a lapse in manners. Always be aware of behavioural changes, because this can sometimes mean that there is an underlying issue, in which case you need to make an appointment with your vet to make sure everything is OK."

Do you have any tips you can pass on to owners of older Cockapoos? "Yes, as a breeder, rescuer and owner of Cockapoos I have dealt with a lot of older Cockapoos. The best advice I can give you with your aging Cockapoo is #1 LOVE them; cherish every moment you have with them.

"Always watch the way they react to make sure you do not miss anything that needs veterinary care. Regularly groom them to keep their skin and coat in good condition and feed quality foods and supplements. Have daily play times to exercise them and daily rub downs and petting sessions to make sure there are no sores, aches and pains or lump and growths.

"Join a Cockapoo online forum or Facebook group for support from other Cockapoo owners. Sometimes you can find local groups who will meet at parks or meeting areas to provide support and socialisation for you and your Cockapoo." Pictured is F1 Cockapoo Liberty Belle, courtesy of Rebecca.

Here's the same interview with Jessica Sampson, of Legacy Cockapoos, Ontario, Canada:

"Many Cockapoos start to slow down between the ages of nine to 10, but some may show no signs of slowing down until 12 to 14 years of age. This is a good indication that it may be time to switch to a senior diet.

"I feed all my dogs, from puppies to seniors, an All Stages diet: Dick Van Patten's Natural Balance. I have had great success with this and my Cockapoos live a long healthy life of 16 to 18 years on average. I follow the careful advice of my veterinarian and she has never seen reason to change any of my dogs to a senior diet as they have all been very healthy and their nutritional needs have always been met by the diet we feed our dogs.

"If you feed your dog an excellent quality food, there really is no need for vitamin or supplements, unless your veterinarian recommends otherwise. Follow your vet's advice. We feed all our dogs, regardless of age, a good quality canine probiotic, as good health starts from the inside.

"Cockapoos generally maintain their good health but, as with all breeds, arthritis can be an issue in older dogs, as well as cataracts and hearing loss.

"In terms of behavioural changes, your Cockapoo will sleep more throughout the day. You will notice he is also not as spry as he once was, but should remain the same happy affectionate dog you know and love. Some elderly dogs may have less tolerance and may become agitated or snappy if they are in pain (this is not normal behaviour). If this is the case, consult your vet as to the course of action to take for pain management.

"An active dog is a healthy dog! My advice to owners is to keep up with regular walks and activities. If your Cockapoo seems like he or she has less energy, adjust your walk and play time to a more suitable level. I have had 16-year-old Cockapoos who have had no trouble keeping up on a two-hour hike in the woods!

"Make more regular visits to your vet and follow his or her advice. Elderly dogs' health can change quickly, so making regular vet visits will help identify any changes in your dog and help you to take the right course of action to maintain your dog's health and comfort through his or her senior years."

Jeanne Davis, Wind Horse Offering, Maryland, USA, adds: "I don't actually have any personal experience with elderly Cockapoo's, as I have only been breeding them for eight years. In terms of age, I have had people contact me who have said that their Cockapoo lived for 15 years, others say 18.

"I would say that any dog has to stay active, properly fed and warm. As far as feeding goes, I am not one for any special supplementation, as long as the food that I am feeding is nutritious and palatable. However, it is important to keep Cockapoos' teeth clean so that they don't get gum disease and then start having tooth problems."

Pictured, courtesy of Jeanne and with plenty of life to look forward to, is Champ by Wind Horse Offering's Stud Muffin out of Wind Horse Offering's Lily.

15. Cockapoos Helping Humans

With their intelligence, happy dispositions, empathy and love of humans, Cockapoos have developed a reputation as excellent therapy and service dogs. They bring joy to the elderly and ill as well as providing a lifeline for people with disabilities. They assist children in the autistic spectrum and can also help youngsters overcome speech and emotional difficulties.

There is a difference between a therapy and a service dog, also called an assistance dog; and Cockapoos are suitable for training as either. A therapy dog visits settings such as retirement and

nursing homes, hospitals, hospices and schools, where they are handled and petted to help provide a calming influence. Scientific evidence has shown that being around and stroking dogs can provide comfort and reduce stress levels. In the UK, therapy dogs are also known as PAT dogs (Pets As Therapy); further information can be found here: www.petsastherapy.org.

The history of the first-ever therapy dog dates back to World War II when a female Yorkshire Terrier was found on the battlefield in New Guinea. She was adopted by US Corporal William Wynne who named her Smoky (pictured). She became the first therapy dog when William was hospitalised for a jungle disease and his friends brought the little Yorkie into the hospital to cheer him up as he was recovering.

Smoky immediately became so popular with the other wounded soldiers that the commanding officer, Dr Charles Mayo (who founded the Mayo Clinic), allowed her to go on ward rounds and to sleep on William's hospital bed. It is also recorded that Smoky helped engineers to get communications up and running at an airbase in the Philippines. She dragged a telegraph wire tied to her collar under a runway and through a 70-foot-long pipe only eight inches high.

Smoky's use as a therapy dog continued for 12 years, during and after World War II. She died in 1957 aged about 14. (History source: Wikipedia)

Wider use of therapy dogs is attributed to American nurse Elaine Smith, who noticed how well patients responded to visits by a chaplain and his Golden Retriever. In 1976, Smith started a programme for training dogs to visit institutions. She later formed Therapy Dogs International, which today has more than 24,000 registered dog and handler pairings.

Service dogs provide a wide range of tasks. They are specifically trained to help people who have disabilities such as visual, mobility or hearing impairments, mental illnesses (like PTSD - post-traumatic stress disorder), seizures and diabetes.

Mary Gosling is co-founder of the British Cockapoo Society. She is also deaf. After a difficult time, her life has been transformed by her Hearing Dog, Harley (pictured). Here is their very moving story, written in Mary's own words for The Cockapoo Handbook:

Mary and Harley's Story

"Before becoming deaf, I was a fairly normal single Mum, living with my teenage daughter. She was gearing up for her GCSE exams and so that was a big thing going on. I had spent time living in Spain and was just readjusting back to living in the UK.

When I became deaf, it literally happened out of the blue; without any warning or apparent reason. I had gone to bed one night feeling fine - my hearing was normal, no headache, earache etc, but when I woke up the next morning, I was completely deaf. I literally couldn't hear a thing. My daughter was having a school exam that morning, so I tried to pretend that everything was fine. I didn't say anything to her, and took her in a cup of tea as usual. I couldn't ring anyone for help because obviously, I couldn't have heard them talking. I couldn't ring the doctor or friends. I became very anxious and started crying and my daughter asked me what the matter was. She then took over and got me to hospital.

I was in hospital for about two weeks. I had nearly every test you can think of - blood tests, MRI scans (to see if I had some sort of tumour), lumbar punctures and hearing assessments. But all the time I was there, I couldn't hear and it wasn't improving. Eventually, they told me that my hearing had gone, and it was going to be permanent. I was one of the people to suffer from Sudden Hearing Loss and they don't know why - it can be viral, but they are not sure.

Of course I was devastated. All of the things we take for granted were gone. I couldn't hear the TV or radio, listen to music, hear my family talk to me, phone family or friends. Everything changed. I became quite good at lip-reading, but I couldn't hear people talk to me in the shops or hear what people were saying in a group conversation, I just couldn't follow what was going on. I felt isolated, even when I was with people, and soon depression set in. I just didn't know how to cope. I felt my life was over and didn't know what the future held. At 45 years of age, this wasn't supposed to be happening.

My daughter saw an advert for Hearing Dogs for Deaf People, a national UK charity that breeds and trains dogs to be Assistance Dogs for deaf adults and children, and mentioned it to me. That was the start of a long and on-going relationship I have had with this great charity. Hearing Dogs take puppies through socialisation and then on to learning what is called 'soundwork' so they can alert their human recipient when the doorbell goes, or the phone rings, or the fire alarm goes off, etc. It really is a wonderful charity. I also love dogs, which helps. So we got in touch and went along to see them at their headquarters in Buckinghamshire, England.

I went through an assessment where the charity gets to know you, sees how much help you need, what your personal circumstances are, what you can hear - or not hear - and so on. Deafness is not a standard thing; different people can hear different tones and sounds. Some people may be able to hear more than others, so each recipient of a Hearing Dog has a dog that is specifically trained for them.

Unfortunately, there is a long waiting list of about five years, and it took a long time before I got my own Hearing Dog, Harley (pictured), a wonderful Cockapoo who has really changed my life. It takes about 18 months to two years to get pups from birth to being fully-fledged Hearing Dogs. They are first given the normal socialisation process, where they live with a volunteer family, get used to all the day-to-day sounds, experiences etc. that a well-grounded dog needs to cope with. They are introduced to babies, children, taken on buses and trains and so on. They then have to learn the basic obedience skills and, if they are deemed suitable, they go on to the final stage of learning; the all- important soundwork. Not all dogs pass this training. Those that don't are called the Fallen Angels, and they are placed with a loving family to be a much-loved family pet.

Harley brought me companionship and restored my confidence. I didn't have to worry about missing a text from family or friends, as he would jump up and alert me about it. And at night, I didn't have to worry if the fire alarm went off, as I knew he would wake me up if I was sleeping. I didn't have to worry if someone was speaking to me in a shop - Harley would let me know!

I had previously had a couple of experiences where someone in a supermarket had literally barged into me with their trolley because I hadn't moved when they had asked to get past me in the aisle - I just hadn't heard them! This doesn't happen now. Everyone in the local shops knows Harley, he is a bit of a local star. On one occasion Harley saved me from serious injury. I was crossing the road when a car jumped the traffic lights and Harley just stopped; he wouldn't move at all, despite me telling him to walk on. By the time I realised why he had deliberately stopped me, I realised the car was inches away from my legs.

I do have some other health issues, and Harley is wonderful at helping me cope with the effects of

those. He is amazing. He now opens the door, brings shoes, helps me undress - he takes my socks off and gives them to me or will put them in a basket. He takes trousers off - this is where his size lets him down. He tries to pick them up off the floor, but ends up standing on them because his legs are so short! He may only be a small dog, but his heart is huge, and he always tries his best to do what is needed or to help."

Mary is pictured here with her Harley on the right and another Cockapoo Hearing Dog, coincidentally also called Harley.

"I'm now in a sheltered housing (assisted living) bungalow, and the property has an emergency cord system you can pull if you are not well or if there is a problem. Pulling the cord triggers an alert system and someone will ring you and speak over an intercom to check you if you need assistance. Obviously this is no good for me because I wouldn't be able to hear anyone if they rang, so Harley has now been taught to bark when they speak. They now know that if the alarm is pulled and he barks, it's a real emergency. He does this on top of all the other help he gives.

I really don't know what I would do without Harley now. I rely on him for his help, his companionship; he gives me the confidence to get out in the world. I am now a volunteer for the Hearing Dogs charity, and fundraise for them as much as I can. It costs about £45,000 to raise and train each dog and to provide lifelong support for the dog and its human recipient, so every penny raised is so important. When we set up the British Cockapoo Society, we were determined that a big part of our remit was going to be to help raise money for Hearing Dogs. We hold competitions online, have a club shop selling items and money is donated to the charity. We produce and sell a yearly Cockapoo calendar, again with profits going to the charity. Every penny counts and I know that these dogs are changing people's lives for the better."

Hearing Dogs for Deaf People has helped thousands of people with hearing impairments in the UK since it was set up in 1982. It currently has some 900 Hearing Dogs, generally Labradors, Cocker Spaniels, Poodles, Golden Retrievers and Cockapoos. The charity has a network of helpers and is always looking for new volunteers, foster carers and fundraisers. People can sponsor a puppy and keep up to date with his or her progress for as little as £3 a month. For more information, visit www.hearingdogs.org.uk

The British Cockapoo Society was set up August 2013 by Mary and Diana Hoskins, who have since been joined by Jane Phillips. The BCS currently has more than 3,000 members and continues to grow. The club's aims include to:

➢ Provide information about how to find a reputable breeder
➢ Give advice on finding breeders who are working to good standards
➢ Provide information and encourage prospective owners to purchase puppies bred from DNA health tested parents
➢ Encourage responsible dog ownership by advocating training using rewards and positive reinforcement

For more information, visit www.britishCockapoosociety.com or the charity's Facebook page at www.facebook.com/britishcockapoosociety

---

Rebecca's Story

In the United States, Cockapoos have worked as service and therapy dogs for decades. Rebecca Mae Goins, of MoonShine Babies Cockapoos, Indiana, first came across them when she was a teenager visiting relatives in assisted living. She said:

"There would be visiting teams of handlers going from room to room; some would have dogs some would have cats, but this sparked an interest for me. As an adult I chose to go to school to be a Pet Care Technician, and Companion Animal Hygienist. At that time in my life I was very active and I was raising and showing Chows. In 2006 my sister gave me the best birthday present - a lovely American Cocker Spaniel, 'Stella Luna.' She came after a very hard hit to my health and she opened the door to what I now know to be my calling: breeding, raising and training Cockapoos to help others,

Our Poodle Sirius was to come a few months later as a gift from my mother and MoonShine Babies Cockapoos was created and we have not stopped providing happy, healthy and loved Cockapoos to the world as assistance dogs and loved pets and family members. Many of our Cockapoo pups have gone into assistance and service homes.

Cockapoos are a very wise choice for an assistance dog, be it Therapy (TD), Service (SD) or Emotional Support Dog (ESD). They are loyal and smart, and easy to train and eager to please; plus the low-shed coat means less dander, and that makes them the perfect choice for work in public where you may encounter people with pet allergies. I have found that children and adults of all ages with mental and physical special needs benefit from the companionship of an assistance dog - and none better than the happy, loving Cockapoo.

Here in the US we have a few different types of assistance dogs. Therapy Dogs assist with companionship and healing in hospitals, nursing and rehab facilities and schools, and Emotional

Support Dogs assist individuals who suffer from mental disabilities, and these dogs can have access to any public areas. I have an F3 (third generation) Cockapoo, Katie Scarlett – pictured - who is my Emotional Support Dog for bipolar disorder and multiple sclerosis. I also have an adult son with autism, and he benefits from the support of his Service Dog/Emotional Support Dog, a wonderful American Cocker Spaniel called Stella Grace. She has opened so many emotional doors and is such a caring and attentive dog. She can even alert people to emotional changes and sugar levels, and has alerted to seizure activity. Both will become mothers for future assistance pups.

At MoonShine Babies, we raise all of our Cockapoo pups with the same training and socialisation techniques used for assistance dogs, and many of our pups go into service homes to help those in need. We are in the process of becoming a breeder of the Pets for Vets program which provides assistance dogs to wounded military veterans suffering from PTSD (Post-Traumatic Stress Disorder) and for whom the dog will become that special companion and protector.

In the US we have many options for training service and therapy dogs. There are foster homes where the pups are cared for before they go on to the professional trainers. The foster parents train the dog to a certain point before sending him or her on to the owner/handler to complete the process. The other option is where the dog is raised and trained by the owner/handler. This is my preference,

because the pup can form a strong bond with the owner/handler and that bond is what counts when you need a service or therapy dog. All dogs have to start off with basic manners and obedience training. During this time they learn the necessary skills to prepare them for the task training, which is where they go out in public places and learn to become a disciplined, calm, well trained, socialized assistance dog.

When it comes to ID tags and badges, it is recommended to have an IN TRAINING badge for those who have not yet completed training, to let people know this is a work in progress. After training, you can either acquire or assemble your Assistance Dog badge and vest or harness. Then when you have issues with people in public that ask you for your proof that your dog is indeed a assistance dog - and sadly this will happen - always remember that, in the US, the ADA (American Disabilities Act) www.ada.gov/service_animals_2010.htm supports you. It is not required for the assistance dog to wear a vest or ID Badge, but it is recommended to avoid confusion. By the way, beware of companies who say "Register your service dog for $$.$$...

To sum up, you cannot go wrong with a Cockapoo as an assistance dog. They will do their job with love and pride."

For further information on therapy and service dogs in the USA, visit the Cockapoo registry at www.americanCockapooclub.com or the following websites: www.ada.gov/archive/qasrvc.htm or https://petpartners.org or www.assistancedogsinternational.org or www.therapydoginfo.net or www.nsarco.com.

With sincere thanks to Rebecca and Mary for sharing their stories

Useful Contacts

British Cockapoo Society www.britishcockapoosociety.com

The Cockapoo Club of Great Britain www.cockapooclubgb.co.uk

Cockapoo Owners Club (UK) www.cockapooowners-club.org.uk

American Cockapoo Club www.americancockapooclub.com

American Cockapoo Club breeders' list http://www.americancockapooclub.com/breeders.asp

Cockapoo Club of America www.cockapooclub.com

Breeders Online (UK) www.breedersonline.co.uk/dogs/cockapoo.asp

The Doodle Trust (UK) www.doodletrust.com

Doodle Rescue Collective (USA) http://doodlerescuecollective.com

www.apdt.co.uk Association of Pet Dog Trainers UK

www.apdt.com Association of Pet Dog Trainers USA

www.cappdt.ca Canadian Association of Professional Pet Dog Trainers

www.dogfoodadvisor.com Useful information on grain-free and hypoallergenic dogs foods

www.akcreunite.org Helps find lost or stolen dogs in USA, register your dog's microchip

Cockapoo internet forums and Facebook groups are also a good source of information from other owners, including:

http://ilovemycockapoo.com/forum.php

http://cockapoocrazy.proboards.com

www.facebook.com/britishcockapoosociety

Contributors

Diana Hoskins and Mary Gosling, co-founders of the British Cockapoo Society

Dave and Linda Zarro, President and Vice President of the American Cockapoo Club, also of

Sugar and Spice Cockapoos, South Carolina, USA www.sugarandspicecockapoos.com

Barb Turnbull of the Doodle Trust

Dr Sara Skiwski of the Western Dragon holistic veterinary practice, San Jose, California, USA

Owners Julie and Nigel Houston, Judy and Greg Moorhouse and all the puppy parents of Karol Watson Todd

Breeders (in alphabetical order)

Jeanne Davis, Wind Horse Offering, Earleville, Maryland, USA www.windhorseoffering.com

Rebecca Mae Goins, MoonShine Babies Cockapoos, www.moonshinebabiescpoo.com

Eileen Jackson, Brimstone Cockapoos, Christchurch, Cambridgeshire, England

Chloe and Pat Pollington, Polycinders Cockapoos, Tiverton, Devon, England www.polycinders.co.uk

Jessica Sampson, Legacy Cockapoos, Beaverton, Ontario, Canada www.legacycockapoos.com

Julie Shearman, Crystalwood Cockapoos, Devon, England www.crystalwoodpuppies.co.uk

Jackie Stafford of Dj's Cockapoo Babies, Rusk, Texas, USA www.moonshinebabies.com

Karol Watson Todd, KaroColin Cockapoos, Sleaford, Lincolnshire, England

Disclaimer

This book has been written to provide helpful information on Cockapoos. It is not meant to be used, nor should it be used, to diagnose or treat any medical condition. For diagnosis or treatment of any animal medical problem, consult a qualified veterinarian. The author is not responsible for any specific health or allergy conditions that may require medical supervision and is not liable for any damages or negative consequences from any treatment, action, application or preparation, to any person reading or following the information in this book. References are provided for informational purposes only and do not constitute endorsement of any websites or other sources.

Author's Note: For ease of reading the masculine pronoun 'he' is intended to represent both male and female dogs.